THE BIG LETDOWN

THE BIG
LETDOWN

•

How Medicine,
Big Business, and Feminism
Undermine Breastfeeding

•

KIMBERLY SEALS ALLERS

ST. MARTIN'S PRESS ⚏ NEW YORK

For information, address St. Martin's Press,
175 Fifth Avenue, New York, N.Y. 10010.

www.stmartins.com

Library of Congress Cataloging-in-Publication Data

Names: Seals-Allers, Kimberly, author.
Title: The big letdown : how medicine, big business, and feminism undermine
  breastfeeding / Kimberly Seals Allers.
Description: First edition. | New York : St. Martin's Press, 2017.
Identifiers: LCCN 2016044039| ISBN 9781250026965 (hardback) | ISBN
  9781250026972 (e-book)
Subjects: LCSH: Breastfeeding. | Breastfeeding—Social aspects. |
  Breastfeeding—Economic aspects. | BISAC: SOCIAL SCIENCE / Women's
  Studies. | SOCIAL SCIENCE / Sociology / Marriage & Family.
Classification: LCC RJ216 .S415 2017 | DDC 649/.33—dc23
LC record available at https://lccn.loc.gov/2016044039

Our books may be purchased in bulk for promotional, educational,
or business use. Please contact your local bookseller or the
Macmillan Corporate and Premium Sales Department at
1-800-221-7945, extension 5442, or by e-mail at
MacmillanSpecialMarkets@macmillan.com.

First Edition: January 2017

P1

*For my children, Kayla and Michael-Jaden,
and for all the little girls who, like me,
found their solace in words and
their power with a pen*

Author's Note

This is a nonfiction work, though the names and descriptions of some individuals have been changed at their request.

I am not a doctor and the information in this book is not intended as a substitute for the advice of the reader's own physician or other medical professional. You should consult a medical professional in matters relating to your health or the health of your baby.

Contents

And I cried . . . For all the women who have ever stretched their bodies out anticipating civilization and finding ruins.

—SONIA SANCHEZ, "JUST DON'T GIVE UP ON LOVE"

THE BIG LETDOWN

Introduction

The beginning is the most important part of any work,
especially in the case of a young and tender thing.

—PLATO

I am driving—correction: speeding—down the Grand Central Parkway in Queens, New York, wearing only a black T-shirt and some brightly colored pajama pants tucked into my Uggs. There's a screaming baby in the back seat. Don't worry, she's mine. Thirteen miles at an unmentionable speed later, I arrive at Long Island Jewish Hospital, where, about six weeks earlier, I delivered my eight-pound, six-ounce daughter by Cesarean section. After fumbling with the car seat, I grab the striped cooler bag from the trunk and move quickly through the lobby, past the gift shop and to the elevator bank, refusing to make eye contact, just in case any of those judgmental "please shut your baby up" types are in the vicinity. At least at the hospital, they may just assume that all the crying is related to a medical problem, not my personal failure. I press the DOOR CLOSE and the floor 3 button simultaneously and so rapidly, I'm sure I've sprained a finger, all the while silently begging God that nobody else gets on. For the ride up, I switch to a swinging, bouncing, and kind of demi-twirling of the car seat combination, hoping this may soothe my child. It doesn't. Just as the elevator doors slowly part, I see my target and make my move, bolting toward my goal: a large door. I turn the doorknob to the left many times and then to the right. I bang and bang on the door. No answer. This is it. My last ditch, desperate attempt for help, quickly followed by the grim realization that there is none to be found. I press my back against the door with all my might and slide slowly to the floor. The feeling of failure is heavy. I pull up my shirt as my braless breast hangs floppily, and make one more, desperate attempt to feed her. She refuses. Her mouth howls. Tears pour down my face. My breasts are engorged and dripping. Nurses, strangers, and hospital personnel step over us. I look around—baby crying, dripping breast exposed and dangling, and me, overwhelmed by failure—and all I see are shoes. Loafers. Heels. Sneakers. It is the visual confirmation that I have hit bottom. And I have milk stains on my shirt.

That door. Behind that blasted door is the place where every other week the breastfeeding support group happens. And even though it is not the day or the time, I was hopeful that someone, anyone would be there and able to help me figure out why I am suddenly and unexplainably failing at breastfeeding. Instead, it is locked and there is not one lacto-friendly-looking person in sight. I reach for the cooler bag. It was given to me when I was discharged from the hospital. There is infant formula in it. Yesterday, it was the devil. Today, it looks like my messiah in plastic packaging. In the days of my breastfeeding zealousness, I refused to even bring it in the house. But a part of me could not, would not throw it away. Just toss it, I said to myself. "It's a subversive tool of the infant formula companies to undermine your breastfeeding success," I ranted to my then husband, who has never been known to turn away any sort of freebie—even a subversive one. But the nice nurse at the hospital had said to take it, "just in case." And perhaps this is my "just in case." How did she know?

I sit there, fumbling to make a bottle of formula with one hand, while my breast continues to leak. My baby needs to eat. I am literally oozing food. Something clearly has gone awry here. And all of it feels like an act of biological treason. My first job as a mother is to feed my baby, and I am failing miserably already, a mere forty-something days in. I educated myself (read all the books and blogs), prepared myself (even toughened up my nipples prebirth by rubbing them with a towel), motivated myself (Chaka Khan's "I'm Every Woman," on repeat), attended the support group, and still these actions aren't enough. At the moment, the experience of breastfeeding just feels absurd and pointless and ridiculously difficult and far more than I expected it to be, and I am profoundly unprepared for all of these emotions. The feeling tumbled me end over end.

Make the bottle. Feed your baby, I say to myself. It's no big deal. Just as I'm ripping off the packaging, I hear someone asking me if I need some help. It's a blurry visage, but the voice is of an older woman, and when I look up I see she is wearing a hospital volunteer smock and pin. I blurt out a two-minute run-on sentence about how my baby won't nurse and she's been crying for hours and I desperately hoped someone from the breastfeeding support group would be here but no one is and I don't know what to do.

In the midst of my rambling and sobbing, she says, "Wait

here. I'll be right back." No mention of the dangling breast or about-to-be-poured formula setup station. She returned with the woman who led our support group.

I was rescued that day, by a kindly older woman. Her name, I learned, was Alice, and while the lactation consultant helps me hand express some milk and get baby Kayla settled and fed, Alice gets me a cup of water, rubs my back, and tells me her own daughter had a similar experience.

In the end, a stranger saves me. Not the pediatrician who is technically responsible for my baby's health and nutrition. Not the ob-gyn who apparently only cares about the contents of my uterus until it is emptied but not thirty minutes more. Not the budget-busting $100-an-hour lactation consultant I paid last week, who was unable to accommodate me on short notice this week. For the next hour, watching Kayla finally calm, suckling on my breast, looking at me, eyes brown and blazing, I can't help thinking about the past three hours and wonder if this is what the experience of feeding our young according to our biological norm is supposed to be like. If breastfeeding is "natural" and "best," then why is it so difficult? Yes, it brings unparalleled moments of joy, but why does it also often include so much emotional anguish and suffering for so many women?

Let's be clear, I am your classic type A superachiever, and I have the stress-induced ulcers to prove it. I eat "difficult" for lunch. I have a master's degree from Columbia University and have worked in some of the world's toughest newsrooms. But everything I ever imagined about myself as a mother slowly disappeared into the cracks of the hospital floor that day. Certainly, doing something that has kept humanity alive since the beginning of the species should not be such a struggle. And it's not just an early-days struggle to learn to breastfeed, but an ongoing social one. Women struggle with nursing in public, being shamed out of retail stores, on airplanes, and even, in one case, out of a lingerie store of all places. Returning to work, we struggle to pump milk for our babies, often being expected to do so in a bathroom stall or other inappropriate place. Employers use terms like "accommodating" nursing mothers, which makes women feel as if they are being done a special favor for being biologically different from men. We battle against social stigma; if we dare to breastfeed beyond twelve months, we are quickly typecast as some alternative parenting weirdo, even though the World Health Organization and UNICEF recommend breastfeeding for two years and the worldwide average age for weaning is close to three years old.

Meanwhile, the messages we receive about breastfeeding are completely disconnected from the actual experience millions of women are having. I mean, let's face it, me sitting braless and crying on a hospital floor does not jibe with any photo you have ever seen in any breastfeeding magazine article or advertisement. Ever. In the images we are shown, there are green meadows. There are colorful flowers and blissfully calm women. Nobody is crying. Or cursing. Or dripping milk on their $250 sheepskin boots. No women on the verge of breakdowns, making over-the-speed-limit dashes for help. But this was me. And, I soon learned, there are millions more like me.

• • •

It's no wonder that, according to the most recent data available from the Centers for Disease Control, while 74 percent of U.S. infants are ever breastfed, only 23 percent are exclusively breastfed at three months and 14.6 percent exclusively breastfed at six months. In the states of Louisiana and West Virginia, the percentage of infants ever breastfed is 56 percent and 59 percent, respectively, with six-month exclusivity rates at a paltry 13 percent and 12 percent. Compare that to Sweden, where the exclusive breastfeeding rate is slightly above 75 percent at three months and around 37 percent at six months. Why in the land where we boast of American exceptionalism do we suck at breastfeeding? And if there is some collective failure among women, is it biological or psychological? Or biological because of a psychological trigger? I found this particularly frustrating because, like many modern parents, I aim for perfection. I was the pregnant woman who sat in my office at *Fortune* magazine with headphones on my belly pumping Mozart into my uterus for the chance that it would improve my child's brain development and intellect. During my pregnancy, I studiously read every fact-filled weekly e-mail from BabyCenter.com (you know those e-mails never stop) alerting me to what was growing and developing during that period, and then I researched what to eat and did it. Need copper for forming of the heart and skeletal and nervous systems? Pass the canned crab meat and raw cashews, please. Big phase of cell development? Bring on the DHA-enriched eggs. And once when I read that talking to your unborn child in operatic tones would enhance brain development, I studied everyone from Elisabeth Schwarzkopf to Leontyne Price and sang arias (badly) for two weeks. Yes, I am that mother. And in some circles, where parenting is viewed as a project to be organized and managed, breastfeeding has become a part of any modern child-maximizing plan. I was guilty of placing myself into this sphere. In many ways breastfeeding has become the measure of the mother, even across socioeconomic lines.

So, of course, I was going to breastfeed. It is best, the doctors say. Breast milk provides unparalleled immunological properties. It is composed of nutrients; enzymes; hormones; growth factors; host defense agents; vitamins A, C, B complex; binding proteins; lysozyme and antibodies; and many other ingredients that build a strong, healthy human being. Unlike any other body fluid, breast milk is actually live. It's not a consistent body fluid such as blood. A secretion of the mammary gland, it constantly changes its composition, dependent on the interaction with the baby and a woman's own body. Breastfed babies have lower risks of stomach viruses and lower respiratory illness, ear infections, and meningitis. Several studies show breastfed babies to be intellectually superior. The American Academy of Pediatrics recommends it. So do the World Health Organization, UNICEF, and Angelina Jolie. And as a sort of healthy-eating enthusiast, it just made sense to me that what nature has provided remains superior to any artificial milk product made in a factory.

But creating a map of those years of breastfeeding, not just with my first child but also four years later nursing my second child, would show a confusing array of lines running in all sorts of directions like the streams of light after a firework explodes. Yet all of those lines could never ever tell the whole story. The map could highlight the warmth and the joy of breastfeeding and that magical connection between me and my child that centered me beyond words. It could possibly pinpoint all the obstacles I ran into at the hospital or at work, but not all of the invisible cultural forces causing them. It certainly wouldn't show my agony as I breastfed despite everything. Despite the pain and the cracked nipples. Despite the emotional exhaustion and the sleep deprivation, the monotony and the resentment, the glory and the ghosts of anxiety-ridden mothers past that haunted me for my first fourteen months of breastfeeding. And then again for the twelve months that I nursed my second-born.

Women deserve to know why we are angry, confused, and struggling for clear answers. We should really dig deep into the why. Why breastfeeding has become such a polarizing issue. Why women are in an information maelstrom when it comes to their infant feeding choices. Why a generation of women who are collectively breaking new barriers in business, science, and the arts also battle feelings of inadequacy about their ability to perform their biological imperative. Why profit motive and other conflicts of interest often cloud what is best for mother and baby. And why the policy changes, scientific innovation, and cultural forces that once aided in our collective advancement as women now seem to be spinning in a powerful and dangerous orbit around us, trapping us inward.

Truth is, the experience of how we feed our young has fundamentally changed in recent history. Somehow our natural instincts to nurse have gone askew, and our views about feeding our children are now more socially and culturally constructed. We no longer rear generations around a single fire or accumulate and share knowledge about how to suckle our young. This isn't necessarily a bad thing, but the impact on public health and female consciousness must be thoughtfully considered. We want convenience and choice and freedom and the best nutrition and the most advanced brain development and bragging rights for motherhood—and maybe that is all too much to ask of a milky composition of proteins, lipids, and oligosaccharides or its artificial substitute. Yes, breastfeeding is only one in a spectrum of motherhood experiences, but examining it provides a powerful lens with which to peer into the conflicts shaping and dividing women's lives. The breastfeeding narrative, both historical and present-day, is a cautionary tale about maternal bodies, good or bad mothers, and how our bodies are measured and assessed. Breastfeeding shows us all the ways, as women, that we have been imagined, constructed, created, and controlled by economics, science, the media, and other so-called authoritative sources. And since, according to some estimates, 80 percent of women will become mothers by age forty-four, we are all affected, childless or not. The breastfeeding narrative is also shaped by the history of the United States from the impact of the Industrial Revolution on women's work patterns to a hypersexualized breast culture and a plastic surgery boom that makes boob jobs as commonplace as tattoos. Evolving feminist ideals and new expectations for marriage based less on economics and procreation and more on love, companionship, and shared parenting also play a part. Not to mention an increasingly industrialized and profit-focused food system where companies like Mead Johnson (maker of Enfamil) target infants from day one and then companies like Monsanto (largest maker of genetically engineered food) pick up the baton not long after. A system where the chairman of multinational food conglomerate Nestlé, the world's largest seller of bottled water as a status symbol for handsome profits, actually appeared several years ago in a video seeming to suggest that treating water as a universal human right was "extreme." Breast milk, like clean water, is a natural resource that should be available and equitably accessible to all. And, like clean water, it should be meticulously protected and preserved for the public good.

For the past five years, I have been on a quest for answers. In the medical world, "letdown" refers to the letdown reflex, triggered by the hormone oxytocin, which causes tiny muscle cells within the breasts to contract and squeeze milk down the milk ducts toward the nipples. For a breastfeeding mother, the letdown is a highly anticipated moment. It is a tingly feeling, possibly painful or even arousing in some women, but it is also a comforting body signal that your milk is flowing to your baby. It is the confirmation that you are fulfilling your biological norm.

For the purposes of this book, it refers to the unseen commercial and social underpinnings that leave women frustrated and confused from the early days of motherhood, battling in so-called "mommy wars" and caught between science wars. Falling back on my journalistic training, I've delved into fields as varied as pediatrics, sociology, history, feminism, economics, and pop culture to better understand the social history and modern influences—some subtle, some blatant—that affect women as infant-feeding decision makers every day. I have visited doctors' offices, hospitals, childbirth educators, and corporate offices. I am less interested in the mechanics of letdown within us—I am not a physician or lactation specialist—than I am with the letdown around us. The mother-child dyad is the most basic yet significant biological unit of humankind, and if something is occurring to contaminate that relationship, on either side, whether that is by well-meaning activists or deep-pocketed drug companies, then it must be thoroughly examined. The outcome has a profound effect on the whole world from the economics of squandering an irreplaceable resource to the personal and societal costs of compromised infant and maternal health outcomes.

Most important, I wanted to know what we can do structurally as a society and collectively as womankind to ensure that fewer and fewer of us find ourselves speeding down that highway in the years to come.

This is what I learned.

1

Doctor Who? The Medical Field's Influence on Mothers

We have not lost faith, but we have transferred it from God to the medical profession.

—GEORGE BERNARD SHAW

I distinctly remember my anxiousness as a new mother just before a pediatrician visit. The visit starts with the inevitable weigh-in and then the height and head circumference, followed by a breakdown of where my daughter sized up on the chart compared with other babies. In our comparison-prone world, growth charts and growth percentiles are like SAT scores for babies. This is how we judge them—by weight gain. Growth percentiles rank your child based on what percent of the reference population your child would equal or exceed. For example, on the weight-for-age growth charts, a two-month-old girl whose weight is at the twenty-fifth percentile weighs the same or more than 25 percent of the reference population of two-month-old girls, and weighs less than 75 percent of the two-month-old girls in the reference population. They are the most commonly used clinical indicator for assessing the size and growth patterns of individual children in the United States. The problem is, the comparison of baby growth becomes, by extension, a comparison of parenting success and then a competitive sport. Having a baby in a high percentile for growth becomes a mommy bragging right—"My Johnny is in the ninety-fifth percentile"—statistical proof positive that you are doing a good job.

If the anxiety of the weigh-in and the peer pressure for big percentile numbers wasn't enough, I had my own fears. From the very beginning of breastfeeding, I worried if my child was getting enough food. Yes, medical experts tell you if you count five to six wet disposable diapers per day and two to five bowel movements every twenty-four hours with the fastidiousness of a city health inspector, then all is well. But still you wonder. You worry. Not to mention that as superachiever moms raised on test scores, GPAs, performance reviews and living in a "supersize" world, we crave high numbers. We want big. Our society sees plump babies as a sign of good mothering. And, let's face it, we want to boast. As the pediatrician placed my baby on the scale, I couldn't help holding my breath and bracing myself just a little.

So you can imagine the blow to the gut when, after two months of feeling like I had finally nailed the breastfeeding thing, my pediatrician said that my daughter's weight was slightly below average and suggested that I might need to supplement with formula if things weren't ticking upward in two weeks. I was heartbroken. Exclusive breastfeeding for six months was my personal goal, and I didn't want to supplement. She said that my milk supply may be dwindling and that this was very common with women. She told me that I shouldn't feel bad if I needed to add formula and that I had "done well."

What she didn't tell me was that the chart that she was using to gauge my child's growth progress was based on an outdated sample of babies who weren't being fed the way my baby was being fed. That's because until 2006, the standard infant growth charts in the United States were based on a sample of formula-fed infants. In 1977 the National Center for Health Statistics (NCHS), which became part of the CDC in 1987, published a set of growth charts based on the Fels Longitudinal Growth Study. These charts eventually became the standard U.S. growth charts and were later used by the World Health Organization and others to develop global growth curves for infants. The U.S. growth charts became the model for the world. The Fels study, however, was based on a sample of formula-fed Caucasian babies born between 1929 and 1975 in Ohio—infants who weren't even being fed according to the globally recommended infant nutrition standard: breast milk. These babies started solid foods before four months and were being measured every three months, which researchers later realized is too long of an interval for gauging the rapid growth periods during infancy. In addition, relying on a sample of infants from one racial, socioeconomic, and geographic background over a short period of time wasn't ideal for measuring a general infant population. So while pediatricians and health officials were promoting breastfeeding as the best nutrition, they were also comparing all babies to formula-fed babies. We now know that breastfed babies and formula-fed babies grow differently. This important fact was missing from the growth charts being used all over the world prior to 2006.

This isn't a small matter. For over two decades, many

governmental and United Nations agencies used the data collected from physicians based on these growth charts to measure the general health and well-being of national populations. That information, in turn, was used to set global infant health policies, determine stages for interventions, and monitor the effectiveness of the recommendations. Growth charts are the core tool of the pediatrician. They are used to determine the degree to which the physiological needs for growth and development are being met during infancy and childhood and to assess a child's nutritional status. Yet generations of mothers and babies were incorrectly subjected to the bottle-based growth charts. Many breastfed infants were misdiagnosed with a failure to thrive and given formula based on these growth charts, causing needless distress to their mothers. I know. I was one of them.

At the same time, inadequate infant growth has been one of the biggest sources of profit for the infant formula industry. One of formula makers' most consistent marketing messages has been that when mother's milk is insufficient, then infant formula is there to ensure optimum growth and wellness. That eventuality could be nearly guaranteed when breastfed babies were measured against charts contradicting their normal growth pattern. It is no wonder that infant formula companies have freely given away growth charts to physicians as promotional material for years. It is a mighty sheet of paper with the power to direct medical advice on infant nutrition and either bolster formula sales or support breastfeeding worldwide. Growth charts are a really big deal.

And for decades they were wrong. It wasn't until the early 1990s that researchers began to document the different growth patterns of breastfed babies and formula-fed babies. Studies show that breastfed babies grow faster during the first few months of life and then tend to "lean out" from month 3 to month 12 when compared with formula-fed babies. Then researchers set out to find if this should be classified as some sort of "faltering" or a normal outcome of breastfeeding even in optimal conditions. One key study by DARLING (Davis Area Research on Lactation, Infant Nutrition and Growth), published in *The Journal of Pediatrics* in 1991, found that the slower growth of breastfed infants did not cause negative consequences for activity level, time spent sleeping, or achievement of developmental milestones. The report concluded, "infants with slower growth velocity were just as active and were ill no more often in subsequent months than infants who were growing more rapidly." Basically, the slower-growing breastfed babies were just fine.

It wasn't until 2006 (six years after I received my supplementation recommendation) that the World Health Organization released its own growth curve charts, using breastfed babies as the standard for growth, changing our understanding of the differences of how breastfed and formula-fed babies grow. The WHO charts were created from a sample of nearly nine thousand babies who were exclusively or near exclusively breastfed for the first six months. The charts established the breastfed child as the normative model for growth and development around the world. Applying them to formula-fed babies can serve as an early warning to doctors if a formula-fed baby is experiencing excessive weight gain and is therefore at greater risk of being overweight or obesity. "Arguably, the current obesity epidemic in many developed countries

would have been detectable earlier if a prescriptive international standard would have been available 20 years ago,"
the WHO admits, acknowledging the role of two decades of
inaccurate growth charts in the course of childhood health.
All over the world, babies were misclassified as underweight
and given infant formula, which is more calorie-dense. The
higher fat content of formula and the propensity to overfeed
when using a bottle has been linked to higher rates of childhood obesity. Infant formula also contains unhealthy sugars,
some of which have been banned in Europe because of their
known link to childhood obesity.

But getting to the critical and yet basic point of having a
valid growth chart that works for all babies and is based on
the diet that public health experts unanimously agree is best
has taken over twenty years. It took less time to put a man
on the moon. The Panama Canal was constructed in ten years.
How did this happen? Child nutrition researchers, who as a
group have been heavily funded by infant formula companies,
accepted formula feeding as the norm for their studies. Physicians, who have historically had a financial relationship
with infant formula companies, relied on researchers for information about how breastfed babies grew. And institutions
responsible for setting guidelines to ensure the health of infants around the world relied, in turn, on those two entities
for data and recommendations.

· · ·

Thirty-two. That's the number of seconds it took for me to
encounter the infant formula marketing at a pediatrician's

office on the outskirts of New York City. I walked about ten feet from the office door to the reception desk and, at the check-in window, I picked up a pen and there it was—the words ROSS LABS emblazoned on one side of the pen and a Rosco teddy bear on the other side. The clipboard matched. That day, I was on a reconnaissance mission—visiting various pediatrician and ob-gyn offices in and around New York City to see how long it would take from the moment I entered the office door before I met infant formula marketing—along with the implied message that infant formula is doctor-approved.

My expedition took me to neighborhoods like the Upper East Side, where there were very few traces of infant formula marketing in the waiting or examining rooms, to some forty miles east to the suburbs of Long Island where, infant formula marketing was even more present in ob-gyn offices than in pediatrician offices. All in all, I visited some thirty offices over the span of my "mission," and I only found one physician with absolutely no visible marketing materials in the office or examining room representing the formula brand or the pharmaceutical company that manufactures it. Only one doctor out of thirty who did not give out magazines or giveaway packs full of infant formula coupons and pamphlets to expecting mothers.

Every year Perrigo Nutritionals, makers of Store Brand Formula, conducts a nationwide "Pulse of Pediatricians" survey—conducted by SERMO, the largest online network for physicians. In their most recent findings, 59 percent of pediatricians reported distributing infant formula samples in their offices—despite the fact that the American Academy of Pediatrics adopted a resolution in 2012 advising pediatricians to stop displaying infant formula marketing materials in their offices and clinics.

The participation of physicians' offices in formula marketing programs, from logo-laden growth charts to formula coupons and freebies, has a strong correlation with breastfeeding outcomes. A 2000 study published in *Obstetrics and Gynecology* showed that mothers who receive formula marketing at the ob-gyn's office have stunted breastfeeding experiences. The randomized, controlled trial of more than five hundred mothers looked at the impact of promotional materials on the first prenatal visit. Mothers received either a formula-company-sponsored information pack on infant feeding or a noncommercial pack. The results showed that among mothers who were uncertain about their plans to breastfeed, those who received the formula marketing packet were 1.7 times more likely to stop breastfeeding before two weeks than those who received the noncommercial information. The study concluded that this was "compelling evidence that obstetric care providers should not participate in formula marketing programs."

Obstetricians and pediatricians exert a powerful influence on women not just because they passively display waiting room materials and give away freebies but because of what they actively say about breastfeeding. In a study of obstetricians and patients at a multispecialty group practice in Massachusetts, just 8 percent of physicians felt their advice on whether and how long to breastfeed was important, but more than one-third of mothers reported that their provider's advice on these topics was very important. This study also found that patient perception of clinicians' opinions is directly correlated with breastfeeding duration. In looking at breastfeeding prevalence at six weeks postpartum, researchers found that 70 percent of women who thought their physician favored breastfeeding were still breastfeeding compared with 54 percent of those who thought their physician had no preference.

Here's what we know thus far: Doctors may not think that mothers are influenced by what they give away or which infant feeding method they support, but mothers are. Their behavior reflects it and that behavior affects infant health and maternal health. In the Store Brand Formula survey, 97 percent of pediatricians said questions about feeding are the most frequently asked category for new parents, with pooping and sleeping coming in second and third place.

If so many parents are asking about feeding, shouldn't pediatricians be the most knowledgeable on all the options, starting with the optimal nutrition as recommended by the American Academy of Pediatrics? And shouldn't the AAP, representing over 64,000 pediatricians and pediatric specialists, be leading the charge for breastfeeding? Instead of being the seemingly strongest and most natural ally, the AAP continues to be heavily supported by infant formula donations, raising questions about its own bias in the infant feeding information it provides to parents. Formula manufacturers have donated $1 million annually to the AAP in the form of a renewable grant that had already netted the AAP $8 million by 1995. The formula industry also contributed at least $3 million toward the building costs of the AAP headquarters. AAP's "Friends of Children Fund" (FCF) is a corporate donor fund used to support "high priority activities" and generate new knowledge about how to care for your children, according to AAP's Web site. In return for a donation, members receive "significant acknowledgment in several AAP publications visible to our 60,000 members," the Web site says. Yet, 89 percent of the top donors—those giving $50,000 or more annually—are infant formula or pharmaceutical companies, including Mead Johnson, Nestlé, Perrigo Nutritionals, Pfizer, and Sanofi Pasteur, one of the largest companies in the world devoted entirely to vaccines. The potential conflicts of interest for parents to receive truly unbiased information from the AAP seem hard to ignore.

Medical schools also play a part. What do doctors learn about breastfeeding in medical school? "Not much," said my current pediatrician. "There was about a day or so on the medical evidence on the benefits of breastfeeding, but nothing about medical problems related to lactation or the science of what's happening in the breast at the anatomical level," he said. Most medical schools don't have any meaningful breastfeeding curriculum that includes in-depth training on the mechanics of breastfeeding, how to identify and treat lactation problems, and how breastfed babies grow and develop. Many of those teaching at medical schools are of the generation that were trained at a time when science aimed to bring better living and the chemistry behind infant formula was thought to trump breast milk. The message at many medical schools is that understanding breastfeeding is not in a physician's job description. In fact, lactation holds the dubious distinction of being the only bodily function for which modern medicine has virtually no training or knowledge. Doctors know how to treat and prescribe for erectile dysfunction, but lactation dysfunction doesn't even exist as a diagnosis. Nevertheless, where medical schools have failed to educate, infant formula companies have been more than happy to fill the gap. In the absence of independent medical training, doctors and mothers alike have relied on the commercial industry—the one supplying and profiting from the substitute product—to provide so-called unbiased education and guidance. Every year, the Abbott Nutrition Institute hosts conferences to "educate" thousands of physicians and nurses on infant nutrition. This is like going to a Toyota car dealer to learn about the benefits of a Buick. Or imagine thousands of licensed dieticians being trained at a McDonald's Nutrition Institute.

Women can't be supported by doctors who themselves need support in receiving independent breastfeeding education. And so a vicious cycle begins. Doctors don't talk much about breastfeeding because they (still) don't know much about breastfeeding. But not talking about breastfeeding leaves mothers with a perception that their physician is not wholly supportive, which influences their feeding behavior. In turn, mothers likely won't talk much about breastfeeding to a doctor they sense isn't supportive of breastfeeding. In the end, nobody is talking about breastfeeding.

But what if we broke the silence? What if physicians were able to admit that they don't know much about breastfeeding although they should and then we actually do something about it? Researchers at the Robert Wood Johnson Medical School set to find out. Their study, published in the journal *Pediatrics,* found that when residency programs implemented a breastfeeding curriculum for interns in pediatrics, family medicine, and obstetrics and gynecology, it improved the knowledge, practice patterns, and confidence in breastfeeding management of the residents. The curriculum included formal interactive teaching sessions, discussion of breastfeeding issues on daily clinical rounds, and patient visits with lactation support personnel. Hospitals that implemented the curriculum found that mothers were more likely to still be exclusively breastfeeding six months after discharge.

That's good news. So is the success of the Academy of Breastfeeding Medicine, an international organization of multispecialty physicians who support lactation science and practice. ABM, founded in 1994, has worked to educate more doctors on breastfeeding, to ensure that lactation questions are included on certain licensure examinations, and to help medical schools improve breastfeeding curricula. ABM's signature one-day professional course, "What Every Physician Needs to Know About Breastfeeding," has been offered at the annual conference and in select cities nationwide. But the overall response from physicians for a physician-led organization to offer evidenced-based breastfeeding education has been tepid, to say the least. ABM hoped to expand course availability by offering it to more cities as a video presentation, but ABM Executive Director Karla Shepard Grubinger said in an interview that the expansion pilot met with mixed success due to varying levels of local leadership and interest in the issue. While the ABM claims 650 members in 2016 from more than fifty countries, there are more than 58,000 general pediatricians in the United States alone, according to the American Medical Association's most recent data. That means about 1 percent of the total number of general pediatricians are actively involved in the organization specifically designed to improve their knowledge of breastfeeding—a top area of questioning from parents. An additional 4,322 physicians were trained jointly in internal medicine–pediatrics, and 19,091 as pediatric subspecialists. On the obstetric side, there are more than 52,000 ob-gyns in the United States, according to recent research by the Vimo Research Group. With a conservative estimate of a combined total of more than 100,000 ob-gyns and pediatricians in the United States alone, and a representation of 650 ABM members *internationally,* if membership in this group is any indication, the physicians primarily responsible for infant feeding discussion and monitoring seem to have a long way to go to make a strong stand for breastfeeding. If breast milk is medically best, then why aren't more of the medical professionals responsible for our births and our babies more actively seeking out education and support so mothers can perform breastfeeding well?

How Did We Get Here?

To fully understand how women came to be so greatly influenced by both the action and inaction of obstetricians and pediatricians requires looking at how money, commerce, and even women themselves conspired to change our relationship to pediatricians and obstetricians. But first, a brief history lesson. For centuries, birthing and infant feeding were women's domain, supervised by nurses and midwives. Birthing was not considered an event requiring constant medical supervision. Obstetricians were jokingly referred to as doctors for "standing by." Pediatricians were in a similar situation. "Treating only children seemed de facto evidence of incompetence," writes sociologist Jacqueline Wolf. "When seeking a physician for a child, parents judged doctors' competence by their ability to heal adults. Medical professionals and laypeople alike consequently scorned pediatricians as 'baby doctors.'"

Mothers breastfed for as long as their babies needed their milk. And when a mother died in childbirth or in the rare instance that breastfeeding was not possible, families hired a wet nurse or they relied on a kind lactating neighbor to feed the baby. However, starting with World War I, family patterns and working habits changed. Women entered the workforce in record numbers. With mothers away from their babies for many hours of the day, artificial milk feeding increased. But without proper pasteurization and refrigeration, homemade human milk substitutes and inadequate sanitation led to gastrointestinal ailments and skyrocketing infant death rates. As municipalities began compiling vital statistics, the high rates of infant mortality became a glaring public health problem that needed to be fixed.

As frequent witnesses to the gruesome deaths of infants from diarrhea caused by being artificially fed, pediatricians in the nineteenth century strongly advocated breastfeeding but also worked to secure the health of artificially fed babies by making breast milk substitutes safer. In addition to their work trying to "humanize" cows' milk, pediatricians inspected dairy farms, lobbied municipal and state governments to pass pure milk laws, and distributed free pasteurized milk in urban neighborhoods. Pediatricians led the charge for milk reform. They spearheaded efforts to impose strict standards on the dairy industry and began to create "scientific" nonmilk substitutes so mothers could avoid the problems of unrefrigerated milk. In fact, the original members of the American Pediatric Society came together in 1888 with the sole mission of applying scientific medicine to artificially fed infants. Creating a replacement for mother's milk was the foundation of the pediatric field.

In the 1890s, the Harvard pediatrician Thomas Rotch used mathematical formulas to instruct chemists how to alter the percentages of fat, protein, and milk sugar in cows' milk according to the needs of a particular baby. This is where the word "formula" came from. These "formulas" incorporated variables such as the baby's weight, energy level, physical ailment, and the smell, color, and texture of the baby's stools. Rotch believed that even minute changes in percentages were significant to the digestion by the infant. The mother had to return every few weeks to have her baby's formula adjusted. The process had the allure of scientific complexity, as each prescription-based "formula" was designed specifically for the needs of that individual infant.

The tide had turned for the pediatric industry—instead of being vilified and viewed as an unnecessary specialty, mothers now considered a pediatrician indispensable. Even breastfed babies were thought to need medical supervision since lactation appeared to be an unreliable body function.

In focusing on the needs of the rich, pediatricians saw the potential to gain respectability and make money. At the time, much of pediatric training centered on the intricacies of formula writing. But the custom-made formula turned out to be impractical, and, as the number of infants put on formula increased, individualizing prescriptions became too inconvenient and costly. In addition, the whole middle market of lower- and middle-class families, who could not afford private physician formulations, was being priced out of the physicians' services.

As the pediatricians focused on the higher-end market, some of the first commercially made infant foods began to hit the stores. Nestlé Milk Food and Horlick's Malted Milk were widely advertised in newspapers and magazines and were easier to prepare than the pediatricians' complicated formulas, as they only needed to be mixed with hot water. As mothers purchased more ready-made milks, repeated doctor visits became unnecessary, and doctors in private practice saw a loss of income. As it turns out, commercial interests were smart to bank on the middle market. But doctors felt cut out of the deal, since they were the first to legitimize formula creation.

This was about power, not babies. It also meant the loss of prestige for pediatricians, who didn't seem as critical to the infant-feeding equation when mothers could make substitute milk without the help of a doctor. In 1893, Dr. Rotch wrote: "The proper authority for establishing rules for substitute feeding should emanate from the medical profession, and not from non-medical capitalists. Yet when we study the history of substitute feeding as it is represented all over the world, the part which the family physician plays, in comparison with numberless patent and proprietary foods administered by the nurses, is a humiliating one, and one which should no longer be tolerated." Doctors wanted to assert their dominance over infant feeding decisions. Meanwhile, public health officials continued to promote breastfeeding as the best alternative to the dirty and deadly cows' milk. But by the mid-1920s, efforts to clean up the dairy industry were successful and many of the most egregious problems associated with substituting cows' milk for human milk had dissipated. With the advent of pasteurization, refrigeration, and the bottling and sealing of milk, infant deaths from diarrhea decreased 84 percent in Chicago alone. It was presumed that cleaner food laws along with the scientific advances of formula put artificial milk on par with breastfeeding. Doctors hailed the cow as "the foster mother of the human race." How children would fare under this "foster care" system was yet to be fully considered.

Meanwhile, the matter of whether medical authorities or commercial entities would drive infant feeding decision making was still unresolved. Manufacturers realized that doctors were more advantageous to their commercial interests as friends and not foes. Physicians realized that they needed to be involved with the mass distribution of artificial milk or miss out on the financial benefits of the work they started. An unholy alliance was formed. And strategic steps were taken to deliberately push mothers out of the process. One step was the mass production and widespread distribution of artificial milks—but with no directions on the package. The instructions simply advised consumers to consult their doctors before using the product. The information was that these commercial foods were dangerous if used without physician instruction, yet distribution was not restricted or controlled. The message sent to mothers was that everything would be fine, if you just went to your doctor first for his direction. In 1923 Mead Johnson, maker of Enfamil, boasted in a corporate document that their "ethical" marketing policy was "responsible in large measure for the advancement of the profession of pediatrics in this country because it brought control of infant feeding under the direction of the medical profession."

The collusion between infant formula manufacturers grew deep. The formula makers used medical doctors for testimonials. Several manufacturers were owned by doctors and pharmacists. They wanted doctors to sanction their products, while doctors wanted to retain control over the distribution of formula and share in the profits from this new market.

With so much riding on doctors, the infant formula makers realized they were a more important target audience than mothers themselves. When the first commercial infant formula was introduced to the United States in the late 1860s, manufacturers advertised their new product directly to consumers in women's magazines. Advertisements implied that babies needed more than just breast milk to achieve optimal health and nourishment, and they emphasized how closely formula approximated breast milk's chemical composition. As is still done today, formula companies attracted new customers with free samples and information on infant feeding and care.

The combination of skillful marketing and promotion efforts combined with physician promotion succeeded in giving artificial feeding an aura of medical legitimacy. Parents grew to believe that a commercial product could be as good as, or better than, the real thing. By the end of World War II, bottle feeding had become the standard method of infant feeding in the United States and, to a lesser extent, in Europe as well. The authors of a 1991 Scandinavian study reviewing hospital procedures surrounding breastfeeding said, "The interference of the medical profession in the twentieth century in the feeding of healthy, term infants may in the future be regarded as a puzzling, uncontrolled, less than well-founded medical experiment."

The Impact of Time

Meanwhile, industrialization brought another revolution to America—mechanization of time. Scheduling became vital to factories and railroads. For much of middle America—used to structuring their lives around natural events like sunrise and sunset—it was an incredible shift to adjust their lives to a mechanical clock. So that babies adapted to this cultural development from birth, most of the infant care manuals of that time instructed mothers to care for infants according to the clock.

Following the advice of the top medical experts of the time, the U.S. Children's Bureau produced a series of informational pamphlets for breastfeeding in the 1910s that included various suggestions and instructions. Included among the recommendations were that to breastfeed successfully a mother must sleep eight hours a night, nap midday, exercise, take fresh air for an hour each morning and evening, and nurse on a strict schedule. Feeding advice was also culturally biased: the nursing mother was instructed to eat a "bland" American diet and to keep a physical distance from her baby—ideas that were antithetical to many immigrant cultures, who ate spicy foods and often slept with their children. The advice offered from physicians also emphasized the need to avoid being nervous, or overcome with "fright, fatigue, grief or passion." This type of physician advice went beyond helping a mother with the mechanics of nursing or suggesting time intervals for feeding and was about regulating women—their emotions, their cultural practices, their diet, and their bodies. These types of strict guidelines put pressure on women and succeeded in sabotaging confidence in breastfeeding.

Lactation is a self-limiting condition. Less breastfeeding meant less breast milk production. Less milk production meant more concerns about insufficient supply. At the time, doctors didn't understand lactation enough to connect the dots between the stringent guidelines and the surge in insufficient milk. They had other theories, including assertions that "over-civilization" forced women to live unnatural lives and, therefore, their bodies were unable to perform natural functions like lactation. With women increasingly unable to breastfeed, pediatricians became even more in control of perfecting a replacement for human milk. Women became more dependent on medical professionals for information just as physicians' knowledge of the science of lactation decreased. They did not know about lactation but about the science behind the formulas their colleagues helped create. Both mothers and doctors had forgotten the importance of human milk. Although in the past mothers consulted other mothers, clergy, kin, manuals, magazines and, as a last resort, physicians, by the early twentieth century the physician's word was law.

From the early twentieth century until the late 1980s, most formula companies abandoned direct-to-consumer advertising and used the medical community as their sole advertising vehicle. Why bother talking to mothers when doctors made the nutrition decisions for their babies? By making sure their products directed women back to the doctor for guidance, the infant formula makers provided a steady flow of income for the physicians. They further engendered physicians' goodwill by sponsoring scientific conferences and research on infant nutrition. Doctors retained their role as the undisputed advisors on infant health and feeding, despite their limited medical knowledge on lactation, while simultaneously providing product referrals for formula purchase and serving as a credible advertising source.

At the same time, big changes in how women gave birth were taking place, which would influence how mothers fed. Remember, for years birth was considered a normal physiologic process; women did not need a doctor with special skills in order to give birth. Delivering babies was viewed as the work of midwives. Obstetricians were laughed at by other doctors for doing "nothing." Giving birth may not always require a doctor, but there is pain. As the women's rights movement picked up steam, in 1913 two wealthy American women took up the cause of urging other women around the country to battle for their right to a painless childbirth, in the form of Twilight Sleep—a way of giving birth in a heavily sedated state that had been developed in Germany. A woman simply woke to a baby—with no memory of the labor of birth. Two female reporters from *McClure's Magazine* in New York, who had been previously denied interviews by German doctors, hatched an undercover plan to send a pregnant friend to Freiburg, Germany, to have a Twilight Sleep birth. The women, staunch feminists, planned to make Americans aware of this "miracle" discovery. The three women decided to liberate American women through Twilight Sleep, urging them to rise up against the oppression of medical men. The 1914 article sparked a call to action among feminists, making the right to a painless birth a key women's rights issue. Feminists saw maternal health care as a significant area that needed improvements. The only problem was that feminists focused on the pain and discomfort of the labor of childbirth. In their minds, the pain was the problem, and freeing women from pain meant liberation from men. Among anti-feminists, the thought was that Twilight Sleep would encourage upper-class women to have more babies. But the pain of laboring was nothing compared with the so-called solution. The sedation of Twilight Sleep was created by two powerful drugs, morphine and scopolamine, which didn't suppress pain but created retroactive memory loss with psychotic side effects. Yes, women woke up with a baby and no memory of the pain of childbirth. But the comfort came at a cost. They also did not remember the psychotic fits and thrashing that were common with these drugs, causing injuries to their heads. So their heads were wrapped with blankets or towels to cushion the blows. The drugs caused women to attempt to claw at the walls or their medical providers, so they were put in straightjackets or their wrists were strapped to the beds. Then, so that they would not fall out of bed, they were put in "labor cribs" and were allowed to go into labor, screaming, tied down, blinded and bound—often in their own urine and feces, and sometimes for days on end, until it was time to give birth. The women had no memory of this. Husbands were not allowed in to see their wives during this era so they didn't know what was happening. Yet, when the woman awoke, everyone was happy. With the advent of Twilight Sleep, the practice of obstetrics suddenly became complex. Every woman desiring Twilight

Sleep had to be hospitalized, anesthetized for days, and monitored closely by a doctor in order to give birth. This was a dramatic shift: birth went from being primarily an event with minimal medical intervention to an event that required days of medical and pharmaceutical supervision. The job of delivering healthy babies shifted to the job of removing pain, avoiding death from drug-related complications, and keeping visible bruises to a minimum. Instead of midwives or regular obstetricians, women needed specialized doctors in order to have the birth experience they wanted. Despite doctors' antipathy toward Twilight Sleep and their outrage at women's demands, Twilight Sleep was an avenue for the attention and respect that previously eluded obstetricians.

Most U.S. doctors were anti–Twilight Sleep and angry at the avalanche of demand from women's magazines like *McClure's*, *Reader's Digest,* and *Ladies' Home Journal.* While the media raved, the 1914 *New York Medical Journal* warned that doctors were being rushed into "indiscriminate administration" of a procedure "tested and found wanting." But the speed of demand was unstoppable, as the popular media simultaneously presented only huge local successes. Between 1914 and 1945, America became a Twilight nation. Movies such as *Science's Greatest Triumph* were shown throughout the U.S. and the National Twilight Sleep Association was formed. With enormous public pressure and potential loss of clients who were switching to doctors offering the "Freiburg Miracle," hospitals from New York to San Francisco began scrambling together Twilight Sleep units. The pressure continued until one of the movement's staunchest advocates, who organized rallies for the procedure, died during her Twilight Sleep childbirth.

Although there had been numerous women who had died under Twilight Sleep, the woman, Frances Carmody, was the wife of a Brooklyn lawyer. Her husband and her obstetrician assured everyone that her death had nothing to do with Twilight Sleep. But with a key organizer of Twilight Sleep dead, likely because of the procedure itself, support for it began to fall apart.

The organized crusade for Twilight Sleep was relatively short, but the damage to women and the birth process was done. The change in how obstetricians were perceived, how they treated the birth process, and how American women experienced birth were dramatic. It accelerated the trend to hospital birth, where, with newly elevated status, doctors gained control of the birthing room. Ironically, women were the catalysts for this change, showing the power of the consumer to shape medical practice. Doctors also saw the profitable side of birthing, and, even though Twilight Sleep wasn't the answer, they continued to look for safer ways to have a medicated birth—from ether to epidurals. The desire for painless childbirth continued and led to more assembly-line, hospital-based programs of heavy sedation. This created a symbiotic relationship between the medical field and the pharmaceutical industry, which supplied the sedatives.

As births moved from the home to the hospital, something else happened—the practice and sensibility of obstetricians changed. Instead of sitting at a woman's beside in her home for hours, they were shuttling between patients in a hospital, moving one along to deal with the next. They lost familiarity with and concern for the rhythms and nuances of labor and the needs of the mother. Prior to this cultural shift, comfort and reassurance was often the most necessary or only "treatment" needed during birth. Now medical interventions were created to interfere with a natural process. Chemically inducing labor, heavily drugging laboring women, and separating mothers and newborns became commonplace—all of these are counterproductive to breastfeeding. In 1971, the year I was born, only 24.7 percent of babies were ever breastfed.

Even this brief look into the development of the practices of the physicians who guide us through pregnancy, birth, and infant health shows the close influence of consumer demands and commercial interests regardless of health implications. Pediatrics and obstetrics grew larger and more popular at the expense of women. As pediatrics cozied up to the infant formula industry, obstetricians began to rely on pharmaceuticals to enhance credibility. So the two medical practices that women rely on at one of their most vulnerable periods have earned their reputation by presuming the female reproductive system is so wrought with problems it needs constant monitoring, sedatives, and frequent medical intervention. In 1996, the C-section rate in the U.S. was 21 percent; in 2015 it was 32.7 percent, a 53 percent increase well above the "medically necessary" target of 10–15 percent WHO recommends. The disturbing trend of a male-dominated field controlling where and how women give birth and how women feed should concern all women. How these practices impact lactation were never considered. As lactation became the least appreciated and least understood reproductive function by the very physicians who should've understood it best, it became the function most dispensable, the easiest to cast aside. Human milk substitutes, however, became indispensable. And therefore, unbelievably profitable.

2

Milk Money: The Big Business of Bodies, Breasts, and Babies

Soda companies, infant formula makers—these are not so-cial service agencies. They are businesses whose primary job is to produce dividends for investors. Once that is under-stood, corporate marketing becomes understandable.

—MARION NESTLE, AUTHOR AND PROFESSOR OF
NUTRITION AT NEW YORK UNIVERSITY

Before there was industrial agriculture, processed foods, McDonald's, high fructose corn syrup, and TV dinners, people ate real food. Those people included infants and tod-dlers. Babies ate breast milk until they moved on to home-made baby foods. If a baby could not be breastfed by its own mother or another mother, he or she was fed breast milk sub-stitutes made according to recipes shared between mothers or published in the common household advice manuals. "If the [cow's] milk cannot be obtained," said Joseph B. Lyman and Laura E. Lyman, in their *Philosophy of House-Keeping* (1869), "water in which cracker or good wheat bread has been soaked with sugar added to it is very nutritive and di-gestible." In the 1920s and 1930s, evaporated milk became widely available at low prices, evolving into the number one ingredient in homemade infant formula. While crackers and evaporated milk weren't ideal food options for infants—and many babies who ate those substitutes developed diet-related illnesses—they were used as emergency solutions for the rare occurrences when a baby couldn't be breastfed.

What began as a homemade product used rarely, for pre-term infants who were too ill to nurse or when a mother's milk was not available, grew into a mass-produced, worldwide product meant to replace mother's milk even when it was available. By the end of World War II, bottle feeding had become the standard method of infant feeding in the United States and, to a lesser extent, in Europe as well. The shift from occasional use of formula to the ubiquitous use of formula was driven by the profit-making potential of infant formula, not the nutritional needs of babies. The important shift from thinking of formula as a second-rate, backup product that should be used only when needed to considering it on par with mother's milk and using it as the first option forever changed infant feeding patterns across the globe—and, therefore, our collective health trajectory.

All of the science says that a baby's best interests are met when they receive the nutritional, developmental, and immunological benefits of breastfeeding. On the other hand, the goal of the formula industry and its bumper crop of ancillary bottle-feeding products is to maximize market size by increasing the number of mothers who buy these products and the length of time they use them. Infant formulas are the only source of nutrition for many infants during the first months of life. They are critical to infant health since they must safely support proper growth and development during a period when the consequences of inadequate nutrition are most severe. Ultimately, public health and private profit are at odds because the formula industry profits from the failure of breastfeeding. And the failure of breastfeeding among a generation of women is a fatal blow to the health and wellness of future generations.

Few products other than infant formula undermine a normal bodily function in order to create a physical need for a commercial product in order to replace it. Formula samples cause the mother to need formula: once formula feeding starts, the lactation process, which slows with less frequent nursing, actually begins to dry up. When the free sample of formula is used, and there has been less nursing at the breast, there is an actual need to buy more formula.

It's not an accident that big business is interested in what we eat on the very first day of life. The collision of medical needs, parenting trends, and the historical undermining of women provided business and marketing opportunities. By the mid-nineteenth century, formula companies saw a commercial opportunity and seized it. Processed infant food reduced parental anxieties about nutrition (which was fanned by male physicians) and later, offered women entering the workforce the appearance of an irresistible convenience. Manufactured and well-advertised, infant formula was admired by doctors and health professionals and welcomed by mothers. Fueled by changing ideas about infant feeding and a budding advertising industry, infant formula grew in popularity.

Commercially made milk emerged as an ideal industrial product: a standardized creation with predictable tastes, tex-

tures, and qualities. But because formula is easy to mass manufacture doesn't necessarily make it the healthiest option for
babies. Food is programming. What we eat every day, good
and bad, sends messages to our body. That makes our earliest
diet especially critical. Introducing babies to minimally nutritious, calorie-dense products, laden with sugar and salt, lays
the groundwork for a lifetime of overeating processed foods
since our sensory preferences for tastes are developing in
infancy.

· · ·

It's a clear brisk day when I meet with Dr. Julie Mennella of
the Monell Chemical Senses Center, a nonprofit research
center in Philadelphia. Mennella, a biopsychologist and researcher, has produced a large body of work examining the
genetic influences and sensory development of taste preferences in utero and the early months of life. Mennella's work
found that babies born to mothers who eat a diverse and varied diet while pregnant and breastfeeding are more open
to a wide range of flavors. She's also found that babies who
follow that diet after weaning carry those preferences into
childhood and adulthood. Researchers believe that the taste
preferences that develop at crucial periods in infancy have
lasting effects for life and actually predict what they'll eat
later. In fact, changing food preferences beyond toddler-
hood appears to be extremely difficult. "Where you start is
where you end up," Mennella says.

The Monell researchers identified three key periods for
developing taste preferences: in utero; in early infancy, before

three and a half months of age; and at weaning, which makes what the mother eats during pregnancy and breastfeeding critically important. The flavors we are exposed to in mother's milk are the flavors we find acceptable as we grow up. Studies show that breastfed babies are more likely to try new foods later on in life because, unlike formula, which tastes the same every time, breast milk varies daily in flavor and taste. "Infants exposed to a variety of flavors in infancy are more willing to accept a variety of flavors, including flavors that are associated with various vegetables and so forth and that might lead to a healthier eating style later on," says Gary Beauchamp, the director of the Monell Center.

This work has profound implications for understanding how critical early food experiences are to our future health. It also explains why there is profit potential for pharmaceutical companies in determining an infant's diet and future health trajectory. Take sugar intake, for example. Independent laboratory testing has found alarmingly high levels of corn syrup and sugar in popular infant formula brands. The formula companies aren't required by law to disclose sugar levels, but some independent studies have found shocking results. One independent analysis by an NBC news affiliate in Chicago and Deibel Laboratories found as many as 13.5 grams of sugar per serving in some infant formula brands, including Enfamil Premium. That's about the same amount of sugar as an eight-ounce Vitamin Water and about half the sugar in an eight-ounce Red Bull, but a newborn baby is consuming that serving three to six times a day. That amounts to roughly fifty-four grams of sugar per day with only four feedings—almost the same amount of sugar in one twenty-ounce Coke. Imagine giving your newborn a bottle of Coke or two Red Bulls every day. When I eat sugary snacks, I can balance my diet by drinking more water, eating more vegetables later, or consuming less sugar for the rest of the week, but for infants, formula is their sole diet—their only source of nutrition. This makes the ingredients in what they eat every day, several times a day, worthy of even deeper scrutiny. Instead, we have the opposite.

Deibel's analysis found Similac Advance Organic Complete Nutrition to have 3.5 grams per serving of sucrose—the most potent and addictive form of sugar. Because of its potency, sucrose has already been banned from infant formula in Europe in conjunction with antiobesity efforts. The top five ingredients listed for Similac Sensitive Formula for Fussiness and Gas are corn syrup solids, sugar (sucrose), milk protein isolate, high oleic safflower oil, and soy oil. Enfamil's Soy Toddler formula also lists corn syrup solids as the initial ingredient, followed by vegetable oil (palm olein, coconut, soy and high oleic sunflower oils), soy protein isolate and calcium phosphate. These dangerous sugars, including sucrose, remain in infant formula in the United States. The Infant Nutrition Council, the trade association for the infant formula manufacturers, says the ingredients are safe: "All of these carbohydrates have been shown in clinical studies and many years of consumer use to be safe and support normal growth development in infants." Infant formula makers conduct their own research and then, in effect, road test it on babies and wait for adverse results. They are automatically considered safe until proven otherwise. Meanwhile, for years, scientific journals on nutrition, going back to a 1995 study in the

American Journal of Clinical Nutrition, have published ongoing findings linking the consumption of large quantities of sugar and high fructose corn syrup to behavioral disorders such as ADD as well as anxiety, hyperactivity, distractibility, and nighttime insomnia. An infant diet that is high in sugar and corn syrup also increases the risk for a wide spectrum of other health problems ranging from dental cavities to nutritional deficiencies, according to published studies. The American Academy of Pediatrics has published multiple health warnings about the dangers of sugar-sweetened sodas, sports drinks, and fruit juices. In her groundbreaking book *Soda Politics: Taking on Big Soda and Winning,* Marion Nestle, a nutrition professor and founder of the food studies program at New York University, deconstructs the impact of soda drinking on public health. "Soda is sugars, water, and nothing else of redeeming nutritional value. They account for between a third and half of all sugar intake. Substantial research indicates an association between habitual soda drinking and obesity, type 2 diabetes, and other chronic conditions," Nestle noted in an interview. While sodas have come under intense scrutiny for their dangerous sugar content, most parents are unaware of the sugar content of infant formula. The health impact of a generation of infants being fed a high-sugar diet is hard to ignore. According to a 2000 report by the American Diabetes Association, type 2 diabetes, which used to largely affect adults, is the "new epidemic" in the American pediatric population, with a 33 percent increase in incidence and prevalence among young children and adolescents. A decade before the study, this disease was rare in the American youth population. According to a report by Dr. Francine

Ratner Kaufman, much of the increased prevalence is attributed to excess caloric intake and childhood obesity. There is no question that consuming high levels of sugar from birth is woefully dangerous. Yet consumers are unaware of the true content of sugar in formula, and manufacturers are not required by the government to disclose it. In the meantime, formula feeding primes millions of infants for a lifetime of unhealthy taste preferences.

As a result, big pharma is shaping and controlling America's eating habits from birth. That means they ultimately influence everyone's health, priming our population for diet-related diseases, like diabetes. Simultaneously, they are selling the drugs that treat those diseases. Healthy infant nutrition, it turns out, is ultimately a form of preventive medicine, and that is at odds with the profit-driven model of big pharma. They will make less money down the line if people don't need their medications. In other words, it is in their commercial interest to directly and indirectly create the conditions that generate demand for their products in later years. To fully achieve that objective, their work begins at birth, in an all-out profit battle to be every newborn's first food.

An industry accomplishment of this scale is the stuff of business-school case studies. Imagine this MBA project: invent a product that will compete with another product already in worldwide use, a product that is perfectly designed, impossible to replicate, responds directly to the needs of its recipients, is convenient, and mostly enjoyable to use. Then add this humdinger: this product is also free. Not only should your invention compete with this established product (and cost a lot), but it should also push the perfect, established, free product out of the market, making it unnecessary and obsolete. In fact, users of the established product should be ridiculed or treated like weirdos or fanatics. This is the story behind the business of infant formula.

While agribusiness behemoths like Monsanto dominate the commercial food industry with mass-production must-haves such as genetically modified seeds and bovine growth hormones in cows, pharmaceutical companies dominate the market for liquid nutritional supplements and infant formula. Today, infant formula is a global industry with $11 billion in annual sales and represents the largest segment of the baby food market. Wall Street analysts estimate that the total world-wide market for infant formula could reach as high as $80 billion. Therefore, the current estimated world sales of formula of $11 billion represents only 14 percent of the total potential sales. For drug companies, infant formula is the cash cow of pediatric "drugs." No other product has such profit potential and guaranteed supply of potential users. While adult drugs make millions, big pharma doesn't have any incredibly lucrative drugs in the pediatric arena. Many analysts say the market for expensive pediatric ADHD drugs has peaked with more than 4.5 million children diagnosed. But with infant formula, the potential market is replenished daily, justifying an annual marketing budget of $500 million to $1 billion.

Two pharma giants, Abbott Laboratories (whose drug portfolio includes Humira for rheumatoid arthritis and the HIV drug, Norvir) and Bristol-Myers Squibb dominate the infant formula industry, creating a virtual oligopoly. In addition to their large stake in Mead Johnson, Bristol-Myers Squibb's portfolio includes the blockbuster drugs Plavix, a blood thinner; and Abilify, for schizophrenia; and Reyataz, for HIV. The largest formula maker, with 50 percent of the market share, is Ross Labs, a unit of Abbott that makes Similac (named for being "similar to lactation") and Isomil, a soy-based formula. Infant formula sales account for up to 50 percent of the total profit of Abbott. Second, with about 35 percent of the market, is Mead Johnson, maker of Enfamil. And while Bristol-Myers Squibb sold Mead Johnson back in 2008 in an initial public offering that raised over $560 million, it still owns over 150 million shares of the company, valued at over $14.5 billion. Carnation, maker of Good Start formula, the third largest player, has been a subsidiary of Nestlé since the Swiss giant purchased it in 1988.

The infant formula business is booming. Companies like Abbott and Mead Johnson can spend $1 billion on marketing or research and development because of the high profit margins that come with mass-producing formula. A Florida attorney general estimated that for every dollar formula companies charge for wholesale baby milk, only 16 cents is spent on production and delivery. That's a huge margin between costs and sales, allowing Mead Johnson to maintain eye-popping profit margins that are over 60 percent. Compare that to the retail behemoth Walmart, whose profit margins are closer to 24 percent. Apple's 2015 profit margin was 39 percent. Infant formula is extremely profitable. In 2015 Mead Johnson reported net sales of $4 billion, while Abbott's sales topped $5 billion for the year. And Abbott Laboratories has been able to post 15 percent profit increases every year for over two decades.

With billions of dollars in sales and double-digit revenue

growth every year, it begs the question of where companies cross the line between making profits and profiteering. How much profit is too much for a company mass-producing an inferior diet for babies? And at what point is what is required to maintain such profit growth unethical? Yes, infant formula is a necessity for the babies who need it, but the economics benefit only infant formula makers. Billions could be saved by families, taxpayers, and corporations by encouraging more breastfeeding. In New York City, ready-to-feed infant formula costs about twenty-one cents per ounce with an average baby consuming twenty-five ounces per day. In one year, that's 9,125 ounces at the price of $1,916 (the actual cost is even higher when you add in bottles, nipples, water, and time spent traveling to and from the store). That's a huge cost to families but a huge windfall for the manufacturers. Those manufacturers are not focused on what's best for babies. They are publicly traded companies with demanding shareholders and earnings-watching Wall Street analysts who want to see continued revenue growth. Satisfying these interests involves employing practices that ultimately mislead women and compromise infant health.

On June 15, 2016, Kasper Jakobsen, the president and CEO of Mead Johnson Nutrition, presented at a Deutsche Bank analyst conference. The opening slide was of a bright-eyed, smiling Asian baby and the Mead Johnson tagline, "Nourishing the Best Start in Life." The tagline itself is telling as the infant formula company uses the language of a "best start" in life, which has been primarily used in reference to breast milk. According to the edited call transcript posted on the company's Web site, Jakobsen spoke about their strong focus on digital and social media and their analytics, particularly their robust database of pregnant women.

Some of you may not be aware that out of all women who give birth in the United States of America, we have the names and addresses of approximately 70 percent of them in advance of them giving birth. So, that's a fantastic asset for the company to be able to interact with consumers at the most critical time when they are thinking . . . "What are we going to do about feeding our child? . . . What questions do we have about feeding methods and problems and how to overcome them?"

Jakobsen does not reveal if women knowingly share their information with infant formula companies or through what mechanism the company receives this information and if there is consent. Jakobsen continued:

I think it's an asset that we've really just begun to leverage and I'm excited about the potential to grow that further. There are all kinds of things that we can do with these digital assets if we begin to think about it in a more entrepreneurial fashion . . . and we don't think about it simply as an add-on to how we do marketing for infant formula . . . but we think in a more entrepreneurial fashion about how we could behave like a start-up.

"Behave like a start-up"? In most business-management literature, behaving like a start-up is synonymous with taking risks, always finding new market opportunities and going for the win, at any cost. Jakobsen also said, "This idea about how do you go about disrupting yourself is increasingly becoming important for companies in the consumer products industry, no matter whether you sell infant formula or you sell beer." I'd like to think the approaches to selling these products—while both damaging to your health—should actually be very, very different.

A year earlier, on February 17, 2015, Jakobsen openly acknowledged exploiting economic and social trends for profit gain in his presentation to the Consumer Analyst Conference.

> The U.S. is an approximately $4 billion [infant formula] market. It's a very large market and I think there were three factors that fueled our growth in the U.S. market in 2014 and then there was one offset. So, let me begin with the offset. . . . [W]e continue to see breastfeeding rates in the U.S. climb through 2014. Now we'll be watching very closely as we go through 2015 to see whether the improvement in unemployment trends will cause this trend to abate somewhat. It's our hope and expectation that that will be the case.

The hope expressed by Mead Johnson's CEO, that the structural barriers that make breastfeeding and employment very difficult for mothers will cause them to abandon breastfeeding in favor of formula feeding, highlights the unethical strategies and trends that infant formula makers exploit for their success. When a CEO directly connects improving employment numbers to less breastfeeding and more formula purchases, then the breastfeeding and work problem is far from resolved. It recognizes that exclusive breastfeeding for any meaningful duration has become the luxury of those not returning to work or those who can employ themselves. It also proves that the formula company has a vested interest in employers and federal policies not allowing more paid time to breastfeed. This borders on the exploitive.

But pays off handsomely for the CEOs. Miles D. White, the CEO of Abbott Labs, maker of Similac, was one of the highest paid CEOs in 2016, earning $19.4 million in total compensation, according to the Equilar/Associated Press S&P 500 CEO Pay Study for 2016. The study said that figure represented a 16 percent increase over his previous year's salary. By way of comparison, Wall Street CEOs, who have some of the highest salaries, saw their pay rise an average of just under 10 percent in 2015. According to the most recent jobs numbers, the wages of the average American worker rose by just 1.6 percent in 2016.

Let's be clear, under our capitalist system, businesses exploit supply shortages, disasters, inefficiencies, and wars all the time. CEOs in the U.S often have fat contracts and even fatter golden parachutes. Companies benefit from unfair incarceration laws. While people died during the Iraq and Afghanistan wars, billions were made by military contractors, construction companies, and ammunition suppliers. But the current war on women and mothers earns its billions at the expense of voiceless babies. And the spectrum of indirect beneficiaries spreads far, including large investment companies, such as The Vanguard Group, a mutual fund giant with over $3 trillion in assets, including billions in employer-sponsored retirement plans. As of March 2016, Vanguard owned more than 96 million shares of Abbott Labs valued at over $4 billion, making it one of the largest shareholders of infant formula stock. Billionaire investing giant Warren Buffett, owns a 25 percent stake (valued at over $22 billion in March 2016) in Kraft Heinz, the huge consumer foods conglomerate that also makes the Nurture brand of infant formula and a variety of baby foods. Nestlé is technically still under an international boycott for its egregious infant formula marketing practices of the past.

To create these mind-blowing returns for shareholders, pharmaceutical companies often use psychological warfare—another profiteering-like tool. To start, they use a common business ploy of creating the appearance of a problem. After all, the most successful products and services are created to solve a problem. For instance, cars were invented to get people from one place to another more quickly. "Problems" are relative. One person's problem may not be that of another. Problems can be personal. Problems can be perceived. The problem of waiting too long for a cab or not having the physical cash to pay for one led to the growth of Uber. Problems can even be manufactured. I did not know that room-temperature baby wipes were a problem until I was being sold a $21.99 wipe warmer. In order for the business of infant feeding to be financially viable, there had to be a problem that can be solved by a commercial product. Years ago, before pasteurization, there was a very real problem: infants who could not be breastfed often died from contaminated milk and unsuitable substitutes. But for the business of infant formula to thrive, sick and orphaned babies could not be the only problem in need of a solution. The business model needed a wider audience for commercial success. Breastfeeding itself needed to be a problem. A woman's lactating breasts needed to be perceived as unreliable, and a mother's milk supply needed to be questioned so that artificial milks could solve the problem.

After casting uncertain lactation as a problem, the formula industry generated profits through fearmongering. One go-to maneuver of the industry is a strategic marketing staple, courtesy of Gene Amdahl, an IBM executive turned multi-million-dollar tech entrepreneur. Amdahl famously coined the term FUD to refer to IBM's killer business tactics. FUD stands for "fear, uncertainty, and doubt"—exactly what IBM salespeople instilled in the minds of potential customers considering other products. The goal was to persuade buyers to be "safe" by buying IBM products rather than to risk a computer crash, virus, or server disruption with a competitor's equipment. After 1991, the term became more generalized to refer to any kind of misinformation used as a competitive weapon. From a strategic marketing perspective, the objective is to amplify your prospective customer's FUD toward your competitor's product and alleviate it for yours.

Infant formula makers have exploited the FUD tactic to market to vulnerable parents for years. Mothers already doubt that they have sufficient milk, and heightening that fear can actually hinder the biological process of breastfeeding. That fear is naturally present. I've said many times that lactation is a self-limiting condition. Fear and anxiety can stifle the let-down reflex and, therefore, lactation, so companies purposefully design marketing strategies to aggravate existing worries about infant feeding. In that way, they actually stymie their greatest competitor—the biological process of lactation and the breastfeeding mother. This practice has been a marketing staple in the formula industry worldwide. As far back as the 1940s, manufacturers of Borden KLIM evaporated milk ran a radio jingle in the Congo that stoked mothers' fears over insufficient milk:

> *The child is going to die*
> *Because the mother's breast has given out*
> *Mama o Mama the child cries*
> *If you want your child to get well*
> *Give it KLIM milk*

In Africa in the 1950s, Nestlé's Lactogen was advertised for "when breast milk fails." Today, the infant formula industry consistently sends the message that breast is best but that, if breastfeeding fails, formula is there. While mentioning that breastfeeding often fails, the formula makers, at the same time, create certainty about their own product, adding ingredients that sound similar to breast milk and touting it as "closest" to mother's milk.

At times, their tactics have included egregious acts explicitly designed to fool mothers, starting with the most vulnerable ones: those in developing countries.

• • •

In the 1960s, the increasing birthrate and rapid urbanization of Third World countries made the developing world a ripe market for infant formula manufacturers. In places like Africa, relatively weak professional and social institutions, fewer legal hurdles to doing business, and understaffed government departments helped create a fertile ground for expansion and unregulated marketing. For mothers in those countries, formula invoked images of modernization and an appealing Western lifestyle. Infant formula companies went as far as employing "milk nurses," women dressed in nurse-like uniforms who distributed formula samples and information to mothers, showing up at their homes unannounced or waiting in clinic lobbies. Women assumed they were medical professionals offering infant nutrition advice when they were actually salespersons there to push a product. Nestlé was considered the most aggressive offender. Its marketing practices in the developing world were exposed in a scathing report in *The New Internationalist* in 1973, called "Babies Mean Business." Nestlé's activities were deemed so egregious that they became the rallying point for the largest-ever international campaign to end the commercial exploitation of infant feeding practices, led by the group Baby Milk Action. Another infant formula brand, Dumex, had milk nurses, who were banned from entering maternity wards directly in Singapore and would instead wait outside the hospital gates to catch new mothers with free samples on their way home, *The New Internationalist* reported. In Jamaica, Bristol-Myers milk nurses allegedly entered public maternity hospitals and copied names and addresses of new mothers in order to visit them at home. These allegations led to a hearing in the U.S. Senate and prompted the World Health Organization to develop an international code of marketing rules. By then, the commercial success was undeniable. By 1980, Nestlé, Unigate, Bristol-Myers, Abbott, Wyeth, Glaxo, and several other formula companies were bringing in multimillion-dollar profits globally for products that, in most instances, the mothers did not need. A Nestlé boycott still exists in some form in several countries today.

From a business perspective, the profiteering was a huge success—especially for Nestlé. In 1977 *Fortune* magazine estimated that Nestlé was the most profitable food company in the world. It dominated the global baby milk market and was also considered the most aggressive promoter of formula feeding. Even when international health advocates, starting in 1974, mounted shareholder resolutions against American companies to curb inappropriate sales practices, particularly in Africa, Nestlé had de facto immunity. Only Swiss nationals could own shares in the company, so U.S. citizens could not use investor influence to push for change. It was virtually untouchable in the United States. By the mid-1970s, over 75 percent of American babies were fed on formula—a historical low for breastfeeding.

• • •

While big business has dominated the market using fear and uncertainty to churn profits, a new crop of smaller businesses is adding another dimension to the scaremongering. The fear of not having enough milk has been coupled with worries about milk quality. One such business is called Happy Vitals, which offers direct-to-consumer breast-milk testing kits that are touted as "easy-to-use" but come with hard-to-swallow prices. According to the Web site, "mothers can learn for the first time about the nutrient makeup of their breast milk, improve their diet and nutrition, and safeguard against exposure to heavy metals and other toxins that are harmful to a child's growth and development." This is classic pandering to a mother's doubts that their milk is not good enough for their baby. You can alleviate your fears, but it will cost you $169.95. That will get you a simple analysis of a sample of breast milk for four key nutrients: glucose, lactose, protein, and fat. For the much larger price tag of $659.95, they will also test for "indicators of immunity": cortisol, IgA antibodies, IgG antibodies, IgM antibodies. Eleven micronutrients: calcium, folate, iron, vitamin D, vitamin A, ferritin, magnesium, phosphorous, sodium, potassium, and vitamin B12. And four heavy metal toxins: arsenic, lead, mercury, and cadmium (based on samples of an infant's hair and nails). These unnecessary kits capitalize on women's fears and confusion around science that makes mothers think their milk may be tainted.

From home kits to mind tricks, focusing on the subliminal works. Drawing on cues from society in general, formula makers also skillfully use the fear of being judged as a "bad" mother to peddle their products. Since breastfeeding is unfairly used as one of the measures of a good or bad mother, companies have leveraged that fear of being judged into a reason to support formula feeding. Women are forced into so-called choices, such as returning to work too soon. When their lactation slows as a result and they turn to formula feeding, they fight back against being judged as "bad" for their decisions. No mother should be judged for the choices she makes or the lack of choices she has concerning working or infant feeding. But women feel a need to defend themselves. And thus ensued the so-called mommy wars—women judging women for choices and, sometimes, things that really aren't choices at all. The mommy wars are leveraged as marketing tools by infant formula makers and other business interests by creating mom types and then pitting one against the other. Each mom type then buys the product associated with her type. For years, minivans were marketed to soccer moms. Creating mom silos works great for marketers. Mead Johnson and Abbott have also plowed millions of dollars into marketing campaigns that co-opt the language of mommy wars and "judgment" just to create more divisions. In 2015 Similac hit the viral mother lode with its "Sisterhood of Motherhood" YouTube video commercial. The opening scene shows a series of mom stereotypes—from working mothers to "granola" types, "breast police," and stay-at-home dads—who come together in a park for a standoff. "Nipple up," says one mom in the breastfeeding posse as the sides get ready for a West Side Story–like showdown. Suddenly, one of the mothers loses hold of her baby's stroller, and it goes rolling down the hill. With a baby facing danger, everyone runs after the stroller, abandoning their "sides" to save the child. You can't help but feel a tug at the heartstrings. The Internet and social media circles exploded with warm and fuzzy comments applauding the "feel good" commercial for showing how all moms and dads are in this together. But exactly when weren't we?

Let's be honest, marketers don't make commercials to make you feel good; they make commercials to sell their product. And telling a story is a powerful selling tool. What's the underlying story of this commercial? There is a war. The war is being waged by judgmental, sanctimonious parents, who are the enemies. When fighting occurs, random bad things happen. These bad things can only be stopped and lives saved when all the warring factions come together to do what is right in a crisis situation. And since a very cute baby was saved, no one can say that the choice was wrong. This is the exact same narrative of failed breastfeeding. Everyone should be okay with any route mothers take without any mention of medical knowledge or the social or public health consequences because using formula ultimately saves a baby and that can't be wrong. The subtext is that if a parent uses formula, any mention of breastfeeding or scientific facts is just judgey.

The commercial also begins with a flawed premise—the mommy wars must exist or why else would there be a commercial urging them to end? Instead, the ad actually perpetuates the same war that it pretends to end. In this narrative, breastfeeding is just another choice—like cloth diapering or which color to paint your kid's room—but one that completely ignores the medical and scientific fact that breastfeeding provides optimal nutrition for babies. Instead, the commercial says, It's all the same, don't judge. And if you do, you are a bad mom, a confrontational one. It's the corporate vision of a united world—one big happy marketplace. It also implies that mothers should save their energy for the really big, life-threatening stuff that really matters. These are underhanded ways of sending mothers mixed messages that rouse emotions but don't address the structural barriers that need to be dismantled for all women and babies to thrive. Creating emotional campaigns to encourage formula feeding while executives count on employment limiting breastfeeding to boost profits shows the profit-seeking behavior that has continued for years.

· · ·

The co-opting of language includes the co-opting of consumer marketing trends. For example, when cola giant, Coke (formerly a longtime, major donor to the American Academy of Pediatrics) realized they were on the wrong side of the growing eat-healthier movement and the mounting evidence directly linking sugar consumption to obesity, they decided that instead of trying to buck the trend or constantly defend their product, that it was better to actually follow the consumer. In effect, if you can't beat 'em, join 'em. Don't want aspartame? Fine, Coca-Cola now markets an all-natural stevia-based low-calorie cola called Coca-Cola Life. Advertisements use the language of "moderation," encouraging customers to have a little rather than none at all.

Monsanto, the world's largest maker of genetically modified seeds, now markets itself as being "part of the bigger conversation about food," even while actively working behind the scenes to stop widespread consumer efforts for GMO labeling legislation. Following the consumer means that in 2015 Abbott introduced the first non-GMO infant formula in the U.S, in response to growing demand for GMO-free products. This is smart consumer marketing but it is still marketing junk food to babies.

While closely following lifestyle trends for their consumer marketing efforts, they also closely watch medical professionals to gauge their latest needs. Since doctors cannot be directly paid to endorse infant formula, drug companies moved to less obvious forms of compensation: subsidizing office furnishings, research projects, conferences, publications, and travel junkets for medical professionals. There were the infamous "ski and learn" conferences, and less expensive maneuvers like bringing free coffee and donuts and other food to the hardworking, time-strapped nursing staff as a way to curry favor. The most insidious of these perks was a free service to renovate or build newborn facilities in hospitals around the world. A 1982 report by the Action for Corporate Accountability found that Abbott Laboratories helped design at least two hundred maternity departments a year in the United States alone. Abbott is still involved with hospital design, engaging in humanitarian efforts, such as Design 4 Others (D4O), which uses volunteers to design and build health care facilities for communities with limited resources across Africa and Asia. In the United States, the Abbott-designed wards included central nurseries that place mothers far away from babies, a practice that disrupts the natural rhythm of breastfeeding. A mother's physical contact with her baby stimulates the production of prolactin, the milk-making hormone. With babies separated from mothers, important unique feeding cues can also become illusory. Babies may turn their head, open their mouth, stick out their tongue, or even make small noises to indicate they are ready to feed. These relatively small movements often go unnoticed by nurses attending to several babies. If a baby has to resort to crying in order to communicate hunger, he or she may be too exhausted to nurse properly. But in order to pick up on these cues, mothers need to be near their babies. Infant formula marketers know this and used this knowledge and their deep pockets to their commercial advantage.

One proposal from Ross Laboratories revealed by the Action for Corporate Accountability in the late 1980s showed that a New York City hospital would be paid $1 million to use Ross's architectural services for its nurseries. In exchange for the payment, the hospital would be required to provide gift

packs with formula to all new mothers. The proposal also required the hospital to use promotional videos made by Ross
for any of its prenatal childbirth and breastfeeding classes at
the hospital. These videos were known to have flawed information and send subliminal messages that breastfeeding is
difficult and often fails while promoting the convenience of
bottle feeding. The video packaging also contained formula
samples and coupons. Beyond the general maternity wards,
formula manufacturers also seek to infiltrate where the sickest
babies are kept. In 1991 the Ross Products division of Abbott
Labs convened twenty-five physicians, nurses, planning officials, and architects to discuss the role of the neonatal intensive care unit (NICU) design environment on very low birth
weight babies (VLBW). This group's findings, again convened
by the infant formula maker, became design recommendations that were presented to and later incorporated into
the Federal Guideline Institute's *Guidelines for Design and
Construction of Health Care Facilities*. According to FGI, a nonprofit founded in 1988 to guide the health-care built environment, the guidelines have long been a document written
jointly by federal and private agencies. However, somehow
the process was infiltrated by infant formula companies,
who have been directly involved in creating the national
recommendations for the NICU environment. This is particularly concerning since low birth weight and preterm infants are the ones who need breast milk the most—for
them it is lifesaving. The two leading causes of infant death
among preterm babies—necrotizing enterocolitis and lower
respiratory infections—are significantly lower among breastfed infants.

While infant formula manufacturers plow money into defining the physical space at hospitals and influencing the cultural environment when you leave one, hospitals are woefully understaffed with lactation consultants, and lactation consultants are often underpaid. In the United States there were 15,144 International Board Certified Lactation Consultants (IBCLC) as of 2015. But, according to preliminary numbers for 2015 from the National Vital Statistics Report, more than 3.9 million babies were born. Let's dig a little deeper into some state data. In California, there were 2,258 IBCLCs in 2015. According to the preliminary birth data available for California, there were 491,487 live births in 2015. That means there were approximately 217 mother-baby couplets for each IBCLC. But in Mississippi there are only 74 IBCLCs, where in 2015 there were some 38,390 live births. That's about 518 babies for each IBCLC. Across the country, there's a huge gap in the number of professionals providing lactation support compared with the number of mothers who need support. While there may not be enough money or staff for every mother to receive the time and quality of breastfeeding help she needs, there is always a discharge bag or formula freebies in the mail for every mother who leaves a hospital.

Today, the practice of direct promotion to doctors and nurses in the hospital is no longer allowed. Hospitals, in response to pressure from breastfeeding advocates and the Baby-Friendly Hospital Initiative—a campaign and ten-step hospital accreditation backed by the WHO to reduce infant formula influences in hospitals and create more breastfeeding support—have voluntarily changed their policies for formula reps on the maternity wards. Instead, infant formula reps use social media and other tactics to reach doctors and nurses directly. Nurses often tell me that they miss the free donuts or free lunch. Yet, infant formula companies still pay million-dollar rebates to hospitals and provide equipment and training for medical staff. But there is no such thing as a free lunch or donut. When companies are willing to put so much money on the table and into hospital coffers, it is clear the discharge packs are anything but benign. The payoff is worth it. As one Abbott training manual from the early 2000s put it, "When one considers that for every 100 infants discharged on a particular formula brand, approximately 93 infants remain on that brand, the importance of hospital selling becomes obvious." It's also obvious how hospital balance sheets have grown to rely on the refunds, rebates, and other incentives that formula companies pay.

These discharge bags insinuate that the hospital endorses formula as a general practice and a specific brand in particular. Compelling research proves that women who receive formula discharge bags at the hospital do not meet their stated breastfeeding goals. Studies published in the *American Journal of Public Health*, the *Journal of Human Lactation*, and *Pediatrics* (see especially the comprehensive 2010 analysis "The Burden of Suboptimal Breastfeeding in the United States: A Pediatric Cost Analysis") document the link between formula samples and reduced breastfeeding. Yet hospital decision making about whether or not to give away formula is mostly driven by finances—can they afford to financially function without the handsome rebates, refunds, and other incentives that the infant formula companies provide? The implications of infant and maternal health are often an afterthought to hospital profitability.

It's no wonder that since 2006 there has been a nationwide effort to "Ban the Bag." Among the nation's forty-five top-ranked hospitals, 67 percent have stopped distributing formula samples and formula-company-sponsored discharge bags, according to a recent analysis by Public Citizen, a nonprofit advocacy organization. All mothers who medically need formula receive it, but it is not given away at discharge as a default. Massachusetts and Rhode Island have statewide bans on formula discharge bags. All public hospitals run by the New York City Health and Hospitals Corporation banned formula bags and promotional materials in 2007 because of their negative impact on breastfeeding rates. Twelve private New York City hospitals made the same move when they voluntarily signed on to the city's Latch On initiative. Latch On doesn't go as far in eradicating formula use in hospitals or as far as a Baby-Friendly hospital designation, but it is a step in the right direction toward removing the financial incentives of formula marketing in hospitals.

Hospitals aren't the only organizations benefiting financially from the profit making of infant formula companies. The pharmaceutical companies also work indirectly through physician organizations, such as the American Academy of Pediatrics (AAP) and the American College of Obstetrics and Gynecology (ACOG). In 2013 the Academy of Breastfeeding Medicine and several women's health and breastfeeding organizations joined forces to petition the AAP—an organization representing over sixty thousand pediatricians whose recommendations form the basis of pediatric preventive health care—to terminate its ongoing financial relationships with infant formula manufacturers. In the summer of 2012, the AAP entered into a sales agreement with Mead Johnson, the maker of Enfamil formula, to put the AAP logo on the tags of formula discharge bags. The Enfamil bags with AAP materials give an implied endorsement by the academy—the agency trusted to champion infant and child health. Parents turn to the AAP expecting unbiased advice, not conflicts of interest, when it comes to infant health. However, the commercial prowess of infant formula manufacturers has allowed them to pay their way into hospitals, professional organizations, and the hearts and minds of doctors and nurses with offerings as expensive as new hospital wings and conferences and gifts as cheap as donuts.

But the business environment favoring infant formula companies goes even higher up the chain of command. This kind of billion-dollar success couldn't occur and continue for decades without the right regulatory environment and government collusion. Third World countries are not the only places with severe cracks in their regulatory controls. In this case, a key factor supporting the success of infant formula in the United States is the FDA's odd designation of infant formula as a food versus a drug. This designation was changed in 1992. It should be noted that infant formula is made mostly by pharmaceutical companies and being able to land clearly in the food camp may explain the Bristol-Myers spin-off of Mead Johnson. Being in the food category means any ingredient added to food, including infant formula, must only be "generally recognized as safe" (GRAS) for its intended use. A drug would have to be tested for its safety and

effectiveness—that is, does it do what it says it does?—but infant formula, as a food, does not have to meet this measure.
Manufacturers must only provide the FDA with "assurances"
and "reasonable certainty," attested to by competent scientists,
that the requirements specific to infant formula have been
met for each new infant formula and that the ingredients are
"safe" before it is sold to the public. Those competent scientists
can be selected by the manufacturer. In the end, manufacturers use their own scientists, who assure the FDA that their
products are safe and then technically "test" their products
on infants and wait for adverse responses to make adjust-
ments. Therefore, infant formulas are not FDA approved.
There is no test for nutritional adequacy, only a requirement
to comply with a list of required ingredients, such as protein,
B12, and vitamin D. Infant formula is judged by the government only on its composition and not on its nutritional benefit
to a child. This simplistic approach to something as important as infant formula is particularly concerning. The underlying assumption that any infant formula that simply contains
the specified ingredients in the required amounts is both
safe and nutritionally adequate grossly underestimates the
complexities of breast milk, which is more than the sum of
its components. Throwing a bunch of ingredients into a
blender is not the same as preparing each ingredient in the
way that maximizes its nutritional content; how those ingredients are processed is critical to their nutritional value.
Eating a protein bar is not the same as getting protein naturally from food. Infant formula lists its fat content, but it is
usually from beef tallow—not the same as the complex fats
in mother's milk. Food scientists have acknowledged that

breaking food down into its chemical components and simply marketing those components is dangerous for public health. Allowing food manufacturers to swap out one ingredient and add others ignores the processing that occurs. "Identification of food mainly with its chemical constituents at best has limited value, and in general has proved to be unhelpful, misleading, and harmful to public health," wrote Carlos Monteiro, a professor at the Center for Epidemiological Studies in Health and Nutrition at the University of São Paolo and a leading expert on processed foods.

A popular November 2010 editorial in the online *Journal of the World Public Health Nutrition Association,* argued that nutritionists' focus on nutrients, rather than foods, has led to the assumption that if foods contain the same nutrients, they are the same—even though it is never possible to fully replicate the nutritional content of foods because too much about their chemical composition is still unknown. "This notion is an exquisite combination of stupidity and arrogance, or else of intelligence and cunning. For a start, similar results can only be of those chemical constituents that are at the time known, and actually measured," the unsigned editorial said. If this "stupidity" can be acknowledged when thinking about basic nutrients such as protein, how much more so must it be considered with the complexities of breast milk. If the danger of ignoring "process" is a concern that nutritionists have for the general public, it should be an even greater concern for infants. Infant formula may contain nutrients, but they are processed in an unhealthy way and then marketed as being similar to breast milk.

Scientists have argued for years that infant formula actually needs more regulation than regular food because it is the sole source of nutrition for many infants during such a developmentally critical time. But the FDA has been slow to act on the recommendations of several professional task forces to create more controls. Several meetings of the Food Advisory Committee on Infant Formula took place from 1996 to 2002, but the FDA did nothing until September 2014, when the agency published the final rule regarding standards for infant formula manufacturers. After being virtually unregulated for over forty years, the formula industry was forced to comply with the first infant formula law, passed in 1980. The law was finally passed after somewhere between 20,000 and 50,000 infants were exposed to chloride-deficient soy formula and thirty children were diagnosed with hypochloremic metabolic acidosis because of chloride deficiency in the late 1970s. These infants developed loss of appetite, muscular weakness, vomiting, and failure to gain weight, among other problems. Four to nine years later, the same infants were found to have cognitive impairments, including attention deficit disorders with repetitive behaviors, problems with word finding, and autism-like behaviors. That's when additional, federally enforceable requirements were enacted, including required testing for harmful pathogens, such as salmonella. Infant formula manufacturers also had to prove that the formulas support normal physical growth and to test for nutrient content in the final product stage, before entering the market and at the end of the product's shelf life. But these regulations have no punitive measures and don't include all infant formulas.

Meanwhile, if infant formula has been basically nutritionally adequate (as determined by the government) since the

1980s, how do you explain the countless number of variations of infant formula on the market? Lactose-free, ones for allergy-prone infants, and soy-based formulas. New varieties of formula with all sorts of additives come to market all the time, without any independent clinical data that these different components improve infant health. Are these improvements in nutrition made to benefit babies or are they just small variations to enhance profits? "We are constantly adjusting the quality of our products and the components in our products in order to make them more attractive to consumers," Mead Johnson CEO Jakobsen said in the June 2016 conference call with analysts. No mention of babies. "The overarching theme is that we're trying to add value to ensure that we can build on the inherent volume growth in the category by gradually persuading consumers that they should be willing to pay more per serving. And that's a theme [that] plays out differently in different countries. In the U.S., we might execute this by persuading consumers to move from powder form to liquid form, or we might ask them to move from non-hydrolyzed formula to easier-to-digest, partially hydrolyzed products." No mention of why the easier-to-digest isn't their only product.

Since 2000 the price of regular infant formula has increased 100 percent from about eleven cents per ounce to a recent 2016 price of twenty-two cents per ounce, while the base product has essentially remained the same.

Profits are made not just for the infant formula makers but by the ancillary industries they support, from the dairy industry and soybean growers to bottle and nipple manufacturers. As with many innovations, new products arise out of the desire to profit from waste or surplus. In the late nineteenth and early twentieth centuries, the mechanization of the dairy industry resulted in large surpluses of whey from an increase in butter and cheese production. The dairy industry needed new outlets for this surplus in milk and milk waste. As human milk substitutes began to be developed and with government subsidies propping up the dairy industry, cows' milk became the foundation of the baby milk industry. Cows' milk was not used because research proved it the most suitable substitute for breast milk, but because it was plentiful and cheap. Improved mechanization led to dried milk powder, produced through roller and spray drying, which added to the availability of inexpensive and transportable milk. The dairy industry would continue to grow, with much government support.

Much of that industry's initial growth was buoyed by the new market among infants. Dairy industry subsidies totaled $5.6 billion from 1995 to 2014. Today, the dairy industry is one of the most powerful lobbies in Washington, D.C., and a strident and visible supporter of infant formula. However, we only have to look back at the government's role in subsidizing tobacco farmers and the federal and state tax revenues from cigarette sales to see how the government has supported and profited from a dangerous product. It is clear that even the government does not always put public health ahead of financial interests.

· · ·

It's a rainy day in early May 2016 and I'm in Washington, D.C., headed to the Hubert H. Humphrey Building for a landmark event. The U.S. Department of Health and Human Services (HHS) Office of Global Affairs is preparing to represent the U.S. Government at the 68th World Health Assembly in Geneva in a few weeks where it will vote, among other agenda items, on the WHO's "Guidance on Ending the Inappropriate Promotion of Foods for Infants and Young Children." The guidance document would be a clarification and update to complement the WHO code's existing recommendations. HHS has invited input from stakeholders to help shape the U.S. position on whether to endorse the guidance and is hosting a public, informal stakeholder listening session.

The room is fairly full for such a convening. Weeks earlier, e-mails went out that comments would be reduced from five minutes to two minutes to accommodate the long list of speaking requests. As expected, the Infant Nutrition Council of North America, the industry association of infant formula manufacturers, was in attendance. But what was surprising was the number of large dairy-related trade groups that offered comments, obviously encouraging a vote against the measure. Representatives of the International Dairy Foods Association (IDFA), the National Milk Producers Federation, and the U.S. Dairy Export Council took turns calling the guidance "draconian," "highly flawed," and "lacking an impact assessment," and warning that it would "limit families' ability to make informed decisions."

To understand the scope of this presence, consider this: The IDFA, which represents the nation's dairy and manufacturing and marketing industries, has over 530 member companies. IDFA's 220 dairy-processing members run more than 600 plant operations, and range from large multinational organizations to single-plant companies. Together they represent more than 85 percent of the milk, cultured products, cheese, and frozen desserts produced and marketed in the United States. When an organization of that size and scope sends a vice president to offer comments on a guidance document on infant formula promotion, you know the stakes are high.

The guidance passed in Geneva. But in response to the vote, IDFA issued a press release. "We were very disappointed that the guidance was still accepted as is by WHO members, in spite of the significant deficiencies we uncovered regarding the evidence base and procedures used by WHO," said John Allan, IDFA vice president of regulatory affairs and international standards, who helped lead industry efforts to build awareness of the guidance's shortcomings and request changes before it was adopted. "Thanks to the strong stand taken by the U.S. delegation and several other countries, the adopted resolution does provide significant protections for nutritious dairy products," Allan said in the release.

The press release also alluded to months of behind-the-scenes lobbying efforts to derail the resolution. "Since January, when the guidance was introduced, IDFA has been coordinating with member companies and other trade associations to educate members of Congress and officials from U.S. agencies and foreign governments on the weaknesses of the guidance, as well as the potential for unintended health consequences for young children and violations of international trade obligations." By acknowledging coordinated industry efforts to influence elected and government officials on a policy to improve infant health by a global health organization, the dairy industry shows how lucrative the infant formula business is to their future fortunes.

• • •

If you can't digest dairy-based infant formula, there are soy-based formulas. This is not because a preponderance of evidence shows that soy is the best nondairy protein source for babies, but because the influential and profitable soybean industry aggressively sought out new outlets for its products. The soybean industry is a critical sector for the U.S. agriculture market. U.S. soybeans have been a subsidized commodity since 1941. Even food giant Monsanto has a large stake in the sale of soy. At nearly every turn, infant formula is connected to the big business of food.

These competing economic interests have directly affected the variations of infant formula and their profitability but not necessarily their benefit to babies. But there are other contributing factors to the business of undermining breast-feeding. By nature, breast milk has an intrinsic packaging and distribution system—the breast and nipple. Infant formula does not. Big business needed to solve that problem, and companies needed to figure out how to package formula in an appealing and cost-effective way. The "solution" was a bumper crop of other commercial products, such as bottles, containers, and artificial nipples. Nestlé was a big player in the bottle world. Invented in 1860, the long-tube feeding bottle responded to this demand: the glass flask equipped with a rubber tube allowed the infant to more or less feed itself. Although initially acclaimed for its practical nature, this "killer tube" was banned in 1910 because it proved a real breeding ground for bacteria. In 1897 a bottle was patented that hung over the crib so a baby could feed alone, and another was released that stood on a baby's chest. The introduction of artificial milk and then bottles and nipples disrupted the normal feeding process, and the natural bonding that occurs between most infants and mothers was also strained as a result.

While much effort was put into creating the perfect feeding receptacle, re-creating a woman's nipple proved an ongoing technological challenge. The human nipple is pliable and can reach two to three times its normal size when sucked on by an infant. It contains fifteen to thirty pores, each of which spurts milk in a fine stream in different directions. These spurts occur rhythmically when a baby is nursing. After experimenting with different forms and materials, including glass and the actual teats of a cow soaked in preservatives, the first rubber nipple was patented in 1845 by Elijah Pratt. It was not well received. Only after several modifications was the ring and teat improved and accepted. It took until the twentieth century before the materials and technology improved enough to produce a soft nipple that could withstand the heat of sterilization. Today, the market for bottles and rubber nipples is worth $2 billion annually.

While billions are being made selling and delivering artificial mother's milk, the social costs of becoming a predominantly bottle feeding nation continues to rise. In 2016 the WHO released a report that concluded that if every child were breastfed within an hour of birth, given only breast milk for the first six months of life, and continued breastfeeding up to the age of two years, about 800,000 children's lives would be saved globally every year. A recent study in the journal *Pediatrics* found that "the United States incurs $13 billion in excess costs annually and suffers 911 preventable deaths per year because our breastfeeding rates fall far below medical recommendations." The researchers calculated $10.56 billion for the estimated 741 infant deaths, based on 80 percent of families complying with the medical recommendation of six months of exclusive breastfeeding. Ninety-five percent of infant deaths are attributed to the following three causes: sudden infant death syndrome (SIDS), necrotizing enterocolitis (a devastating intestinal disease), and lower respiratory infections, like pneumonia. Breastfeeding has been shown to reduce the risk of all of these and seven other illnesses covered by the study. In that study, the researchers also included the direct costs of health care and parents' time missed from work. Their tally did not include the cost of formula, another added cost for families that don't breastfeed. Although the United States spends more on health care than any other country in the world, a baby born in the United States is less likely to see his or her first birthday than one born in Hungary, Poland, or Slovakia. According to the CDC, the United States has a higher infant mortality rate than any of the other twenty-seven wealthiest countries.

Breastfeeding also provides health benefits for mothers. It burns extra calories, so mothers often lose pregnancy weight faster. Retaining that extra weight can lead to heart disease and high blood pressure, doctors say. Nursing also releases the hormone oxytocin, which helps the uterus return to normal size and may reduce uterine bleeding after birth. Breastfeeding lowers the risk of breast and ovarian cancer. It may also lower risks of osteoporosis. All of these benefits are lost when women do not breastfeed. That same study in *Pediatrics* found that a 90 percent breastfeeding rate could prevent over 53,000 cases of hypertension, over 13,900 heart attacks, and nearly 5,000 cases of breast cancer among women. That's because breastfeeding reduces these risks. The study in *Pediatrics* also estimated that society would save $18.3 billion if mothers were prevented from dying from these diseases.

Not only is breastfeeding a cost saving, it's a powerful investment in the foundation for a healthier future. In fact, an economist from the World Bank, the world's largest source of multilateral development finance for developing countries, recently presented to the Academy of Breastfeeding Medicine on how and why the bank views breastfeeding promotion as a powerful economic investment. "We feel this is one of the premier potential altering transformational investments that developing countries can make and that is currently being underused, to say the least. We are emphasizing breastfeeding more and more in our support to countries, not just as a health investment but as a true powerful economic investment in their futures," said Keith Hansen, Global Practices Vice President at the World Bank, which invests in everything from agriculture and water to urban development and education, with the goal of eliminating extreme poverty. Hansen said the World Bank has set a goal to eliminate extreme poverty and boost what they call "shared prosperity" by the year 2030.

Hansen noted that while many development goals, from bridges and roads that have to be rebuilt following natural disasters to the construction of new buildings, "the gains from early childhood nutrition are forever. And to a large extent, many of them are free because they have come prepackaged in this unbelievable intervention called breastfeeding. This is, of course, what defines us as a mammalian species. And the proof of this is in the lifelong impacts." Hansen says that children who avoid undernutrition are not only much more likely to survive but also to stay in school and are therefore more likely to escape poverty—about 33 percent more likely on average. "And their wages are anywhere from 5 percent to 50 percent higher than their peers who were not able to escape. These data are from very rigorous longitudinal studies . . . studies that have been done over decades now with fairly substantial cohorts and very robustly tested, and the impact, correlations, and causations are very strongly established."

From the position of the World Bank, breastfeeding is an important foundation for economic development and one of the most critical investments a country can make for good nutrition and child health. With the advantages of breastfeeding proven in cost saving, economic development, and human capital gains, it would seem that the only entities that benefit from the commercialization and widespread use of infant formula are the manufacturers.

•   •   •

When commercial interests dominate the infant feeding market, women pay not just with their health but with their confidence: women's ability to perform their unique biological function is undermined during the particularly vulnerable days of early motherhood, which is extremely disempowering. Instead of having a positive, supportive experience at the start of motherhood, women find themselves in a maelstrom of mixed messages, confusing information, and profit-driven propaganda.

The toxic environment can frame our later parenting experiences and determine where and how we get support. It creates more obstacles, and women deserve better. Our babies have become profit centers for hospitals and physicians. Our breasts have become profit centers for pharmaceutical companies and breast-milk substitute manufacturers who benefit from selling us messages that we will fail. What do women gain from this exchange? Not much.

· 3 ·

Scientific Breakthroughs
or Breakdowns?

Doubt is our product, since it is the best means of competing with the "body of fact" that exists in the minds of the general public.

—FROM A 1969 MEMO WRITTEN BY A TOBACCO
INDUSTRY EXECUTIVE

If you're like me, you have at least one friend in your social circle who is always quoting some new scientific study to defend their latest diet, exercise routine, parenting style, or something else. You can barely get through the morning news or the home page of your favorite Web site without learning about a recent study proclaiming some new health benefit or disputing a previously identified one. A reliance on scientific research is now deeply embedded in American culture, and we are simply infatuated with scientific innovation. In a 2015 survey by the Pew Research Center, 79 percent of those surveyed said that science has made life easier for most people, while just 15 percent said that it has made life more difficult. Meanwhile, parents are increasingly relying on science to help guide their decision making about everything from nutrition and vaccinations to social development and preventive health measures. Yet when parents turn to science for evidence that infant formula is inferior, they find a confusing landscape of information that has been muddled by faux science, questionable funding sources, inconsistent research methodologies, outdated protocols, and the media's hunger for the next provocative "breakthrough" headline. This search for science is another byproduct of the structural and economic forces that undermine breastfeeding. When breastfeeding is extremely difficult because of the structural barriers, parents feel that the preponderance of scientific evidence that breastfeeding is superior must be indisputable to justify the time, effort, and potential shaming involved. With that in mind, the infant formula companies have a vested interest in keeping the scientific landscape muddled by industry-sponsored studies and questionable protocols that lead to sensational anti-breastfeeding headlines. In the end, science is yet another source of unclear information for mothers, letting them down.

Meanwhile, the process of science is far less linear than the media's coverage suggests, and the media often gives no account of the trials and errors that actually occur along the way. This creates unrealistic expectations that the scientific community is good at self-policing and that science always gets it right, without providing the tools to decipher the good science from the bad. That, in turn, perpetuates the illusion that the scientific body of evidence proving that breastfed babies are healthier is conflicting and inconclusive, when all of it is not. There is strong science, weak science, and junk science on both sides of the issues. In the end, a scientific conclusion is like a prosecutor's indictment; it's really the beginning of a long process. After an indictment, we expect a prosecutor to provide detailed and consistent evidence that must stand up to a jury of peers, who should be able to take as much time as they need to review it. Science is similar, but in science a community of peer reviewers are simply assessing the evidence to see if it is sufficient to accept the claim. But this does not make it fact. There are always uncertainties in science, because science is a process of discovery. The good news is that the uncertainty keeps scientists questioning and propels the science forward. The bad news is people are generally looking to science for cold, hard facts—which are really hard to find.

The Internet certainly has not helped. The Internet was meant to lead to the great democratization of information—the opportunity for billions of people to reclaim control of expertise from the elitist clutches of research institutes, universities, consultancies, big corporations, and the mainstream press. This was supposed to raise the quality, usefulness, and relevance of expert advice; instead, we find bad information masquerading as fact everywhere. We find faux science looking and sounding exactly like the real thing.

The truth is, there's good science and there's bad science—but often bad or questionable science lands in the same credible science category simply because it is called a "study." Are there weak pro-breastfeeding studies? Absolutely, but that weakness is usually in the methodology, such as the sample size, and typically not because it was funded by a for-profit company with a vested interest in a certain outcome. Unfortunately, most of us typically don't have the know-how to properly unpack the research before us. What we do have are attention-grabbing headlines or the assertion that a news item about a research study was "most shared" on Facebook. In this environment, important distinctions and gaping research holes get lost in the media clamor about provocative findings. Important questions about the kind of study or how was it conducted often fall to the wayside in favor of the flashy headline—even when the research is flimsy. We may think "the latest" research means better research, but in doing so we are throwing out the bathwater of years of scientific evidence in favor of one new baby.

The "bathwater" of scientific research on breastfeeding, now decades deep, actually contains infallible proof of the disadvantages of formula feeding. The evidence in favor of breastfeeding as the optimal nutrition for infants is strong enough to convince the World Health Organization, the Centers for Disease Control and Prevention, the United Nations, UNICEF, the Academy of Pediatrics, and countless other international bodies to resolutely support it. The United Arab Emirates made it mandatory by law to breastfeed for two years, noting the health benefits and cost savings. While the science of breastfeeding has thoroughly convinced health authorities, government agencies, and policy makers, it remains widely disputed on the individual level, mostly by those left with the burden of actually doing it—women.

The public's failure to understand that it is scientifically undisputed that breast milk is the best way to feed an infant is the result of our changing relationship to science, a general misunderstanding of what science should be, and the increasing influence of money and society on the direction of scientific research.

To better understand the body of evidence supporting breastfeeding, we go to the Big Bertha of breastfeeding studies—one of the most systematic and comprehensive reviews of breastfeeding research, conducted by the Agency for Healthcare Research and Quality (AHRQ), one of the twelve agencies within the U.S. Department of Health and Human Services. The depth of this study takes into account the full body of scientific evidence—including any studies that only proved weak associations. For their study, AHRQ convened eight investigators from the Tufts–New England Medical Center Evidence-Based Practice Center along with a fourteen-member technical expert team. The landmark four-hundred-page report screened over nine thousand abstracts and identified forty-three primary studies on infant health outcomes, forty-three primary studies on maternal health outcomes, and twenty-nine systematic reviews or meta-analyses that covered approximately four hundred individual studies. They looked at short-term infant health outcomes, such as infectious diseases (including ear infections, diarrhea, and lower respiratory tract infections), sudden infant death syndrome (SIDS) and infant mortality, and longer-term outcomes such as cognitive development, childhood cancer (including leukemia), types 1 and 2 diabetes, asthma, eczema, cardiovascular disease (including hypertension), hyperlipidemia, and obesity. For mothers, the researchers examined the findings on short-term outcomes such as postpartum depression and return to prepregnancy weight, and long-term outcomes, such as breast cancer, ovarian cancer, diabetes, and osteoporosis.

In this review, not all science was equally weighted or even deemed worthy of consideration. To make sure the results were applicable to the U.S. market and clearly understood by researchers, only studies conducted in developed countries and published in English were included. In the case of studies on infant feeding, studies must have had a comparative arm of formula feeding or different durations of breastfeeding included. Studies that examined only formula-fed infants were excluded. Then the expert panel developed an approach to grade the studies that made the first cut based on their methodological quality. Primary studies and meta-analyses were graded A for good, B for fair to moderate, and C for poor. "A" studies presented the least bias and the most valid results. "B" studies were susceptible to some bias but were still considered valid, and the "C" studies had significant biases that may have resulted in invalid results. There was also a checklist developed specifically for this review to evaluate the quality of the reviews of observational studies. The checklist included such questions as whether the study included an appropriate search strategy, justification for inclusion and exclusion criteria for studies, and a description of a well-defined population. The definition of breastfeeding (either at the breast or expressed milk fed with a bottle) varied across the studies reviewed, so the authors elected to use the definition of exclusive breastfeeding as provided by the authors of the studies reviewed and to qualify the conclusions based on these definitions.

What did this megareview of scientific research of various

breastfeeding studies reveal regarding the body of research on breastfeeding and infant and maternal outcomes? In full-term infants, the exhaustive literature review found that a history of breastfeeding was highly associated with a reduction in the risk of acute otitis media (ear infections), nonspecific gastroenteritis, severe lower respiratory tract infections, atopic dermatitis (severe eczema), asthma in young children, obesity, types 1 and 2 diabetes, childhood leukemia, sudden infant death syndrome (SIDS), and necrotizing enterocolitis (NEC), a serious and often fatal intestinal disease. There was no substantive relationship between breastfeeding in full-term infants and cognitive performance. The relationship between breastfeeding and cardiovascular diseases was also unclear.

The specific associations range in significance. For example, the study found that there was a 23 percent reduction of otitis media when breastfeeding. When exclusive breastfeeding for three or six months' duration was compared to exclusive formula feeding, there was a reduction of otitis media of 50 percent. For atopic dermatitis, there was a reduced risk of 42 percent in children with a family history of atopy eczema and exclusively breastfed for at least three months compared with those who were breastfed for less than three months.

For gastrointestinal infections, one case-control study analyzed and rated as good found that infants who were breastfeeding had a 64 percent reduction in the risk of nonspecific gastroenteritis compared with nonbreastfeeding infants. Furthermore, an updated meta-analysis by the authors found the risk of asthma is reduced by 27 percent in infants breastfeeding for at least three months compared with nonbreastfed infants. If there was a family history of asthma, the risk was reduced by 40 percent. The authors also conducted their own meta-analysis on seven case-control studies and found that a history of breastfeeding reduced the risk of SIDS by 36 percent. In three meta-analyses that were rated as good and moderate regarding methodological quality, breastfeeding was associated with a reduced risk of obesity in adolescence and adult life when compared with those not breastfed. The reduction ranged from 7 percent to 24 percent. For the preterm infant, the authors performed a meta-analysis of four randomized controlled trials of necrotizing enterocolitis (NEC) and found an absolute risk reduction of 5 percent. The authors point out that this small difference is significant given the high fatality rate of NEC, one of the leading causes of infant death.

The infant health outcomes where there was little or no evidence of positive outcomes related to breastfeeding included full-term and preterm cognitive development, risk of cardiovascular diseases, and types 1 and 2 diabetes.

For maternal outcomes, a history of lactation was associated with a reduced risk of breast and ovarian cancer and of type 2 diabetes. Early cessation of breastfeeding or not breastfeeding was associated with an increased risk of maternal postpartum depression. There was no relationship shown between a history of lactation and the risk of osteoporosis. The effect of breastfeeding in mothers on return-to-prepregnancy weight was negligible, and the effect of breastfeeding on postpartum weight loss was unclear.

The health implications of these findings are hard to ignore. For example, acute otitis media (AOM) is a very common childhood infection that begins with an upper respiratory tract infection and spreads to the inner ear. Meanwhile, the prevalence of a first attack of AOM in children under one year of age is estimated to be 44 percent, according to the report. Given that 80 percent of children have had an episode of a serious ear infection by the age of three, therefore, a 23 to 50 percent reduction in this infection, depending on duration of breastfeeding, would affect a large number of children. Among mothers, the report found the reduction in breast cancer risk was 4.3 percent for each year of breastfeeding in one meta-analysis and 28 percent for twelve or more months of breastfeeding in the other. With one in eight U.S. women, about 12 percent, estimated to develop invasive breast cancer over the course of her lifetime, the protective benefits of breastfeeding are critical.

So if a high percentage of the actual science favoring breastfeeding is so clear on eight health indicators for infants and four indicators for mothers, why does the science of breastfeeding continue to appear confusing?

Part of the problem is how the research is being conducted. The common protocol for breastfeeding research is literally stacked against breastfeeding. In public health research, it is the biological norm, not the cultural norm, that is used as the baseline control group to compare against the "treatment." The health comparison should note whether the deviation from the baseline is helpful or harmful. Nonsmokers are compared to smokers, showing that smokers are more ill. This happens everywhere, except in breastfeeding research. Instead of using breastfeeding as the baseline, researchers have fallen into the trap of using formula feeding as the baseline and breastfeeding as the treatment. In a proper scientific landscape, it would be incumbent on infant formula manufacturers to prove that there are no or minimal risks when formula feeding is used compared with the biological baseline of breastfeeding. Instead, breast milk is studied in order to prove it to be better than formula. This backwards science creates backwards language. Because breastfeeding is the biological norm, breastfed babies should not be noted as "healthier"; artificially fed babies should be described as ill, and that they are more often and more seriously ill.

Another way the science industry has undermined breastfeeding research is with a historic overreliance on the randomized controlled trial (RCT). The RCT is widely considered science's gold standard for study design because little is left to chance. In an RCT, subjects are assigned to treatment groups at random. One group is treated and the outcome is compared to an identical group (the control group) that did not receive treatment. Of course, this is impossible to achieve in breastfeeding. You can't randomize who is breastfeeding—you will know you are doing it—and it would be unethical to stop a woman from breastfeeding for the sake of research. But Dr. Michael Kramer, a highly respected researcher at McGill University in Montreal, came as close as possible to achieving an RCT in breastfeeding when he released a series of groundbreaking breastfeeding studies in 2001. Kramer found a unique way to randomize his study; instead of telling each woman how to feed her child, Kramer studied women who began breastfeeding at birth on their own. Half of the mothers, however, were encouraged to breastfeed exclusively by a health professional and received ongoing supportive interventions modeled on the World Health Organization's Baby-Friendly Hospital Initiative. The other half did not receive the supportive intervention. He followed 17,046 healthy mothers and infants born in Belarus throughout their childhood, and the resulting Promotion of Breastfeeding Intervention Trial, or PROBIT, is the largest cluster-randomized controlled trial ever conducted in the area of human lactation during infancy. The study randomized thirty-one maternity hospitals and their affiliated health centers (where children are followed for their routine health care) to either receive the experimental intervention of breastfeeding promotion or the control arm of continuing the common breastfeeding practices, which does not include, for example, postnatal home visits from health professionals. It also produced two randomized cohorts with a substantially different exposure to breastfeeding. The women who received more information and support breastfed their children for much longer, allowing researchers to study the impact of extended exposure to breast milk. Kramer's most notable finding was that breastfed children scored 7.5 points higher on tests measuring verbal intelligence and 2.9 points higher on tests measuring nonverbal intelligence at the age of six and a half. The PROBIT study has, over the years, produced other findings about breastfeeding—some showing strong positive associations, such as a reduced risk of gastrointestinal infections and atopic eczema in the first year of life, some showing weak to minimal associations with conditions such as obesity.

Kramer's work was significant and remains highly referenced. The lack of an RCT for breastfeeding given the difficulty of creating one has often been used to discredit the volumes of research that do exist. But RCTs cannot be the only gold standard. RCTs are not perfect, and many things simply can't be studied using this approach, mostly because of ethical issues. And while no one suggests abandoning the RCT, more and more scientists are supplementing RCTs with other forms of evidence.

These other study designs have a widely accepted hierarchy of credibility that can help us determine the good science from the not so good. But first, a few questions that are critical in recognizing good science: What was the sample size? Bigger is always better. And, what was the methodology—how was the study designed and how was it executed? In other words, was it an RCT or a cohort study? What about the funding source? Look beyond the prestigious sounding "institute" to see who is actually funding the research. Science funded by formula companies, baby food manufacturers, and those who have commercial interests in selling other processed infant foods deserve our immediate scrutiny. I also take interest in how the study is reported by the researchers themselves and by the general public. In other words, be leery of inflammatory headlines and sensational claims.

At the top of the science heap are systematic reviews, which are considered the most reliable evidence, followed by evidence from randomized controlled clinical trials, cohort studies, and then case-control studies. A meta-analysis, or review study, is a common statistical technique for combining the findings of other independent studies over a period of time. These are considered most trustworthy when rigor has been applied to assessing the methodological quality of the design and execution of each study included in the review. Most research falls into two categories: observational studies or experimental studies. In experimental studies such as an RCT or a controlled clinical trial (CCT), researchers introduce an intervention and study the effects. Experimental studies are usually randomized. In observational studies, which include cohort studies and case-control studies, a large group of people are followed over months, years, or decades in an effort to identify associations between behaviors and certain health markers or a specific treatment. These studies are usually more "retrospective"—using data based on events that have already happened. Observational studies have become a staple of many research journals, but they are often hotly debated when it comes to breastfeeding because it is argued that some benefits may not be attributed to breastfeeding alone. For example, if a cohort study found that women who breastfed lost postpregnancy weight faster than mothers who did not, it could be questioned whether the effect was solely due to breastfeeding since women who breastfeed may be more likely to eat healthier while they do so.

Another problem with analyzing breastfeeding data is the definition of "breastfeeding" itself. Does it mean a child is fed exclusively at the breast or can it include bottle-fed breast milk? And what frequency of breastfeeding is required to be included in the cohort? Breast milk is a delicate, living fluid, and breastfeeding benefits increase with duration. So a child who was breastfed for one month may not have the same health benefits as a child breastfed for twelve months—but most studies never make the distinction. In 2012 the American Academy of Pediatrics acknowledged that among several ongoing methodological issues in breastfeeding research is "the absence of distinguishing between 'any' and 'exclusive' breastfeeding." In evaluating outcomes, it is important for breastfeeding studies to account for the frequency of breastfeeding and for whether the baby was fed at the breast or by bottle. Yet these distinctions are lacking in many of the high-profile studies that streak across social media and that women use as decision-making tools.

Dr. Miriam Labbok, former director of the Carolina Global Breastfeeding Institute at the University of North Carolina at Chapel Hill said in an interview that she'd been encouraging a standard definition of breastfeeding for research protocols since 1988—to no avail. Labbok, an epidemiologist, said the CDC and the WHO include babies fed both expressed milk and at the breast in their breastfeeding definitions, adding that policy makers at both institutions come from a perspective of nutrition, where the focus is only on receiving the food. Researchers from maternal and child health departments, who are more likely to have a deeper understanding of the nuances of lactation science, would be more concerned with method of delivery, Labbok noted. But the distinction is critical. Studies show that babies only fed by bottle eat more and thus grow differently. A 2010 analysis shows that babies fed breast milk by bottle in early infancy were more likely to empty their bottles later in infancy than their breastfeeding counterparts, which could impact weight gain. Infants fed both at the breast and with bottles of expressed milk gained weight at a similar rate to those only breastfed, but infants gained more weight per month when fed only by bottle. There are a couple explanations why: babies can get milk out of bottles quicker than from breasts, and breastfed babies eat from their feeding cues and then stop when they feel full, but caregivers tend to see an empty bottle as the sign of a completed meal.

Even the positioning that occurs during feeding at the breast is important. Breastfeeding protects against ear infections not just because of breast milk's anti-infective elements, but because of the posture of the baby's head and the dynamics of the cycle of sucking, swallowing, and breathing while nursing. Bottle-fed infants may miss out on these protective elements. The quality and content of the breast milk can also differ when it is exclusively pumped. A mother's breast milk changes according to a baby's needs, as it ages, as well as throughout the course of a day and even the course of each feeding session. Research has confirmed that the fat concentration of expressed milk increases with the baby's age in the same way that breastfed milk does. But if mothers don't pump for long enough at each session, their infants may receive predominantly foremilk (which is high in carbohydrates) and not get enough hindmilk (which is high in fat). The fat is the good stuff. Even how you store pumped milk may limit its beneficial properties, according to some research. Freezing can break down its immunological cells and lipids (but doesn't affect its antimicrobial proteins), refrigeration reduces ascorbic acid concentrations, and both storage methods reduce antioxidant activity, some studies show. You get the idea. Breast milk is a delicate substance, and lumping all breastfed children in one category and then claiming that the results represent breastfeeding in its totality is dangerous and misleading. We would never give any credit to a study that claimed to show that lowering fat in your diet did not improve long-term heart health if the study mostly included people who only decreased their fat intake for one day or even one week. But this is exactly what happens with some breastfeeding studies. In 2014 a highly publicized sibling study by Cynthia Colen, assistant professor of sociology at Ohio State University, made big headlines. "Is Breastfeeding Really Better?" asked the March 2014 *New York Times* article. A follow-up appeared on Slate, with a headline that had over 81,000 Facebook shares within two days: "New Study Confirms It: Breastfeeding Benefits Have Been Drastically Overstated." It was a classic example of simplistic reporting going for the "breakthrough" headline that distorts reality.

Colen's study, comparing siblings within the same family who were fed differently during infancy, suggests that breastfeeding might be no more beneficial than bottle feeding for ten of eleven long-term health and well-being outcomes in children ages four to fourteen. Those outcomes included body mass index, obesity, and hyperactivity. When restricting the sample to siblings who were fed differently within the same families, Colen and her coauthor found that the scores reflecting breastfeeding's positive effects on ten of the eleven indicators of child health and well-being were closer to zero and not statistically significant—meaning that any differences could have occurred by chance alone. The study shows that the long-term beneficial effects of breastfeeding may be overstated, Colen said, and that other family conditions may contribute more to health outcomes in the absence of breastfeeding.

To get her findings, Colen used data from the 1979 cohort

of the National Longitudinal Survey of Youth (NLSY), a nationally representative sample of young men and women who were between ages fourteen and twenty-two in 1979, as well as results from NLSY surveys between 1986 and 2010 of children born to women in the 1979 cohort. The group analyzed 1,773 "discordant" sibling pairs, or children from 665 surveyed families in which at least one child was breastfed and at least one other child was bottle-fed. The study authors examined behavioral assessments of children born between 1978 and 2006 and looked at outcomes from ages four to fourteen. They include three measures of physical health (body mass index, obesity, and asthma diagnosis), three behavioral indicators (hyperactivity, parental attachment, and behavioral compliance), and five outcomes specifically designed to predict academic achievement.

The data being used for the research comes from a twenty-eight-year study that included more than eight thousand children, yet Colen ends up with 1,773 individuals, or 22 percent of the original sample size. Kramer's PROBIT study followed over seventeen thousand healthy mothers, more than double the sample size of the NLSY study.

The problems with the Colen sibling study are varied. I'll start by following the money. After putting in a public records request to Ohio State University for their corporate funding sources, the query revealed that in 2014, the same year Colen's study was released, Abbott Labs, the maker of Similac, contributed between $250,000 and $499,000 to the school. A spokesperson confirmed that the school had not received funds from Mead Johnson or Nestlé in the last three to five years; however, drug companies such as Bristol-Myers Squibb and Novartis pharmaceuticals are hefty contributors. Beyond missing these important linkages, the sensational headlines missed the fact that Colen and her coauthor, David Ramey, deliberately skipped over the infant and toddler years, where breastfeeding has the greatest impact, reducing incidences of respiratory and ear infections, diarrhea, and sudden infant death syndrome. To establish breastfeeding duration, mothers who responded yes to the "Did you breastfeed?" question were simply asked the age of the baby when they stopped breastfeeding completely. The survey made no distinction between exclusive breastfeeding and mixed feeding, nor did it ascertain whether the breastfeeding occurred by bottle or only at the breast. For the body mass index definitions and conclusion, the study authors were using data based on CDC growth charts that, as discussed in an earlier chapter, misrepresent the normal growth pattern of babies. These distinctions have major ramifications for outcomes, particularly obesity measures. For example, Colen's sibling study found breastfeeding's beneficial influence on body mass index decreased by 66 percent between siblings across families and siblings within families—an outcome that could be affected by how the child was breastfed and for how long. But these important details about methodology are not discussed when flashy study headlines hit the media.

Probe a little deeper and you'll find that 32 percent of the mothers in Colen's sample smoked during pregnancy, 43 percent said they drank during pregnancy, and the mean family income of her group was $60,000, slightly above the $53,657 median household income for the U.S. Yet there's no discussion of how the potential effects of smoking, alcohol use, and socioeconomics may impact results. For the behavioral assessments, the authors relied mostly on data from interviews, where mothers were asked questions about whether their child has difficulty concentrating, is easily confused, or obeys when told to eat. There was no mention of how the researchers accounted for bias in the responses. Knowing the immense pressure women feel to breastfeed and the immense guilt they have when they don't, is a mother more likely to represent her formula-fed child as equally competent as her breastfed child? It's an important question. In addition, the footnotes to the NLSY data sets show that the siblings can be biological, step, or adopted, which raises a number of questions about how the siblings may be genetically different beyond whether they were breastfed or not. Yet the authors of the sibling study analyzed all pairs in the same way.

The most problematic aspect of the study is the authors' questionable assumption that all sibling pairs were born into and developed in the same environment, where nothing was different except whether they were breastfed or not. Anyone who has multiple children can tell you that from the arrival of one child to the next, life circumstances can be very different: parental employment, health, and marital status all change, and thus so do priorities, stress levels, and other factors. Let's look at the experiences of my two children, who are four years apart. Even though both were breastfed exclusively for twelve months, what happened after the breastfeeding period was very different for each child. For example, I freelanced and worked at home until my first child, my daughter, was three years old. That means that after being weaned, my daughter ate mostly homemade food that I dutifully prepared with fresh and organic ingredients; I had time to devote to cooking nutritious family meals. She also had my undivided attention for reading, music lessons, playdates, and other developmental activities. By the time my son arrived, our family financial situation dictated that I return to work after taking off one year (the maximum time my company would hold your job). After my son's breastfeeding period and after I returned to work, my son was in the care of a nanny. I did not prepare homemade baby foods the way I used to. I simply did not have the time. He ate more store-bought baby foods. In fact, the whole family ate more store-bought, processed foods. And while I did my best to find a caregiver who agreed to follow the strict schedule I left for reading, music, playtime, and limiting television, I was not in control of his daily activities. I am completely aware that my second child's lived experience was very different than that of my first. And it didn't have anything to do with breastfeeding. This is the nature of life. Anytime we are comparing siblings over an extended period of time beyond the breastfeeding years, it is unfair and slightly irresponsible to conclude that the reason for any difference in their health or developmental outcomes should be attributed to breastfeeding alone or examined only within the context of breastfeeding.

Things get even more dangerous when scientific reporting focuses solely on the findings with little regard for the researchers and funders involved. At times, we need to analyze the scientists delivering the decision-guiding information the way we analyze politicians and CEOs—with a critical eye. In January 2013, *The New England Journal of Medicine* published a headline-grabbing report, "Myths, Presumptions and Facts about Obesity," which disputed, among other factors, links between breastfeeding and a lower risk of childhood obesity. The media enthusiastically spread the word, saying the study debunked any association between breastfeeding and a lower risk of obesity later in life. The media did not cover the many holes in the *NEJM* study, such as the lack of systematic review—a type of literature review that critically analyzes multiple research studies or papers. Nor did the media dig into where or why those holes existed. But the most glaring problem was the funding source of the research and the numerous conflicts of interests of the study authors. The authors disclosed receiving compensation, travel reimbursement, lecture fees, and consulting fees from several groups, including Mead Johnson (makers of Enfamil infant formula), the Global Dairy Platform and other dairy associations (most infant formula is made from dairy products), and various drug makers. The authors also received funding from Kraft Foods, McDonald's, Coca-Cola, PepsiCo, and Jenny Craig—all huge processed-food makers—which studies have found markedly decrease scientific objectivity. In fact, the disclosures took up a half page of fine print of the journal. And these were not one-off, here-and-there payments. For example, a lead author, Arne Astrup, disclosed receiving payment for board membership from the Global Dairy Platform, Kraft Foods, Knowledge Institute for Beer, McDonald's Global Advisory Council, Arena Pharmaceuticals, Basic Research, Novo Nordisk, Pathway Genomics, Jenny Craig, and Vivus; receiving lecture fees from the Global Dairy Platform, Novo Nordisk, Danish Brewers Association, GlaxoSmithKline, Danish Dairy Association,

International Dairy Foundation, European Dairy Foundation, and AstraZeneca; owning stock in Mobile Fitness; holding patents regarding the use of flaxseed mucilage or its active component for suppression of hunger and reduction of prospective consumption and other patents, including one for a method to regulate energy balance for weight management.

The disclosure section continued: "Dr. Pate reported receiving consulting fees from Kraft Foods. Dr. Rolls reports having a licensing agreement for the Volumetrics trademark with Jenny Craig. Dr. Thomas reports receiving consulting fees from Jenny Craig. Dr. Allison reports serving as an unpaid board member for the International Life Sciences Institute of North America; receiving payment for board membership from Kraft Foods; receiving consulting fees from Vivus, Ulmer and Berne, Paul, Weiss, Rifkind, Wharton, Garrison, Chandler Chicco, Arena Pharmaceuticals, Pfizer, National Cattlemen's Association, Mead Johnson Nutrition, Frontiers Foundation, Orexigen Therapeutics, and Jason Pharmaceuticals; receiving lecture fees from Porter Novelli and the Almond Board of California; receiving payment for manuscript preparation from Vivus; receiving travel reimbursement from International Life Sciences Institute of North America; receiving other support from the United Soybean Board and the Northarvest Bean Growers Association; receiving grant support through his institution from Wrigley, Kraft Foods, Coca-Cola, Vivus, Jason Pharmaceuticals, Aetna Foundation, and McNeil Nutritionals; and receiving other funding through his institution from the Coca-Cola Foundation." The list went on.

Marion Nestle, a New York University professor of nutrition

and food studies, was quoted as saying in a news interview: "I can't understand the point of the paper unless it's to say that the only things that work to prevent obesity are drugs, bariatric surgery, and meal replacements, all of which are made by companies with financial ties to the authors."

That the authors received ongoing compensation from food and drug companies is a conflict of interest and puts the study results in serious question. Are we really to believe that these authors are objectively evaluating the science? Was this conflict of interest ever raised during what we would expect to be a rigorous peer review process? Peer review is at the heart of the processes of not just medical journals but of all of science. The peer review was conceived to improve the merit of papers actually being published and was supposed to be an objective process. Considered the sacred cow of science, it is the method by which grants are allocated, papers published, academics promoted, and Nobel Prizes won. Articles in peer-reviewed journals are considered to have more scientific integrity than those appearing in publications without peer review, which are seen as less rigorous and so not taken as seriously. The general public has come to rely on these markers to help them weed out valuable research findings from the questionable ones. But the peer review process has also come under intense scrutiny in recent years, particularly after several notable cases of reviewer bias and even fabricated peer review reports. "In August 2015, the publisher Springer retracted sixty-four articles from ten different subscription journals 'after editorial checks spotted fake e-mail addresses, and subsequent internal investigations uncovered fabricated peer review reports,' according to a statement on their Web site. The retractions came only months after BioMed Central, an open-access publisher also owned by Springer, retracted forty-three articles for the same reason," wrote one author on a commentary on peer review fraud published in *NEJM* in December 2015. Turns out, some of the quality measures we've been taught to rely on aren't as infallible as we would like to believe. And many are using these scientific findings to make significant health decisions. Even if you can possibly look beyond the financial entanglements of the study authors, it was clear that the authors ignored a growing body of research on the connection between breastfeeding and obesity. There are several studies that show that breast milk contains complex nutrient combinations that may influence insulin resistance and metabolic responses. One study comparing the milk of humans and other species suggested that the high lactose and cholesterol content of human milk supports growth of the central nervous system, whereas the high protein and mineral content of other species' milk supports rapid gains in physical size.

Feeding at the breast also creates a unique habit of self-regulation. Studies show breastfed infants are more quickly able to recognize feelings of satiety. They nurse until they feel full and then they stop. Imagine eating a plate of food with your eyes closed—with only your stomach to tell you when you've had enough. Therefore, a breastfed baby is less likely to be obese because from birth he learns to eat from his internal feeding cues to determine if he is full or not. In contrast, formula feeding is a more parent-driven feeding activity, with the regulation of intake directed by the parents rather than the infant. Compared with nursing infants, bottle-fed infants are fed on a more regular schedule, and the average number of feeds consistently suggests that parents are driving intake patterns. Subsequent research has shown that common bottle feeding practices, such as "emptying the bottle" and serving larger volumes of formula at feedings, are associated with excess weight gain in the first six months of life. In one study published in the journal *Pediatrics,* infants whose mothers were randomized to consume carrot juice during the third trimester or during the first two months of lactation consumed greater amounts of, and showed fewer negative facial responses in response to, a carrot-flavored cereal compared with infants whose mothers did not drink carrot juice or eat carrots during pregnancy and lactation. The study suggests that flavors within both the amniotic fluid and breast milk may help guide infants toward flavors and shape early preferences. These are powerful nuances to the linkages between obesity and breastfeeding that may not fit into a simple "breakthrough" headline. The 2013 *NEJM* study authors did not acknowledge any of this growing body of research and none of the reporting covered the omission.

This type of simplistic reporting is dangerous and irresponsible. And there are four players in these fiascos: scientists, who face an increasingly competitive grant environment and are looking for media attention but don't have the time to help the public or policy makers understand the science; the media, with editors who insist on story hooks and reporters who are looking for short headlines and sound bites but rarely educate readers on the scientific process; doctors who unknowingly tout faulty science; and the general public, particularly women, who are leaning on science to help justify the false "choices" they make about how to feed their babies. Science is no longer just a tool for decision making. Or a way to better inform mothering. Science has also become a WMD—a weapon for mom destruction. When Colen's study and its provocative headline were released, the writer of the Slate piece concluded her professionally written and scientifically researched column with, "Hopefully this study will give women who can't or don't want to breast feed for whatever reason more ammunition to tell the breast-is-best purists to piss off." The gloves were off. Science—and, in this case, a questionable study—was the "ammunition" of choice. Women took to the comment section of the post and hit social media to bash and attack each other in the name of new research. Desperate to defend their choices, women use any science that sounds good to build a case to support a position and destroy the counternarrative. Mothers who have likely spent hours vetting physicians, a child care provider, or a stroller are willing to take most science by the headline, without the tools and resources to probe deeper.

Quite frankly, we don't understand the process. Scientific discovery is not a onetime event; it's a complex winding road with many trials and errors along the way. Instead, most of us expect each new study and each new headline to bring final certainty, but science is cumulative. "Only one in fifty reported scientific breakthroughs is a real breakthrough," noted one science journalism professor in Germany. What science does provide is a consensus of experts, based on the evidence they've accumulated and analyzed. Take smoking. Even now, certain elements of tobacco science remain unclear, such as why some smokers get lung cancer and others do not. Yet as a complete scientific body of knowledge, we know that cigarettes cause cancer and even secondhand smoke is harmful. No one doubts that fact today, regardless of the elements of uncertainty that remain unproved by science. The consensus of expert advice favors breast milk as the normal food for babies.

Doubt-mongering works—as it did in the past for smoking and does now with climate change—in part because we don't understand what it means to say something is a cause. We think it means that if A causes B, then if you do A, you will get B. As in, if smoking causes cancer, then if you smoke, you will get cancer. But that is not the case. We all know someone who smoked for years and never got cancer. In science, there can also be a statistical cause, in the sense that if you smoke you are more likely to get cancer. Or if you breastfeed, your infant is less likely to have severe infections. Uncertainty is a part of science. But it also makes it vulnerable to being misrepresented. Knowing this, infant formula companies and the ancillary industries repeatedly twist normal scientific uncertainty into a way to undermine the validity of actual scientific knowledge. This is dangerous and wrong.

Meanwhile, despite the efforts to manufacture uncertainty about the power of breast milk and to show there are insignificant differences in breastfed and formula-fed babies, infant formulas spend a lot of money and time seeking patents for human milk composition and stockpiling breast milk with plans to emulate it as best as possible. In a recent analyst conference call, Mead Johnson CEO Jakobsen, boasted that at Mead Johnson "we operate the largest breast milk bank in the world where we regularly collect breast milk from all over the world." Even with their patents and thousands of gallons of mother's milk for research, there has not been one study proving infant formula to be better than breast milk. There is absolutely no evidence that infant formula improves the health of mothers or babies. As Dr. Kramer said to me in a 2013 interview: "The bottom line is that nobody has shown that formula feeding is better for any health outcome in the mother or the baby. If you take that as the bottom line—that nobody has demonstrated that formula is better for the mother or the baby for anything—then the rest, in a way, is irrelevant."

The Infant Formula Breakthrough

The dangerous relationship between science and breastfeeding is not just about breast-milk research. The field of science has worked tirelessly and benefited handsomely from applying scientific innovation to the quest to replicate and replace mother's milk. One of the biggest wins for infant formula was the development of synthetic versions of DHA and ARA, two long-chain fatty acids found naturally in breast milk that are known for their benefit to brain and eye development. DHA, which stands for docosahexaenoic acid, is a polyunsaturated fatty acid of the omega-3 family. This particular fatty acid is concentrated in the cells of the human brain and in the membranes of the retinal photoreceptors in the eyes. ARA is short for arachidonic acid, which is an omega-6 fatty acid.

The synthetic version of the DHA and ARA oils were first created in 1999 by Martek Biosciences Corporation and were quickly introduced as an additive to infant formula. Their patented, genetically modified oils are called DHASCO (docosahexaenoic acid-rich single-cell oil) for the synthetic DHA and ARASCO (arachidonic acid-rich single-cell oil) for ARA, both marketed under the brand name Life's DHA. The breakthrough created a financial windfall for the infant formula makers as they laid claim to actually mimicking the complexities of mother's milk. Even before the additive oil made it into a bottle, Martek was clear about the marketing potential for convincing parents that infant formula was close to breast milk. The company's own 1996 investment promotional materials said, "Even if [the DHA/ARA blend] has no benefit, we think it would be widely incorporated into formulas as a marketing tool and to allow companies to promote their formula as 'closest to human milk.'" Since officially hitting the market in 2002, almost all brands of formula sold in the United States are now fortified with DHASCO and ARASCO oils.

Turns out, the process for replicating what naturally occurs in breast milk is not very natural at all. The breasts do not need anything to make DHA and ARA. But in a lab, the DHA is extracted from fermented microalgae and the ARA is extracted from soil fungus—items that are not even part of a human diet. To be exact, Martek ferments laboratory-grown algae and fungus, extracting the DHA with hexane, a neurotoxic petroleum-based solvent, then bleaching and deodorizing it before making it into powder form. The AHA additive, ARASCO, is obtained from the *Pythium insidiosum* or *Mortierella alpine* species of fungus, using a similar production and extraction process. Not very natural. Fungal food sources have the potential of acting as opportunistic pathogens in individuals with compromised immune systems, doctors say. Hexane is considered a neurotoxin and a hazardous air pollutant. It is a chemical by-product of gasoline refining and is also used as a solvent for glues, varnishes, and inks and as a cleaning agent in the printing industry. The possible long-term dangers of algae, fungus, and rocket fuels in our babies are not yet known, but most formula-fed babies ingest it every time they have a bottle. The benefits to babies is still unclear.

An extensive review of synthetic DHA and ARA research was published in the *Journal of Nutrition.* As far back as 1997, the research concluded that there was not enough evidence to support the addition of these fatty acids to formula. In animal studies, there were reported side effects such as oily, soft stool and oily hair. After four weeks, rat pups had higher liver weights; after three months, they showed elevated serum alkaline phosphatase (ALP) levels, which are linked to liver and bone disease.

The algae DHA is not identical to what is found in human milk. Human fatty acids are structurally different from those manufactured from plant sources, and the acids interact with one another in a very special matrix. Just because human fatty acids perform as they do in human milk does not mean they will perform the same way in an artificial construct.

The Food and Drug Administration, charged with keeping our food supply safe, accepted Martek's claims about the safety and effectiveness of its synthetic fatty acids instead of making its own independent assessments. The oils were allowed onto the market with the stipulation that they would be monitored and a caution that the scientific evidence on the benefits of these additives was mixed. This means "give the formula to as many babies as possible and see what happens." Since the clinical trials (experiments on babies) were done on small numbers, this allows the formula companies to have access to the entire population of babies born in the United States every year: four million unsuspecting infants and their misinformed parents.

According to a panel of independent scientists convened by the Institute of Medicine, premarket safety tests for these DHA/ARA oils were inadequate. The panel concluded that insufficient safety tests were performed. Certain tests were performed only on rats, when they should have been performed on nonhuman primates as well. No chronic toxicity or chronic carcinogenicity studies were performed, not even on rats. In fact, none of the "long-term" safety tests lasted for more than ninety days. The real testing is being staged on a generation of unsuspecting babies—putting infant health on the line to boost profits. This represents an enormous uncontrolled experiment that bypasses informed consent and is being supported by many health care professionals who are wedded to the infant formula industry. Infant formula with DHASCO/ARASCO is priced at 15 to 30 percent more than standard formula. The International Baby Food Action Network (IBFAN) estimates that infant formula supplemented with DHASCO/ARASCO costs parents an additional $200 per year. There is no way to quantify how the misleading marketing of infant formula as having breast-milk-like qualities contributes to low breastfeeding rates in this country.

The biggest financial benefactor has been Enfamil, made by Mead Johnson, which was the first to add artificial DHA and ARA and market them as magical nutrients in their formula. Enfamil advertisements declared "Enfamil LIPIL improves brain development. No other formula gives your baby the best start in life." The fact that infant formula makers plow millions into simulating the components of breast milk and use breast milk as the substance they seek to emulate should speak volumes about the superiority of breast milk. Pepsi would never say it is trying to be as good as Coke—that is a de facto endorsement of Coke.

Another advertisement said, "Enfamil PREMIUM is clinically proven to result in IQ scores that are similar to those of breastfed infants." In order to be "clinically proven," findings from a clinical trial must be repeated and corroborated by other scientists. This did not happen. Mead Johnson based its IQ claims on the results of one clinical trial, conducted by scientists affiliated with the Dallas-based Southwest Retina Foundation. In a 2007 publication, they shared their results: children who were fed formula with DHA and ARA during the first seventeen weeks of life had visual acuity and IQ scores similar to breastfed infants. This team of scientists was sponsored by Mead Johnson (maker of Enfamil), which has, over the years, supplied free formula for trials and granted more than $1 million to support research. Since that sponsored study, no other clinical trial to date has found any benefit to these synthetic additives. In fact, almost twenty other clinical trials found that adding synthetic DHA and ARA in formula provides no benefit in mental and visual development.

Meanwhile, parents and medical professionals continue to report negative reactions in babies fed with formula products containing synthetic DHA and ARA. In 2011 the FDA announced it would investigate claims that DHA-ARA infant formulas support brain and eye development.

In the meantime, Life's DHA is still being sold in many regular and so-called organic brands, which many consumers trust. From Martek's own Web site, here is a list of infant formulas containing their product, which is both genetically modified and typically manufactured using a known toxin:

Earth's Best Organic Soy with DHA & ARA (Hain Celestial Group)

Enfamil LIPIL (Mead Johnson)

Enfamil Next Step (Mead Johnson)

Isomil 2 Advance (Abbott)

Nestlé Good Start Supreme with DHA & ARA (Nestlé USA)

Parent's Choice Organic (Wal-Mart)

Similac Advance (Abbott)

Ultra Bright Beginnings Lipids (PBM Products, LLC)

These brands are included in at least ninety-eight reports of adverse reactions filed with the FDA by parents and doctors. The Cornucopia Institute, a nonprofit focused on social justice in the food chain, requested copies of the reports through a Freedom of Information Act request, as part of their Organic Integrity Project. The adverse reports ranged from constipation and bowel obstruction to vomiting and diarrhea, as infants endure months of pain and fussiness and parents face months of anxiety and distress. In some cases it was not possible to determine if the reported problems were due to bacterial contamination of the formula, lactose intolerance or allergies, or other problems commonly experienced with infant formula. Although a clear link could not be established, there is still the potential that DHA and ARA oils are implicated in some of these cases. The adverse-reaction reports represent only the tip of the iceberg, especially since most parents remain unaware that Martek's DHA and ARA oils may be the cause of their infant's problems. Some parents and their babies have endured symptoms for weeks or months before identifying the cause, believing it was simply colic or unexplained fussiness. In reality, babies are needlessly sick in part because of a scientific endeavor to mimic mother's milk for the sake of greater profits. Imagine if the millions wasted on developing and marketing a potentially dangerous substitute was spent on creating the policies and resources mothers needed to easily nurse their own babies and then making sure any necessary substitutes were as rigorously tested as possible. Instead, misleading infant formula production and marketing is often viewed as a victimless crime and therefore not a serious problem.

Whether we are examining the scientific research on breast milk or the application of scientific advances to replicating breast milk, it seems that mothers and infants lose. Do we know everything about breast milk? No. Breast milk is a complex, living substance brimming with live cells, enzymes, and bioactive compounds. Lactation and human milk remain some of the least researched aspects of human functions. Have some advocates overemphasized the health benefits that have been proved by science? Probably. Even Kramer noted this dangerous misstep in our interview. "There's no question that the science overall supports the benefits of breastfeeding. But the arguments against the research question if all of the benefits attributed to breastfeeding have been equally well-documented scientifically. And the answer is no," Kramer says.

Here's what we do know: doubt-mongering works, commercial interests thwart what's best for public health, and our concept of what scientific evidence means can be severely flawed. We only need to look at our failures to act decisively in response to the body of scientific evidence on tobacco, acid rain, and global warming. Go back to 1969, and the now infamous memo written by an executive from the tobacco giant Brown & Williamson: "Doubt is our product." Thirty-seven years later, U.S. district judge Gladys Kessler found that the tobacco industry had "devised and executed a scheme to defraud consumers and potential consumers" about the hazards of cigarettes. These were hazards that their own internal company documents proved they had known since as early as 1953 and yet they consistently conspired to suppress this knowledge. Their indictment, under the RICO Act (Racketeer Influenced and Corrupt Organizations) was based on overwhelming evidence that they led an intentional campaign, initially spearheaded by the high-powered public-relations firm they hired, to fight the facts and to sell doubt. Their chief objective was to protect the highly profitable business of tobacco sales. The health of Americans was never a consideration.

Their insidious campaign relied heavily on industry-sponsored science—hiring scientists and funding research to create their own so-called evidence. The tobacco industry's position was that there was "no proof" that tobacco was bad, and they fostered that position by manufacturing a "debate," creating their own research and then convincing the mass media that responsible journalists had an obligation to present "both sides" of the issues. As part of their doubt-mongering strategy, tobacco companies used scientists who appeared to be independent, when, in fact, many of the payments from tobacco companies were channeled through other organizations and special-interest groups. External research was used to bolster the industry's position that the public should decide for themselves and that government was interfering in the personal lives of Americans. Then they created front groups with names suggestive of public-interest groups and began what became a standard industry practice of hiring various think tanks and consulting firms to defend their products. Does any of this ring a bell? The whole strategy is eerily similar to the tactics deployed by the infant formula companies. The plan to create doubt that breast milk is actually better than formula is a business strategy. It is not a public health directive or the result of the actual scientific body of evidence. Much of the so-called scientific debate over the benefits of breast milk is not waged for the sake of women's ability to choose, it is for a company's ability to churn profits, which they plow back into industry-sponsored research to bolster the likelihood of outcomes that serve their profit-making needs. Over time, this faulty science becomes part of systematic reviews and other study methodologies.

This science can be used to shape national policy. Consider the government's dietary guidelines (DGA). According to the *1990 National Nutrition Monitoring and Relation Research Act*, every five years, the Department of Health and Human Services (HHS) and the U.S. Department of Agriculture must jointly publish nutritional and dietary information and guidelines for the general public based on current scientific and medical knowledge. The guidelines are used to shape the makeup of federal food assistance programs, such as the Special Supplemental Nutrition Program for Women, Infants and Children (WIC), and help determine which foods are chosen for the USDA's National School Lunch Program and School Breakfast Program. These guidelines are the basis for federal food programs, recommended diets for pregnant women, and are used to set health policies as well as serve as the foundation of national nutrition education for the public. In a nutshell, they are powerful and influence the diets of millions of Americans. At least for Americans over the age of two. For years, the guidelines have ignored the youngest Americans, skipping over the critical period of infancy to twenty-four months.

The gaping omission was mostly due to a limited understanding of how important the birth to twenty-four-month period was to a person's future health and well-being. That all changed when David Barker, a doctor and research scientist in England, was among the first to tie chronic disease in adulthood to growth patterns in early life. His work began in the 1980s while studying birth and death records in England, where he noticed a link between low birth weight and a risk of dying from coronary heart disease as an adult. He developed a hypothesis that early-life nutrition and growth is an important factor in determining whether a baby will grow up to be more or less vulnerable to chronic diseases like heart disease, high blood pressure, diabetes, and obesity later in life. This finding led to a new understanding that chronic adult diseases are "programmed" in the womb by malnutrition and other harmful influences and gave birth to what has become a major global research area referred to as Developmental Origins of Health and Disease (DoHaD). "Over the years there has been a growing demand to address the relationship of early nutrition to health outcomes throughout the life span due to its importance in public health. Dietary intake during the earliest stages of life requires an increased demand for nutrients to support growth and development and prevent long-term health problems," said Angie Tagtow, executive director of the Center for Nutrition and Policy and Promotion, USDA, in an e-mail interview. "At CNPP, we are committed to our mission of improving the health and well-being of Americans by developing and promoting dietary guidance that links scientific research to the nutrition needs of consumers," Tagtow said. The B-24 advisory committee, made up primarily of doctors, scientists, and nutritionists, has been charged with first reviewing the body of scientific and medical evidence in nutrition and then making recommendations. But the uptick in industry-sponsored research and the insidious practices of the infant formula companies has many wondering how objective these recommendations will be.

If the most recent DGA is any indication, concerns may be justified. In January 2016, when the 2015–2020 DGA were released, nutritionists and food advocates expressed serious concern that the USDA eliminated restrictions on eggs and red meat—a decision, some food experts say, that was due to the influence of powerful food lobbies for dairy and beef and the growing amount of research that is sponsored by the egg industry. For forty years the government had cautioned against egg intake since eggs are the largest single source of cholesterol. Elevated cholesterol levels have been linked to coronary heart disease, type 2 diabetes, high blood pressure, and stroke. However, when governmental agencies are basing national nutrition recommendations on a body of scientific evidence that has been increasingly industry-sponsored, the potential for skewed research and therefore damaging policies are present.

This is exactly what breastfeeding advocates fear with the so-called B-24 project (the plan to include birth to 24 months now in the dietary guidelines). That somewhere between the impact of industry-sponsored research muddling the landscape and the pattern of infant formula companies insinuating themselves into policy decisions regarding infant feeding, the end result won't be optimal. Another policy letdown. Tagtow would not comment on the specifics of the process or any protections to prevent undue influence from breast milk substitute companies, only stating in her e-mailed comments, "We are proud to be embarking on this endeavor and paving the way to better health for our most vulnerable populations." On a personal level, women look to science and important tools like the DGA to assist with decision making. They are often unaware of the behind-the-scenes factors that compromise the quality of the science and therefore the integrity of policy guidance. Without our traditional support circles or generations of women with breastfeeding knowledge, we increasingly turn to science for evidence to feed based on our biological norm.

It should concern all women to see our natural instincts about our bodies and our children pushed to the background in favor of "science." Yes, we live in a complex world without easy answers, so we can expect missteps and a body of expert knowledge that develops as it makes its way through difficult questions and unusual circumstances. But feeding based on our biological norm shouldn't be one of those complex issues. Feeding children the way infants have been fed and the way that the species has survived for millions of years should not be one of the questions we have to turn to science to answer. Let's leave those winding journeys to the real mysteries of our society, like figuring out cancer.

Our trust in science needs to be particular and focused as we improve our ability to decipher good science from the bad. Even our reliance on good science should be balanced with other knowledge, including our natural mechanisms and our confidence in our maternal authority in regard to our family's health. The current predicament of women, blindly relying on any science and making knee-jerk reactions to so-called breakthroughs about breastfeeding, even while infant formula has never been proved to be advantageous, is not solely our own doing. Women have been pushed into this corner by commercial interests, societal pressures, and a confounding lack of support. When women return to work two or three weeks after giving birth and then stop breastfeeding (or don't bother starting) because it's too difficult to pump and work, they end up using science to justify their infant formula use. After running up against a barrage of structural and social barriers, women use science to defend the circumstances they are forced into.

The Things Unseen:
Battling Structural Barriers

Out of sight, out of mind.

—PROVERB

The nurse told her that it wasn't her fault.

On July 18, 2013, Allison Montgomery gave birth to a beautiful eight-pound, four-ounce baby girl at a large New York City hospital. Her husband, Steven, was by her side. Thirty-seven minutes after giving birth, she was wheeled down a twenty-five-foot corridor to her room, while her baby, Jane, was taken to the nursery. Exhausted from seventeen hours of labor, Allison simply wanted to rest with her baby on her bosom. Instead, nurses whirled about, taking her vital signs. Machines beeped. Her baby was down the hall having all the state-required newborn screenings. The pink crib card on baby Jane's bassinet said "I am breastfed." What seemed like hours later, the nurse wheeled a crying baby Jane to her mother for feeding. Allison can still recall the feeling of placing her baby on her breast, remembering the books she read and the YouTube videos she watched about latch. Baby Jane sucked a few times and cried even harder. The mild-mannered nurse with her hair in a tidy bun gently told Allison not to feel bad. "Your milk probably hasn't come in yet," she said, and offered to bring her a bottle of formula to feed her with in the meantime. "You can try again when the lactation consultant is here tomorrow," she said. And she did. And baby Jane nursed. When Allison was discharged, she was given a bag with free formula, formula coupons, and a booklet from the American Academy of Pediatrics.

Two weeks later, the pediatrician blamed it on her breasts.

It was Allison's first time out of the house since delivery, and she had spent most of that time sitting on the couch constantly nursing. In the morning before he left for the office, Steven would prepare Allison's lunch, either a salad, sandwich, or a plate that could be easily microwaved. He would also fill up the water pitcher next to the couch, so she could stay hydrated while nursing. When her husband came home from the office, she would take a ten-minute shower break, and then it seemed as if Baby Jane would start crying again, and Allison was right back to sitting and breastfeeding. She was determined to get it right. She had read the breastfeeding books, saw the pictures in glossy magazines, and bought the cute nursing bras and tanks. But nothing could prepare her for what happened at the doctor's visit. There were lots of questions for the new parents, and then Baby Jane was weighed and measured. She had lost three pounds. At first, from the matter-of-fact way the doctor said it, Allison wasn't sure if that was normal or a cause for concern, but she sensed it was the latter. Allison was devastated. She didn't want to look at her husband. She said she feared she was not producing enough milk. That Jane was nursing constantly. Without any further questions, the pediatrician accepted Allison's self-diagnosis and simply suggested that she supplement with formula. "This is very common with women. Many mothers don't have enough milk to breastfeed. Don't feel bad," he said consolingly. But she did feel bad. On the way out, she noticed the familiar brown teddy bear logo on the weight chart. It was the same logo on the discharge bag she received from the hospital. She began to supplement once, then twice a day. Three weeks later, she was no longer breastfeeding at all.

On August 19, 2013, more than three thousand miles across the Atlantic Ocean, Christina Cooper gave birth to a healthy ten-pound, eleven-ounce baby girl named Grace in a hospital outside London. She delivered with a midwife, as is the custom in England unless there are medical complications. Two weeks later, Grace's weight had dipped to seven pounds, nine ounces—slightly more than the usual postbirth weight loss. The visiting nurse told her to consider supplementing because her breasts may not be producing enough milk. But Christina was also determined to get it right. She walked down the block to the local health center for a breastfeeding support group two or three times a week. From other women Christina learned what breastfeeding looked and felt like. And she began to sense something was wrong. And then Christina began to notice it with her own eyes. One of her breasts just didn't look like the other. The right breast was conspicuously smaller than the left. Even at times when both breasts should be full and leaking—only one was. She noticed her baby didn't have the satisfied "milk coma" look on her face when she fed off the right breast. When she squeezed her right nipple to express milk, very little came out. Christina didn't know the medical term for her lactation failure, but she knew that one breast was not producing. The doctor had never seen this before but repeatedly told her that one breast could never produce enough milk to sustain a child. The nurses told her to supplement, "just to be sure." Her mother-in-law pressured her to formula feed. But Christina was determined and confident. She asked the other mothers and read everything she could to learn about increasing and fortifying her milk supply. She ate halva, a Middle Eastern dessert, and drank lots of water. It was the next doctor's visit that she will never forget. Grace had gained two pounds. It was just the boost of confidence she needed. Sixteen months later, Christina was still breastfeeding her plump and thriving daughter with only one properly lactating breast. Three years later, she gave birth to her son, and breastfed him, too, for eighteen months with one breast.

There's a reason why one woman with two functioning breasts is convinced she has insufficient milk while another woman successfully breastfeeds for over a year with only one properly lactating breast. Studies show that less than 5 percent of women are actually physically incapable of breastfeeding—a negligible number compared with the many women who are diagnosed with low milk supply. If you look at more traditional societies, the rate of mothers successfully breastfeeding their babies is near 100 percent. The so-called insufficient milk phenomenon is primarily a plague of "modern" societies, most notably in the United States. The problem has very little to do with a biological or physiological failure and almost everything to do with the psychological, social, and cultural forces that suffocate our normal infant feeding rhythms.

I often say that women don't breastfeed, cultures do. The prevailing cultural norms create an environment that either supports breastfeeding or discourages it. That is why talking about breastfeeding ultimately leads to talking about the structure of society. That includes hospital maternity care, the quality of maternity leave policies, and the availability of viable options for flexible work scheduling. Add to that an industrialized infant feeding system, a culture that glorifies breast-baring Victoria's Secret ads but that still deems breast-feeding photos on Facebook to be controversial, and a health care system where infant formula is given out for free at hospitals and a high-quality breast pump costs $350. Then, somehow, mothers or their bodies are blamed for any breastfeeding failure, when, in fact, the odds are stacked against women before they even begin. We may feel we are pushing breast-feeding as a message, but we aren't embracing or supporting it as a culture. The sobering reality is that, given our societal structures and cultural contradictions, breastfeeding is nearly impossible.

In my work traveling and talking to mothers, as a rule I never "sell" breastfeeding on the fact that it is free. Yes, the costs of breastfeeding in terms of a good pump and a few good nursing bras pale in comparison to the costs of a year's worth of formula, but breastfeeding is a huge time commitment. And time is money. A mother who is exclusively breastfeeding can easily spend up to six hours nursing per twenty-four hours.

This doesn't account for those critical two-week and six-week growth spurts where nursing can occur even more frequently. Even at a proposed federal minimum wage of $15 per hour, that's $90 per day, $2,700 per month, or $16,200 for six months of exclusive breastfeeding, if we had to pay for breastfeeding on a time-spent basis. That's up to $32,400 for the year if you meet the American Academy of Pediatrics' recommended twelve months of breastfeeding. That's a basic minimum compensation that nobody is willing to pay mothers yet it is much less than what you will pay for a nanny in places like Brooklyn, New York. According to the Park Slope Parents 2015 Nanny Compensation Survey, the hourly rate paid to nannies ranged from $14 to $20 in that year, with an average of $16.61 per hour, or $34,548 per year based on a forty-hour week. A quick scan of the job-seeking Web site Indeed .com, found salaried positions with a $32,000 annual salary included an ice cream shop manager in Park City, Utah, or an area supervisor for a custodial company in Montgomery, Alabama. Those are real jobs—but mothering and providing the preventive health benefits of breastfeeding isn't viewed as valuable work. No one will pay a woman even minimum wage for mothering.

I also never, ever tell women breastfeeding is easy. Yes, compared to the logistics of mixing formula, sterilizing bottles, and traveling with extra bottles, nipples, and formula cans, the act of breastfeeding is certainly easier to manage. But the lived experience of breastfeeding for any meaningful duration is damn hard given all the structural barriers women face. Those barriers create insurmountable obstacles for many women.

The barriers begin in ob-gyn offices, where obstetricians display magazines laden with formula advertising, offer coupons for formula, and barely educate mothers prenatally on the benefits of breastfeeding. When it's time to deliver, you head to a hospital, where even the process of how we birth our babies poses another barrier. Historically, hospitals have played a pivotal role in supporting or discouraging breastfeeding. Decades ago, the medicalization of birth, a practice led by physicians and supported by pharmaceutical companies, meant the introduction of the clock—timed feedings at prescribed intervals—which completely destroyed the natural flow of nursing and perpetuated incorrect information about how babies eat. Hospitals remain notorious for regularly giving supplemental bottles of formula when a mother's milk supply is dependent on the frequency and amount of suckling, especially in the early days.

Today other common medical practices sabotage breastfeeding. Minutes after giving birth, our newborns are wheeled away for tests that could be completed at other times but aren't, despite overwhelming evidence that those precious moments after birth are critical for immediate skin-to-skin contact and for the newborn to act on its natural instincts to suck and establish the breastfeeding relationship. A mother's physical contact with her baby stimulates the production of prolactin, the milk-making hormone. With babies separated from mothers in hospital maternity wards, important instinctive knowledge is also lost and subtle feeding cues are impossible for nurses attending to several babies to notice.

Not only are mother and baby separated after birth, but their care also is immediately divvied up. The infant goes into the care of a pediatrician. The uterus is assigned to the obstetrician. And our breasts are left to the lactation consultant. (If sometime in the future there is a problem, such as cancer, then that is assigned to a surgeon.) We become the sum of our anatomical parts, but that whole person—that mother—is often left to fend for herself. Women are given a pamphlet; if lucky, a pep talk; a demonstration here or there; and perhaps a warning that her hormones may be out of whack for a little while. Within a day or two, the mother is rushed out of the hospital in order to satisfy the requirements of the health insurance companies. The baby receives attention. The mother receives lectures.

As you are discharged with samples of formula and coupons for more, friends, professionals, and even books warn women not to be too disappointed if they don't succeed at breastfeeding and emphasize how common it is for a woman to not have enough milk. The messages mothers receive around breastfeeding also include notions that nursing will exclude the father and damage any paternal-child bonding. Meanwhile, social media abounds with horror stories of cracked nipples, bloody nipples, and, even worse, children who bite.

The pressure and anxiety of it all causes many women to claim insufficient milk. In fact, when mothers self-diagnose that they have no milk, doctors mostly benignly accept that conclusion—a sudden and odd reversal of who is diagnosing whom. Especially since there is not an established diagnosis for breastfeeding problems. Lactation dysfunction doesn't even exist as a diagnosis and has no accompanying health insurance code for which doctors can bill. Within the database of federally funded medical research for 2014–16, there are fifty-eight studies on erectile dysfunction and thirteen on lactation failure. It doesn't need pointing out that erectile dysfunction is within the purview of many doctors' services and that insurance will cover the cost of Viagra. It is no wonder, then, that far too many women are quickly advised by their physicians to stop breastfeeding at the first sign of problems and consoled that their baby will be "just fine." The complexities of lactation failure are so little studied and so often misunderstood that women often feel that they are at fault, as if they are failing instead of suffering from a medical issue.

Even if breastfeeding is problem-free, just weeks after giving birth women find themselves back at work because they lack meaningful maternity leave: one in four mothers in the United States returns to work within two weeks of childbirth. Compare that to Sweden's sixteen months of paid parental leave or Finland's nine months of paid leave and provision for the mother or father to take—or split—additional paid "child care leave" until the child's third birthday. This is not just the work of socially progressive Nordic countries. With the exception of a few small countries, like Papua New Guinea or Suriname, every other nation, rich or poor, now offers some form of paid maternity leave.

Instead, the United States has the twenty-year-old federal Family and Medical Leave Act (FMLA), an unpaid leave that doesn't apply to 40 percent of the workforce because the law only requires companies with fifty or more employees to comply. To get the unpaid benefit, employees must have worked for the company for at least a year and logged 1,250 hours within the previous twelve months. And, quite frankly, a lot of families simply can't afford to take unpaid leave.

In 2013 two mothers in Congress, Senator Kirsten Gillibrand (a Democrat from New York) and Representative Rosa DeLauro (a Democrat from Connecticut), introduced the FAMILY Act (Family and Medical Insurance Leave Act), which would create a paid family leave fund at the federal level. The bill would provide workers up to twelve weeks of paid leave for their own serious illness; to care for a child, parent, or spouse with a serious illness; or to bond with a new child. Workers and employers would each contribute a very small portion of their wages into this insurance program; the self-sustaining fund would mean workers could receive up to 66 percent of their wages while on leave. "Family leave insurance" would be a more accurate description than "paid family leave," because employees would be paying much of the cost themselves.

California, New Jersey, and Rhode Island have already set up state-run, employee-funded disability- and family-care programs. In New Jersey, new mothers are entitled to reduced wages for six weeks. Rhode Island's law offers most workers with up to four weeks off with about two-thirds of their salaries (up to $752 a week), and it protects employees from being fired and losing their health insurance while they're out. And, though the maximum single leave is four weeks, each parent can take four weeks off to bond with a new baby. A mother recovering from birth could combine that with an additional six weeks paid through an existing state program, bringing her total paid time off to ten weeks. An entire family with a new baby could have fourteen weeks off, paid. Though not as robust as Sweden, these state programs are a start down the right road.

Until Congress moves on the FAMILY Act, women are left returning to work too soon after childbirth. In 2012 nearly one quarter of women who gave birth took off less than ten days, according to one study. In other cultures, the weeks after childbirth are a time when the mother needs to be taken care of and allowed to heal. This is also a precious time for bonding and caring for a new child and establishing a breastfeeding routine. But having time off after childbirth also saves lives. "We know maternity leave is associated with lower infant mortality rates," explains Jody Heymann, dean of the Fielding School of Public Health at the University of California, Los Angeles, and author of *Children's Chances: How Countries Can Move from Surviving to Thriving*. As well as receiving more one-on-one care, infants whose mothers have paid maternity leave are more likely to be breastfed, which lowers illness and hospitalization rates for them and benefits women's health. Beyond the marked health advantages, paid maternity leave creates economic gains in terms of reduced health care costs, reduced recruitment and retraining, and improved long-term earnings for women. It just makes sense.

A mother should not have to choose between her next paycheck and her baby's health and vitality. More striking research shows that paid leave is directly correlated to infant death. By charting the correlation between death rates and paid leave in sixteen European countries, a professor of public policy and economics at the University of Virginia found that a fifty-week extension in paid leave was associated with a 20 percent drop in infant deaths. The biggest drop was in the deaths of babies between one month and one year old—the prime period for breastfeeding—though the mortality of children between one and five years also decreased as paid leave went up.

Mothers benefit too. Longer maternity leaves, whether paid or unpaid, are associated with a decline in depressive symptoms, a reduction in the likelihood of severe depression, and an overall improvement in maternal health, according to a working paper issued by the National Bureau of Economic Research. One national study of 1,762 mothers found that a one-week increase in maternity leave was associated with a 5 to 6 percent reduction in depressive symptoms from six to twenty-four months after birth. Another found that women who took less than eight weeks of paid leave experienced more depression and were in worse health overall than those who had longer leaves. The stress of leaving your baby so soon or trying to pump at work reduces many women to an emotional wreck.

Without any government-mandated policy, women find themselves at the mercy of their employer or hoping to win the good boss lottery. According to the Bureau of Labor Statistics, only about 13 percent of U.S. workers have access to any form of paid family leave, which includes parental leave and other time off to care for a family member. The private sector has stepped in to fill in some of the gaps, recognizing that accommodating family dynamics improves retention and employee satisfaction. Companies like McDonald's, Chipotle, and Change.org have extended their paid maternity leave. In 2007 Google boosted its paid maternity leave from twelve to eighteen weeks. Facebook's policy includes four months of paid leave for new moms and new dads, plus a $4,000 payment for each new child, including adopted children. In 2015 Microsoft announced that mothers can take a total of twenty weeks of fully paid leave and fathers can take twelve weeks of paid leave. Netflix, a pioneer in paid leave policies, announced that new parents, both moms and dads, including adoptive parents, can take as much paid leave as they like for up to a year after the birth or adoption of a child. The Los Gatos–based streaming giant became the first company in the United States to formally institute such a generous paid leave policy.

The burden of paying for parental leave shouldn't be shouldered solely by companies, even rich and generous ones like Netflix and Microsoft. Netflix excluded, the policies at some of the most generous American companies pale in comparison with the thirty-one countries that provide a year or more of paid maternity leave, typically through government-run insurance programs.

And while things are improving for women who work in office environments, many of these policies don't trickle down to hourly employees such as factory and retail workers. Nearly 90 percent of workers in private companies are left with no paid parental leave. The lack of a federal policy in the United States widens the socioeconomic disparity that affects which infants are breastfed and for how long. The highest-paid workers are most likely to have paid family leave, according to Bureau of Labor Statistics numbers, with more than one in five of the top 10 percent of earners getting paid family leave, compared to one in twenty in the bottom quartile. Unionized workers are also more likely to get benefits than nonunionized workers.

With no set standard for all, women find themselves cobbling together maternity leave by using vacation and sick days or opting into an employer's disability insurance policy, which may pay a percentage of their salary for some of those twelve unpaid weeks. Teachers and college professors aim for summer break. These days, the concept of family planning does not refer to birth control but to figuring out how to maximize time with a newborn while staying financially solvent, employed, and sane. That is, until the unplannable happens.

Leigh Benrahou was one of those women. Benrahou and her husband carefully and methodically planned the timing of their second child to meet the twelve-month employment eligibility for FMLA at her new job as a registrar at a small college. They constantly reviewed their budget; factored in that Benrahou's mother, who works at an elementary school, would be off during the summer to babysit; and bought into Benrahou's company's disability plan so she could receive a percentage of pay during the twelve unpaid weeks of FMLA. But their carefully laid plans started to go awry in her twentieth week, when she was diagnosed with placenta previa, which can result in early delivery. Benrahou shared her story in a 2015 issue of *In These Times,* the nonprofit online magazine. Despite some bleeding and cramping, and several brief hospital stays that used up her sick days, Benrahou stuck to her plan, working as much as possible after her diagnosis in order to save her precious vacation time, the article continued. But, in late December, her water broke. Though her due date was April 1, Leigh Benrahou gave birth by C-section on Christmas Eve—too soon to qualify for FMLA leave or any payoff from her disability insurance.

Her son, Ramzi, was born at twenty-six weeks and just over two pounds. Knowing that 20 percent of babies born at his gestational age don't survive, Leigh spent the first hours after the delivery singularly focused on her tiny son's survival. He needed oxygen, since his lungs weren't fully developed. And, after he was whisked away for medical attention, Benrahou had to attend to another crisis: her carefully constructed paid maternity leave had disintegrated. So, freshly stitched up and still groggy from anesthesia, she spread out her medical fact sheets, insurance policy papers, and lists of phone numbers on her hospital bed and began to grapple with her new reality. Though her college was on winter break, which put off her return by about a week, Benrahou, who has a master's in non-profit management, realized she'd have to go back to work when classes resumed on January 6, less than two weeks after giving birth.

When women do return to work, many find themselves in a work environment that is unwelcoming or downright hostile to breastfeeding, with few legal protections to rely on. The Americans with Disabilities Act Amendments Act (ADAAA) and the Patient Protection and Affordable Care Act give pregnant women and mothers the rights to accommodations of pregnancy and breastfeeding they lacked in the past. However, interpretations vary and discrimination toward pregnant women and mothers remains a systemic problem.

Sashay Allen-Brown, a police officer with the District of Columbia Metropolitan Police Department (MPD) since 2006, returned to work twelve weeks after the birth of her son in 2011 and had decided to continue breastfeeding her child for one year. As a patrol officer she was required to wear a bulletproof vest but declined because, according to her complaint, "it was incompatible with lactation, caused pain to the breastfeeding mother, and could lead to blocked ducts and infection." According to the court documents, Allen-Brown also e-mailed her supervisor in June 2011 to express her concerns over the condition of lactation facilities, which included offices, semi-public areas, and part of a restroom. After the e-mail, she was sent to the Police and Fire Clinic to undergo a "fitness for duty" evaluation. Because she was unable to wear a vest she was put on an extended limited-duty status by the examining doctor, but shortly thereafter, Allen-Brown was placed on involuntary sick leave by an MPD human resource official. Her request for a limited-duty accommodation beyond the initial six weeks offered to all returning mothers was denied. After her sick leave expired, she was placed on "leave without pay" for approximately nine months, which was the remainder of the time she was breastfeeding. After returning to work Allen-Brown sued MPD on six counts of gender and family responsibility discrimination, pregnancy discrimination, and retaliation. After five years, and several legal setbacks, Allen-Brown was eventually granted back pay for the time she was on involuntary leave without pay, her attorney said in an interview. Allen-Brown's victory—five years later—shows the scope of the legal letdown women face when attempting to use the justice system for their reproductive rights.

Alas, new protections under the 2010 Affordable Care Act, an amendment to the Fair Labor Standards Act, now offer a federal provision that allows mothers to take unpaid, fifteen-minute breaks to pump their milk. In accordance with the

Break Time for Nursing Mothers law, employers must provide a clean, private, and nonbathroom space for mothers to express their milk and allow reasonable breaks to do so. The provision also prohibits retaliation by companies against employees who file complaints. However, the law affects only hourly workers, and none of the policies has punitive measures for lack of enforcement.

New laws mean that they have yet to be road tested. "These laws are still very new in general so the cases are a little bit all over the place at the moment," said Kathy Diane Bailey, attorney for police officer Allen-Brown, in an interview. "I don't know how it is going to sort out to tell you the truth."

In 2014 the American Civil Liberties Union (ACLU) and the Equal Employment Opportunity Commission (EEOC) took the unprecedented step of filing a lactation discrimination suit against Saint-Gobain Verallia North America, the company where thirty-one-year-old new mom Bobbi Bockoras worked for six years before having a child. Bockoras claimed that when she returned to work as a palletizer operator at a glass factory in Port Allegany, Pennsylvania, in June 2013 after giving birth, she planned to pump breast milk during breaks so she could continue nursing her infant daughter, Lyla.

But Bockoras says her supervisors first told her to pump in a bathroom; after she protested, they suggested other alternatives that also failed to meet federal requirements. Bockoras agreed to use a locker room but says it was covered in dirt and dead bugs and lacked air-conditioning. She also said that colleagues harassed her and banged on the door when she was pumping. When she complained, Bockoras says her shifts were reassigned to alternating day and overnight shifts that interfered with her feeding schedule and impeded her milk production—which her lawyers argued was tantamount to retaliation.

Bockoras's case illustrates the insurmountable obstacles women face while breastfeeding at work. Stories like Bockoras's show why women are afraid to speak out. As the ACLU senior attorney representing Bockoras said, "[T]hese obstacles . . . can make [mothers] choose between their jobs and what is in the best interest of their babies." Given the current economic climate, that is no choice at all.

In Michigan, a former employee of big-box retailer Meijer filed suit against the company in June 2016 alleging that the company failed to accommodate her need to pump milk and created a sexually hostile work environment. The mother, Rachel Keesling, who worked at a Meijer store in Genesee County, was hired in 2013 when she was nursing a three-month-old. According to Keesling's complaint, over the next year Meijer's failure to dedicate a legally required lactation room sent Keesling bouncing between a conference room, the store's bathroom, and a closet-like room that housed the store's computer server and other communications hardware. At one point, Keesling was docked pay because of delays in finding a place to express milk, her complaint states. When a union steward intervened, Meijer wiped the disciplinary actions from Keesling's personnel file, and the corporate office sent out a letter to all store managers about the store's duty under federal law with regard to nursing mothers. But in May 2014, according to the complaint, things took another turn when Keesling was told she could no longer use the server room she had been using. That day, Keesling alleges, a supervisor told her "there were monitored security cameras inside the room." Apparently a store manager had learned that Keesling was using the room "and had objected to its continued use because . . . 'you can see everything,'" Keesling was told. "There's probably a video of you on the Internet," another supervisor allegedly told Keesling. "Distraught and humiliated," Keesling says she and her fiance sought answers from the store director, but the director was "dismissive" and unapologetic, she claims. Though the director denied that the server room had a camera, Keesling says she refused to let her back into it to check. Later, Keesling requested a transfer to a different store "due to the sexually hostile environment created by the invasion of privacy and jokes about Internet videos, because of what had occurred, the scrutiny of her coworkers and managers, and the emotional distress." The store director denied Keesling a transfer, however, and Meijer fired her the very next day, "allegedly because she could not come back to the same store where her privacy was violated," Keesling says. The suit, which is still pending, seeks more than $25,000 in damages.

These cases only represent the tip of the iceberg in terms of the real-life experiences of mothers in the workplace. The Center for WorkLife Law at the University of California says it has documented a nearly 400 percent increase in caregiver discrimination suits filed between 1999 and 2008 when compared to the previous decade. For over a decade, the law center has run a hotline for caregiver discrimination claims, or "family responsibilities discrimination" claims. The center also maintains a comprehensive case database that includes decisions on almost 3,000 caregiver-discrimination cases. For every woman who does file a discrimination complaint there are countless women who suffer in silence—pumping in bathrooms and other inappropriate places—or are too fearful of retaliation or being fired that they dare not even speak up. This is a huge societal problem for mothers. Gender discrimination against pregnant women and caregivers not only jeopardizes women's careers but also the economic stability of families that increasingly depend on the paychecks of mothers.

Women now make up more than half of the U.S. labor force. Over the past forty years, the share of mothers in the workforce has risen significantly, while men's real wages over the same period have declined, making the income of working mothers an increasingly important component of household stability. For many families, quitting a job or taking an extended unpaid leave from a full-time job is just not financially tenable. What mothers really need are more policies that allow for colocated child care, flexible time, telecommuting options, and compressed workweeks.

Even if families could figure out how to survive with one part-time salary, the market for meaningful part-time work is virtually nonexistent. In recent years, the number of part-time jobs has increased a paltry 1 percent or less per year—with no mention of the actual wages for these part-time jobs. Meanwhile, a study of working mothers by the Pew Research Center showed that 74 percent work full-time while only 26 percent work part-time. Of those working mothers, 62 percent say that they would prefer to work part-time, and only 37 percent say they prefer full-time work. Only about one in ten moms

(12 percent) say that having a mother who works full-time is the ideal situation for a child. By contrast, most working fathers (79 percent) would prefer to work full-time, while only 21 percent say that they would prefer working part-time. Mothers are under pressure to work when they would prefer to do the job of mothering, but they are by and large being forced into other so-called choices and denied the life they desire. Feeling up against the wall, many women simply quit their jobs, which impacts Social Security benefits and career growth. These kinds of roadblocks and forced decisions breed anxiety and frustration—both of which are highly incompatible with a successful breastfeeding experience.

Meanwhile, any mental health expert worth his or her copay can tell you that feeling physically competent is essential to a person's overall self-esteem. So, of course, failing at something as basic as feeding one's own child can affect a woman's psyche and the rest of her motherhood journey. And for every actual failure there are fears of failure in triplicate. Therefore, is our failure at breastfeeding really a biological or physiological failure or a psychological one brought on by social or cultural triggers? And if our instincts about breastfeeding have gone awry, it is plausible and quite probable that they have gone awry for a very specific and consistent set of reasons.

And those reasons aren't just the oft-mentioned problems of a lack of education or even the absence of federal paid maternity leave. Mothers in the UK enjoy up to twelve months of paid maternity leave, yet the country still suffers from some of the lowest breastfeeding rates in the world. Only 0.5 percent of children in Britain are breastfed for twelve months, compared to 27 percent in the U.S, 35 percent in

Norway and 92 percent of children in India. There is more afoot than just policy—although that is a very critical starting point for the U.S. But, as economic pressure mounts and migration and immigration patterns change, mothers are increasingly without their extended family and traditional support circles. A study by two economic researchers at Washington University in St. Louis found that among U.S. couples with college degrees, more than 50 percent live more than thirty miles from both their mothers and only 18 percent live within thirty miles of both mothers. With limited work options and economic demands scattering family members, women are often, literally, on their own at their most vulnerable time as new mothers. With breastfeeding becoming a lost art among women, very few have family members to turn to for help in the absence of sound medical advice. The formula companies know exactly who they are while they are pregnant and are more than happy to fill the gap with their infant feeding information and "community of support."

Fixing America's broken system to be more family-friendly will take some serious political will. Even the proposed federal family leave policy is being criticized by some politicians as bad for business. This isn't the first time that the interests of business have butted heads with what's best for mothers and babies. In fact, America's thirteen-year refusal to sign the World Health Organization's UNICEF International Code of Marketing of Breast-Milk Substitutes (known as the WHO code) was all about economics and political will. Although the Carter administration was generally procode, things changed under Reagan. American industry came out forcefully against the code, saying it was highly restrictive and would "virtually eliminate legitimate competition and promotion of infant formula even to the medical community." As 118 countries approved the code at an infamous meeting in Geneva, the United States was the only opposing vote, sparking outrage among Americans. In this case, despite the voices of its citizens and the advice of the country's top medical experts, the political will of the U.S. government was clearly in the hands of the lobbyists paid handsomely by the baby food corporations. The interests of corporations were put ahead of the health interests of infants. The political climate, which was focused on getting government out of the corporate suites, became the dominant concern despite the public outcry of its own citizens. President Reagan repeatedly refused to meet with a congressional delegation to discuss it further.

The symbolism was catastrophic to women and babies around the world. Though the United States has only one vote, it dominates the world economy and sets the tone for global political priorities. Therefore, when the United States voted to put profit making ahead of mothers and babies, it sent a message that strict enforcement of the voluntary code was not required.

It wasn't until May 9, 1994, when President Bill Clinton reversed course and made the WHO code worldwide policy, joining the other member nations at the World Health Assembly in Geneva. For the first time, there was worldwide unanimity that, in the infant health area, profit should not come before public health.

But agreement doesn't always equal action. The WHO code lacks punitive measures and, in most cases, breastfeeding advocates are the only ones who know what the code really is. As factors such as cultural norms take on greater influence, many health care professionals are even wondering if the WHO code is still relevant, and if so, what is the smartest way to influence compliance. A proprietary report by a large U.S.-based foundation assessed a multidisciplinary group of stakeholders on perceptions of the WHO code and what might be done to spark a conversation about marketing breast-milk substitutes. The report found that most of the stakeholders interviewed did not view the WHO code as a key driver compared to other social and cultural factors influencing infant feeding decisions, that code compliance has lost its urgency among other issues, and that the code is confusing, which contributes to implementation challenges. Even many advocates can't easily state what falls under the code (pumps don't, but the bottles and teats needed when using pumps do). It's very hard to mobilize women around a confusing concept that many professionals don't fully understand.

Politicians will be critical to advancing necessary policy changes to limit infant formula marketing and level the playing field for breastfeeding. But there has to be political will. And political will is often connected to funding. And it's hard to get political commitments to limit infant formula marketing from politicians who receive sizable donations from infant formula companies. In 2016, Abbott Labs contributed $516,625 to various members of the House and Senate.

When not paying politicians directly, infant formula companies invest heavily in influencing politicians and policy with large payments to lobbyists. In 2015, Abbott Labs spent $2.4

million on various lobbying firms, according to the Center for Responsive Politics.

And in the political world, government funding is allocated to finding cures and providing services, not preventive health measures, such as breastfeeding. As one political analyst explained to me, "There's no politics in prevention. Once you have a disease, people want services and a cure and there is a lobby developed to push for that."

And the political discourse around breastfeeding is that the government should stay out of a very private matter instead of looking at it as a public health issue. The government mandates and supports vaccinations and other activities that it deems to be in the interest of public health, but in political circles breastfeeding remains a private issue. In 2012, at an intimate press conference kicking off the second year of her Let's Move campaign to fight childhood obesity, First Lady Michelle Obama stressed the importance of early intervention. And in highlighting steps parents can take, she recommended that women breastfeed their babies, because "kids who are breastfed longer have a lower tendency to be obese." It seemed harmless enough. But the first lady's comments came shortly after the IRS announced that, after lobbying from lawmakers, breast pumps—which can cost upward of $300—and related supplies could now be paid for with pretax Flexible Spending Accounts, or deducted from one's taxes as a medical expense, if one's total out-of-pocket medical costs added up to more than 7.5 percent of one's income. The IRS has already approved other deductible medical expenses, including contact lenses, acupuncture, and vasectomies.

Shortly after, Tea Party darling Michele Bachmann slammed

the first lady and the IRS on the Laura Ingraham radio show: "I've given birth to five babies, and I've breastfed every single one of these babies," Bachmann said. "To think that government has to go out and buy my breast pump for my babies, I mean, you wanna talk about the nanny state—I think you just got the new definition of the nanny state." To be clear, the government isn't "buying" anything for anyone, but the political discourse around breastfeeding remains provocative and volatile.

Next, conservative pundit Michelle Malkin, who also says she breastfed her two kids, chimed in through a blog post and column, attacking the first lady and the federal government for telling women how to live their lives, dubbing the initiative "Big Bosom."

The loud and clear political message that breastfeeding is a private matter prevents movement on the very public and necessary issues of paid family leave, stronger laws to protect pumping in the workplace, and the state of infant health in America. Ironically, breastfeeding is viewed as a private matter until you attempt to do it in public. Then it becomes everybody's business. Venturing out of doors to dare to nurse in public remains another issue, even though the law explicitly protects moms who breastfeed in public in almost all fifty states. Forty-seven states, D.C., and the Virgin Islands have laws that specifically allow moms to breastfeed in any public or private location. Two of the remaining states—South Dakota and Virginia—exempt breastfeeding moms from public indecency or nudity laws, and Idaho is the only state that has yet to pass any similar laws. But the frequency of media stories of women being asked to leave retail stores or airplanes makes it clear that breastfeeding is still considered a public indecency issue rather than a public health issue.

The system is broken. Or the system is fixed, depending on how you look at it. While all women suffer under the weight of the complexities of breastfeeding, some are more over-burdened than others, usually because of racial and socio-economic factors. For over forty years, rates of breastfeeding among African-American women have significantly lagged those of non-Hispanic white women. When it comes to the gold standard of infant nutrition, twelve months of exclusive breastfeeding, rates among black women are about half that of white women. While all women struggle with the structural barriers, the African-American community also battles a host of cultural barriers when attempting to breastfeed. The implications are severe. In the United States the African-American infant mortality is 2.4 times the rate of white non-Hispanic babies. One main reason for these infant deaths is that African-American babies are disproportionately born too small, too sick, or too soon. Black women have some of the highest rates of preterm births and low birth weight babies—the ones who need the protective benefits of breast milk the most. Breast milk is easier to digest for underdeveloped digestive systems and has been proved to reduce the risk of necrolitis, a leading cause of death among preemies. For a large percentage of black infants, access to breast milk can be a life or death matter.

This makes the racial disparity in breastfeeding rates, which has been closing ever so slightly in recent years, even more unacceptable. The reasons for this disparity, which spans socioeconomic status, are varied and nuanced. They range from lack of support from medical professionals to a lack of role models to the historical trauma of black women being used as wet nurses during slavery. Black women in slavery were forced to stop nursing their own children to provide breast milk for the children of the slave owner. "On the one hand, wet nursing claimed the benefits of breastfeeding for the offspring of white masters while denying or limiting those health advantages to slave infants. On the other hand, wet-nursing required slave mothers to transfer to white offspring the nurturing and affection they should have been able to allocate to their own children," writes the historian Wilma A. Dunaway in *The African-American Family in Slavery and Emancipation.* And since breastfeeding reduces fertility, slave owners forced black women to stop breastfeeding early so that they could continue breeding, often to the detriment of their infants' health, Dunaway notes.

This stunted breastfeeding experience created a stunted mothering experience and the commodification of black women as breeders and feeders. As such, white women were crucial to creating a market for black enslaved mothers' breast milk and the nutritive and maternal care black women provided to white children. Through slavery and dynamics of race and class, an enslaved mother's ability to suckle became a form of invisible skilled labor. This led to exploitation. It meant that not only were black women being exploited on the basis of race, they were also being exploited as women who could breed more skilled labor and as tools to enhance the health of the slave owners' children and the quality of life of his wife.

A white woman's decision to borrow, hire, or buy enslaved

wet nurses often broke the already fragile yet sacred bonds enslaved mothers had with their children and must have caused familial trauma beyond our imagination. A black enslaved mother's child could be sold at any time, leaving her bereft. She could be prevented from feeding her own child—stripping from her her key role as mother. This structural interference into a black woman's role as mother is critical to consider. As slaves, black women were never allowed to fully participate in the protecting and nurturing aspects of motherhood, including the act of breastfeeding. Slave mothers often fought for their motherly rights—the same rights white mothers naturally took for granted—and often lost against their domineering slave masters. The power dynamic and the two distinct definitions of motherhood were clear. White women were granted ownership of their children as one of their God-given rights as a mother. This ownership could only be lost through divorce or death. White mothers never lived with a constant fear of separation. On the other hand, the ownership of motherhood was not the right of black slaves and they were consistently deprived of the true meaning of motherhood because they did not "own" their children. As historian Michele Mock notes, "maternal instinct is corrupted when viewed in the context of slavery. For a slave cannot 'own.' " White middle- and upper-class women were able to choose whether to breastfeed their children or turn them over to a wet nurse when they viewed breastfeeding as beneath them. They had a choice that black women did not have. Whatever "sacred" bond was created through breastfeeding one's own child or using your agency to choose to have someone else to do it for you—none of this was possible to achieve for enslaved black women. In the process, African-American babies and children were dehumanized, a de facto necessity in order to legitimize the denial of maternal rights, maternal bonds, and the nurturing that was taken from black babies and given to white children. Devaluing black children also allowed them to be violently disciplined and ultimately sold or otherwise separated from their parents.

Either way, the possibility for a legacy of historical trauma due to the dysfunctional nature of black women's motherhood experience is clear. Over the years since slavery, black women have continued to be perceived as good caretakers for other people's children but distrusted as mothers of their own children. This stereotype also gave rise to the "mammy" archetype, followed by the stereotypes of welfare queens and domineering women. The role of black women as caretakers of white people's children is reinforced in popular culture as seen in the bestselling book and movie *The Help* and a litany of movies and television shows, including *Gimme a Break,* starring Nell Carter, and *Gone with the Wind,* featuring Hattie McDaniel as Mammy (McDaniel became the first African American to win an Academy Award because of that role). These media stereotypes create negative associations with black mothers, and since breastfeeding is generally associated with "good" mothering, there is often an assumption by medical professionals that black women don't breastfeed. Therefore, black women repeatedly overreport that physicians and other health professionals did not educate them about breastfeeding or only mentioned it in a cursory way.

Moreover, the negative association of breastfeeding with slavery and mammy-ism is still very present among the grandmothers and other family matriarchs who are highly influential in modern black family structures. These grand-mothers and great-aunts often pass on a cultural legacy of viewing breastfeeding as something that African Americans were forced to do for others. This leaves black women with a disproportionate lack of multigenerational support and means that, in addition, they receive negative cues about breastfeeding.

Body politics also loom large for African-American mothers when it comes to breastfeeding. They face a particular legacy of embodied exploitation, in which their sexuality and re-production were appropriated by white men or demonized as dangerous and out of control, exotic and primitive. Black women and their bodies have been the subject of much scrutiny—viewed as a threat to the fragile white woman dur-ing slavery and the antithesis of white and wafer-thin stan-dards of beauty. The act of breastfeeding cannot be separated from the narrative of black women's bodies. This is only the tip of the iceberg of the many cultural nuances of breast-feeding. The river of historical trauma among women of color runs deep and wide. Yet there is often a one-size-fits-all message that ignores the nuances of breastfeeding for differ-ent ethnic groups. As a result, racial disparities still linger.

For others, the support you get can come down to your zip code. For the past five years, I've been exploring the phe-nomenon I call "first food deserts"—neighborhoods where mothers cannot easily access the support needed to provide their babies the most healthful first food—breast milk. Think about it as you would real food. For decades, the public health message was eat well and exercise. It was a great-sounding message, but, as it turns out, it was disconnected from the reality of the lives of millions of Americans. As the USDA now documents, some 23.5 million people live in a food desert—a place where it is very hard to access fresh fruit and vegetables and therefore to eat well. Not to mention that there may be no safe place to exercise. Similarly, there are many areas of the United States where mothers struggle to find support to breastfeed. I discovered these environments in Alabama, Mississippi, and Louisiana, among other places. There is no La Leche League or other meaningful support group. Physicians' offices display infant formula advertising. The neighborhoods are flooded with billboards for formula and early baby foods. There are no Baby-Friendly-certified hospitals anywhere in the vicinity. And the cultural invisibility runs high—people just don't see others breastfeeding, which perpetuates the idea that breastfeeding is not the done thing. And while much effort, including the Baby-Friendly Hospital Initiative, has successfully worked to improve the hospital experience for mothers, in this country a hospital is still a two-to-three-day stay for most women. Even if a woman has a supportive experience or a good latch at the hospital, if she leaves the hospital to go home to a community that is a "desert" of support, she is still in a setup for failure. But this is the predicament most women of color find themselves in—regardless of income. That creates layers of missing support from the federal policies to the employer and local community level.

With so many structural barriers and community barriers, treating breastfeeding like a onetime decision that occurs in the hospital and then assumes autopilot commitment is shortsighted. Breastfeeding is not like choosing a job; breast-feeding is more like trying to diet. Every day is a struggle to make the right choice when the less-healthy options seem so much easier. You know how it goes: you see the brownie, you know the brownie is not good for you, you count how many minutes it will take you on the treadmill to burn it off—but you eat the brownie anyway. This everyday decision making is the real struggle of breastfeeding, and it has nothing to do with counting the benefits. The social support women need is the support to maintain the discipline and commitment required to breastfeed. This support would likely come more easily and everywhere if mothering was more properly valued.

· 5 ·

Nipple-omics and the Value of Motherhood

There is no such thing as absolute value in this world.
You can only estimate what a thing is worth to you.

—CHARLES DUDLEY WARNER

In *The Picture of Dorian Gray,* Oscar Wilde wrote, "Nowadays people know the price of everything and the value of nothing." In our society, items are priced but value remains an abstract and often misunderstood concept. When it comes to breastfeeding, the valuations get even trickier. Our idea of value is based on what somebody is willing to pay for something, and that leaves the modern valuation of breastfeeding steeped in confusion. There is the actual cost of breastfeeding-related products and then there is the priceless value of the preventive health benefits and the monetary value of the time it takes a mother to provide it. How we value the huge time commitment for breastfeeding is directly related to the broader issue of valuing mothering in general. As a society, we talk endlessly about the importance of family, yet the time and work it takes to nurture and manage a family is utterly disregarded. Pressed for time and money, unable to find decent affordable day care, racked with guilt at falling short of the mythic supermom ideal—working and nonworking American mothers alike have it harder today than they have in decades, and they are worse off by almost every measure than many of their peers around the world. Capitalist models would tell you that when you "corner the market" on a certain product or service, then by definition your value should increase—but the exact opposite has occurred for women, who have been actually devalued by their ability to bear children and exclusively feed them. Witness the ever-persistent gender gap. Women are paid 23 percent less than men even when we are doing the exact same work as a man. So how could we be properly valued for doing work, such as birthing and breastfeeding, that men cannot do?

It is universally accepted that no one would work for free except mothers, yet no one has enough money to hire a good mom, which, in that framework, actually makes mothers priceless. This does not include Mother's Day—when the commercial interest in celebrating mothers reaches fever pitch. Beyond that, mothering is mostly considered thankless work. In some places, it can even be a penalty. A 2008 study documented the motherhood penalty showing that the bias toward mothers, the so-called "maternal wall," is more of a problem than the glass ceiling is for all women. The study found that when female subjects were given identical resumes, one but not the other a mother, the mother was 79 percent less likely to be hired, 100 percent less likely to be promoted, offered an average of $11,000 less in salary, and held to higher performance and punctuality standards. Mothers are under stress coping with an outdated system built around the idea that families can afford for women not to work, yet mothers are being underpaid and undermined for their secular work *and* their maternal work. The contradictions are complex. So are the implications. The psychological impact of generations of undervalued mothers is hard to ignore.

One is an irrational lack of confidence in our bodies. No woman actively doubts whether her uterus will eventually begin to contract after forty weeks of gestation or that, after birth, it won't return back to size. You don't fret that one day your kidneys will fail or your digestive system won't work. But we consistently doubt that our breasts will perform a basic mammalian function. Lactation holds the award for being the one bodily function that we think of as precarious and likely to fail us. There isn't much remedy to the psychological warfare against women that has turned mothers against mothers and chipped away at our self-confidence in some very basic biological functions.

In other circumstances, the impact is even more severe. I am sitting in the luxurious lobby of the Sofitel Hotel in Lafayette Square, Washington, D.C., waiting to interview a mother we'll call Katherine. Katherine is a friend of a college friend, a highly successful attorney who moves with ease in the Beltway's political power circles. After giving birth to her third child, the Prozac she had been taking for years just wasn't helping like it used to, even with a higher dosage. "I just didn't feel happy. I have a great house, great kids, great husband, and a wonderful career but I just didn't feel satisfied on the inside," she said. Her psychiatrist then added Ritalin. "I felt great," she said. Ritalin is a psychostimulant, similar to an amphetamine, a class of drugs often prescribed to children with ADHD and now used more and more by moms trying to get more done. With one pop of the pill, Katherine said she felt more energetic and able to focus. "I was a better version of myself. I loved how it made me feel, like, I could do anything," she explained, remembering how managing the nanny, rushing home to have dinner, chauffeuring the kids to soccer and dance classes, keeping track of three different activity calendars, and trying to have a "date night" just seemed "easier" with the drug. She also needed less sleep, which allowed her to stay on top of her work responsibilities, and she found keeping her weight at a size 6 was much easier with her "little helper." It seemed like a win-win.

Except that while Ritalin does indeed make productivity soar, it does so along with your heart rate, blood pressure, and body temperature, and it causes an increased risk of stroke and heart attack. In other words, she is putting her future life at risk to deal with her current life.

At the time I met with Katherine, she was developing cravings and obsession around her pharmaceutical "helper." She was taking almost triple the prescribed dose, which had negative side effects. She was lying to herself and her husband about the drug. She was polishing off a one-month prescription in just eleven days. "I get another prescription in my husband's name. If he knew, he would be so mad and disappointed," she said, unable to look me in the eye. "He thinks I take it as prescribed, in my own name." Katherine confided that she felt as if she was on the brink of a full-fledged addiction problem but felt trapped in the cycle of dependency and couldn't figure out how to squeeze more time in her tightly packed schedule for therapy or treatment.

After successfully exclusively breastfeeding her first two children for six months and then pumping while back to work and supplementing occasionally with formula for the next six months, Katherine didn't breastfeed her third child longer than two weeks because she felt she needed the Prozac at a higher dose to cope with the stress. (Zoloft and Paxil are generally considered "more safe" with breastfeeding, but those drugs didn't work for Katherine this time, she said.) Her "failure at breastfeeding" (her words, not mine) fed more guilt, which she feels accelerated her spiral into depression.

Katherine's experience is far too common. Instead of the blissful existence many women thought motherhood, marriage, and career would bring, they find themselves stressed out, anxious, and remarkably unhappy. To cope with the demands of modern motherhood and the quest to have it all, a woman's must-have support list includes not only nanny, SUV, personal trainer, and housekeeper (even if once a month) but also, now, a prescription drug to help you cope with it all. Not exactly the best environment for breastfeeding.

For years, this fog of anxiety and discontent has surrounded mothers so much so that it has become normal and yet unmentionable—the modern-day "problem that has no name." That is, until the July 2010 issue of *New York* magazine featured the eye-grabbing cover headline, "I Love My Children. I Hate My Life. The Misery of the American Parent," by Jennifer Senior. The feature story, "All Joy and No Fun: Why Parents Hate Parenting," finally said the thing no one wanted to say. At least not out loud. However, once it was uttered, it was as if someone took the lid off the pressure cooker and there was the deafening sound of a million moms screaming "Amen" in unison as someone finally put words (three pages of them) to the simmering discontent they were living out every day.

In fact, for many mothers this disappointing experience begins moments after giving birth, when they are faced with their first task of motherhood: feeding their child. The cheery breastfeeding culture and unrealistic images of peaceful breastfeeding and calm mothers sitting in meadows doesn't always jibe with the realities of the experience. And, quite frankly, the experience is stacked against us.

Breastfeeding feels lonely. In more communal societies, breastfeeding is not a lonely activity, but in America it can be an extremely isolating experience. When not being "accommodated," nursing mothers are hiding—behind screens and closed doors. We leave rooms. Cover our babies. At work, we express milk alone without even our babies as company—we have only a machine and hopefully a table lamp or plastic flowers for that forced homely touch. And then there's the pump.

. . .

Imagine yourself at the superprestigious Massachusetts Institute of Technology (MIT) surrounded by tables full of small squeezable breasts, motors, flanges, screwdrivers, and pliers, with the whir of a 3-D printer buzzing in the back of the room. That's where I am—steps from the Charles River, at the MIT Media Lab for the first-ever breast pump hackathon. The official and laudable title is "Make the Breast Pump Not Suck," and the energy in the room is palpable. The coffee is free-flowing. The crowd, mostly young, includes husbands who've witnessed the experience of pumping, moms and future moms and bright-eyed engineering students who traveled from as far as New York, Connecticut, and Rhode Island looking for a new mechanical design challenge. Not to mention the $3,000 cash prize and trip for two to Silicon Valley to pitch the winning idea to investors. To add to the authenticity, there's actually an adorable toddler running around and a nursing mom in the room. The goal of the historic two-day convening, which brought scientists, inventors, designers, engineers, entrepreneurs, parents, lactation consultants, and Silicon Valley funders to a small building in Cambridge, is to hack the hell out of a device that has not had any major improvements in over sixty years. It is a long overdue marriage of the culture of innovation and the maternal and neonatal health field that notoriously lags behind other fields in technological advancement.

Sure, we've made a two-ton hybrid car that revs quietly. We've built powerful motors that propel objects into outer space. We've made cell phones sleek, stylish, and superpowerful. But the breast pump still sadly resembles a mechanical milking device circa 1920. Even Wikipedia describes a breast pump as "analogous to a milking machine used in commercial dairy production."

The first mechanical breast pump was invented by Edward Lasker, an engineer, in the 1920s. In 1956 Einer Egnell, a Swedish engineer, created the Egnell SMB breast pump, a more comfortable and effective version of the original. But, since then, little has changed about the fundamental design.

Since engineers invented this thing, it seems apropos that engineers would reinvent it.

New design ideas ranged from changing the pump from a vacuum to a more comfortable compression model and integrating massaging technology from the sex-toy industry to a hands-free prototype. Others attempted to hack the experience of breastfeeding, with one group hoping to demedicalize the process by adding knitted cozies for the breast pump, making it softer and warmer for a woman's body. Another group created MilkTrack, which uses a smart chip in the lid of supply bottles and incorporates cell phone technology to track and time stamp your milk inventory, check temperature, and track volume. I was full of hope.

But standing in that room, with the smell of creativity pulsating, it all came back to me. The trauma and the shame of my own pumping experiences. The Madonna-shaped cone-like flanges, the see-through funnels that give you the pleasure of seeing your nipples being sucked shapeless. That dreadful sound.

My first introduction to the unwelcome experience of breast pumps came in 2000 when my daughter was born. Before she was one full day old, she started running a fever and had to be put into the neonatal intensive care unit (NICU). All eight pounds of her. It was an odd sight, to have such a large baby among the other NICU babies—mostly preemies or low birth weight babies. In between visiting her isolette, I slowly rolled my IV stand and my still-sore-from-C-section self to a cold, sterile room with cinder-block walls and only a long brown table in it. Then, I hooked myself up to an industrial breast pump, boxy and bigger than a microwave, for what felt like hours, only to produce what looked like puny, insufficient droplets of milk. During those minutes, I prayed fervently, rabidly to the milk god, whatever lacto goddess of Greek or pagan origins there was or might possibly be in the expansive universe. It was traumatizing. It was like I had a great fever that could only be cooled by the sight of my milk freely flowing into the bottle becoming ounces. Meaningful ounces. The line marks, marking the milliliters on the bottle, taunted me. I desperately wanted everything about that experience to be different from how it was. I never touched a breast pump again.

That is, until my son came four years later. After nine months of exclusive breastfeeding, I had to prepare to return to work. And that meant pumping if I wanted to reach my goal of twelve months. After returning to work, I remember how I would close my office door at *Fortune* magazine and turn on some music in the hopes of drowning out the sound—that embarrassing, godforsaken sound—of my breast pump. It dawned on me that in all of those years since my first experience, they had only managed to put the breast pump in a cuter, more stylish tote bag—simply making it easier to carry the degrading experience.

And, while the hackathon made me excited about the long overdue marriage of innovation and breast pumping, there was definitely a twinge of sadness. Okay, more than a twinge. Why hadn't we demanded this sooner? Why have we accepted such a subpar experience? We have run thousands of miles and worn way too much pink to bring attention to improving breast cancer research and care. We've insisted that our slimming undergarments be as close to sexy as possible. But this? Why not this? We have settled on the most horrible experience when it comes to feeding our babies human milk, and we didn't bother to fuss. This made me incredibly sad. It seemed to me that pumping had become very much like the experience of a bikini wax or a mammogram. Not pleasant, but effective. Not good, but void of regret. It was the bad we were willing to tolerate in order to be good. Good to a man. Good for our health. Or good as a mother.

My sadness confused and compelled me as it was replaced by morose unease. Because I was also among the guilty, a mother who suffered but didn't bother to demand more. Even worse, as an advocate with a national platform, actively involved in the movement to increase breastfeeding rates, I have been focused on helping more women access breast pumps, so they could leave the house for an afternoon or return to work and still provide breast milk. I did this not remembering what happens next, the infuriating experience of trying to extract milk from your body for future consumption. Why hadn't I remembered this before? That day, I remembered.

Pumping, as it is right now, is not the happy medium. It is not the perfect way to balance breastfeeding and work demands. It is not part of the liberation we are seeking. Pumping is often just another trap in the ongoing maze of breastfeeding torture chambers. Another element of the experience that is stacked against us. Yet more and more women are being pushed to pump, as more companies offer Ikea-like nursing rooms and more pumping perks. For example, IBM announced that it would pay for mothers to ship expressed milk back to their baby while on business trips. These perks create the dangerous illusion that breastfeeding and work are finally working, which really shouldn't be our only end game—federal paid family leave and workplace policies giving us time to be with our children should. Instead, we settle for being shuttled into lonely rooms away from our babies and then get excited when we are given relatively low-cost perks like free milk shipment.

Are these small perks supposed to compensate for the fact that we don't get to *be* with our babies? Studies show U.S. women still work more hours per week than in any other industrialized country. Many corporate cultures still value time at the office and at the bar after work over actual productivity—a trend that undermines the work of mothering. And making it easier to pump milk or get it home doesn't necessarily help me get home.

Having more time off would actually allow moms to properly establish their breastfeeding routine and extend the time of breastfeeding at the breast before transitioning to pumping. When mothers are returning to work two to three weeks after childbirth, many don't bother to start breastfeeding and others stop so soon because the barriers seem insurmountable.

Meanwhile, turning into a pump nation could reduce some of the health benefits of breastfeeding. Milk that is directly obtained from the breast is better because bottle feeding reduces the effectiveness of antibodies and kills living cells found in breast milk, experts say. Also, pumped milk doesn't have the same fat consistency as milk received directly from the breast and some of the precious fat is lost in the pump parts, said Dr. Miriam Labbok, the former professor at the University of North Carolina Gillings School of Global Public Health as well as former director of the Carolina Global

Breastfeeding Institute. "An increased reliance on pumping, especially early in the breastfeeding relationship, will certainly blunt some of the benefits of breastfeeding," says Labbok.

Ultimately, the breast pump is a fitting metaphor for women's ongoing struggle with breastfeeding: Too many parts that need to be cleaned. Outdated systems. No dignity. And too much noise. In the real world, the dirty parts represent the commercial interests, the policy implications, feminist rhetoric, the role of race and class, and the politics of women's bodies that complicate breastfeeding. Outdated systems include insufficient federal policies and maternity ward protocols that treat birth as a medical event. No dignity refers to nursing mothers being forced to leave public places as if breastfeeding is indecent. And there's plenty and plenty of noise. The marketing noise. The noise of data confusion. The noise of infant formula marketing. The noise of cultural invisibility and societal pressure.

The contradictions of breastfeeding mirror the contradictions of motherhood. Mothers who breastfeed in public are either doing a beautiful, natural, environmentally friendly thing and bolstering their infant's IQ and immune system or they are perverted exhibitionists who judge others, exploit their children, and should be banned from restaurants, run out of grocery stores, and kicked off airplanes.

In a world where we are fixated on time and overwhelmed with overscheduling, breastfeeding is framed as confining and restrictive because it works best unscheduled. Instead, we should challenge why we have no freedom to be temporarily unstructured or unscheduled or made to feel like less of a woman for exercising this freedom. Especially when, in the long run, breastfeeding helps make a mother's and a baby's life much easier. Yes, breastfeeding has nutritional and immunity merits, but it is also offers a way of being close with a baby and that, in itself, is valuable. There are other ways to experience that closeness, of course, and mothers shouldn't be forced to parent in that way if they don't want to, but we shouldn't sabotage those who do.

The whole situation—just like the breast pump—quite frankly sucks. Mostly because women are unaware of the confluence of forces that undermine their efforts. We've drifted far from our biological norms and, without the intergenerational structure of familial support, we are lost and finding our own way. Too many of us end up robbed of the early motherhood experience we desire. Or reliant on an outdated machine to finish the job our culture won't let us completely fulfill on our own.

Believe it or not, there was a time when women were valued as breast milk producers and mother's milk was considered a precious commodity. Unfortunately, it was a very, very long time ago. Wet-nursing began organically and communally and was often the only recourse for an infant whose mother had died, was ill, or could not for some reason be breastfed by its mother. But it did not take long for that genuine act to be commodified and to become a symbol of financial prosperity. Going back as far as ancient Egypt wet nurses were used, mostly by the wealthy, to give their children the benefits rich women considered themselves too posh to provide. Most Egyptians, Babylonians, and Hebrews breastfed their children for about three years, but the wealthier Greeks and Romans hired slaves to wet-nurse. Outside of slavery, wet nurses could only exist because wealthy people could afford them and valued the "product" they could provide.

As George D. Sussman writes in *Selling Mothers' Milk*: "Any mother who could afford to hire a wet nurse would never sacrifice her sleep, her social life, her sexual pleasure (intercourse was supposed to interfere with lactation), or her small earnings in the store or shop in order to suckle and care for her own baby. In traditional society, mothers viewed the development and happiness of infants younger than two with indifference."

However, as children increased in value, the economics of exploiting that increased value by developing substitute milk products eventually led to the devaluation of mother's milk and, ultimately, mothers themselves. In a paradoxical turn of events, as children became more "emotionally priceless," breast milk lost its economic value, even as the direct and indirect social costs of fewer breastfed babies skyrocketed. Children but not the substance that could make them healthier became more valued.

The undervaluation of breastfeeding is directly related to the broader undervaluation of motherhood. And many experts argue that the undervaluation of motherhood is directly connected to how we value children. I spoke with Viviana Zelizer, a sociologist from Princeton University and the author of the landmark book *Pricing the Priceless Child,* which traces the value of children from their focus as sources of labor to becoming of great sentimental value. Zelizer famously surmised that children are "economically useless but emotionally priceless." The transformation of a child's value indicates how cultural norms and conventions can trump economic valuations, Zelizer says. It was this shift in valuing children, from sources of labor to objects to be cultivated and groomed, that led to the legal justification of life insurance policies for children and lawsuits and monetary damages related to the injury or loss of children. While children have transformed in value, the ones bearing the brunt of the responsibility of taking care of them are still suffering from a gross undervaluation. In several modes of valuation, time is as important as money, yet a woman's time away from working has not been properly valued in this country. Zelizer also points out that the messaging of breastfeeding has been one that stresses the emotional and health values of breastfeeding and not the economics of breastfeeding, particularly as it relates to a mother's time.

Revaluing breastfeeding will not be easy. We need a new social contract. One where mothering and caregiving is properly conceptualized as work in and of itself, rather than being forced into a model of work built around men's lives. The time commitment needed for breastfeeding and nurturing our children has value to the economic development and public health of our nation, as well as to the social fabric of our society.

With so much at stake, how did we end up here? Well, we can partly thank feminism.

· 6 ·

The Feminist Fallacy

I have a brain and a uterus, and I use both.

—PATRICIA SCHROEDER, COLORADO'S FIRST FEMALE
MEMBER OF CONGRESS

If women can't turn to physicians or to the scientific community for clear support, then surely a women-led movement can fill in the gap. Instead, the mainstream feminist movement has resisted breastfeeding as a women's rights issue, mostly framing it as a confining, restrictive, unwanted obligation that keeps women at home, tied to the kitchen and, worse, to a demanding baby. Is breastfeeding an empowering act of self-determination—using the woman's body to produce a life-enhancing food, as only women can do? Or does being at the whim of a child's demands feel so very 1950s? The feminist vote, by and large, has been for the latter. Formula feeding, they argued, meant liberating women so they could return to work. With that position, feminist leaders fell into the dangerous trap of looking at breastfeeding as an individual issue while ignoring the unfair, systemic barriers to breastfeeding that would typically have women's rights activists in a tizzy.

Breastfeeding requires rethinking basic feminist issues such as the sexual division of labor, women's productive and reproductive lives, and the role of the physiological process of lactating in the context of societal norms. It is an important issue for reproductive justice, human rights, and women, although it is rarely addressed as such. Much reproductive-justice work has been focused on providing access to safe abortions and affordable birth control. While we should, of course, give these important issues our due energy, we must move beyond the language of only helping those who want to avoid pregnancy, terminate a pregnancy, or carry out a pregnancy. That support must extend to families and the children they are raising *after* pregnancy, and that means talking about breastfeeding.

This misplaced framing of women's rights has had a profound effect on women and their infant feeding decisions. It has distorted the reproductive right of breastfeeding and contributed to a dangerous "push to pump" and the separation of mothers from their milk. To be fair, mainstream feminist ideology has also resisted breastfeeding advocacy because of feminism's aim to reject cultural norms that use guilt and coercion to label a woman's behavior "good" or "bad," and that is often the perception around most breastfeeding-awareness campaigns. This is, indeed, a misstep of the breastfeeding movement. But taking a position to resist breastfeeding advocacy without looking at who, exactly, is peddling guilt among mothers or at the public health consequences does a great disservice to all women.

Instead of the freedom and liberation the feminist movement sought to provide, mothers are more vulnerable, more frustrated, and more overlooked than ever before. Much of that is due to the feminist leadership, who have been focused more on women having a masculinized version of womanhood instead of on revaluing all the roles of a woman— including mothering work—on its own terms.

The second-wave feminist argument about the oppressive nature of breastfeeding is even more confusing when you consider that formula and the entire formula and baby-food industry were built on the perception that mother's milk is deficient, that there's not enough of it, and that the mother isn't good enough to deliver it appropriately. How exactly is that pro-women? Ironically, it bears mentioning that the origins of our formula culture came from male doctors, who pushed formula on mothers as a "superior" option. The slow loss of control over our bodies came with the "medicalization" of birth and infancy by mostly male physicians, who said women weren't smart enough to feed their babies without expert advice. Then there's the medical profession and their collusion and profit sharing with the growing formula industry. By the turn of the twentieth century, a respected physician wrote, "It is easier to control cows than women." By the 1930s, pediatric research was regularly funded by formula producers. Hospitals sabotaged breastfeeding, separating mothers and babies, insisting on strict feeding schedules, and regularly giving supplemental bottles, even though milk supply is dependent on the frequency and amount of suckling. The standard hospital practice was to sanitize and cover the mother's body and breasts and scrub her nipples, which clearly conveyed the message that the woman and her body were unclean. Much of this historical context is lost in the women's movements' simplistic categorization of breastfeeding as oppressive and bottle feeding as liberation.

In her infamous motherhood manifesto, *The Conflict: How Modern Motherhood Undermines the Status of Women*, Élisabeth Badinter speaks vehemently against the popular breastfeeding ideology, which she describes as "Mothers, you owe them everything!" She writes, "A few advocates of breastfeeding do recognize that mothers might feel trapped by political correctness and they challenge the movement's sentimental image of motherhood with its erasure of all other aspects of breastfeeding: the loss of freedom and the despotism of an insatiable child. They recognize that a baby might be a source of happiness, but also a devastating tornado." Picking up the mantle of motherhood means dealing with the challenges, the awkward moments, the struggles, the desperation at all points of the parenting continuum, not just the infant phase. Therefore, hinging the "tyranny of motherhood" on infants and, specifically, on breastfeeding is dangerous messaging for women because the "despotism" of parenting or "loss of freedom" is not confined to infant feeding or infancy. As a parent of a teenager, I speak from experience. And as an adult child who still relies on my mother and father for child care support and, in the past, financial assistance, I am still in need of my own parents. As they age, they are more in need of me. Yet we often talk about dependency as some deviant behavior, a terrible thing to be fought against at all odds. In some feminist circles, having our children dependent on us is considered degrading to us as women. Dependency happens: whether you are elderly, disabled, sick, or recovering—it is life, not a crime against womanhood. The conversation should shift to rethinking how our economy could be molded more fairly around valuing care work and phases of dependency.

Instead, most second-wave feminist scholarship and activism has presented breastfeeding as an "option" or a "choice" that is not very different from formula feeding. A few within the feminist community have recognized breastfeeding as a women's health issue or a reproductive right. By and large, support for women's rights generally ignores the rights and importance associated with *all* of women's roles, including that of mothers, opting instead to concentrate primarily on other issues such as wage equality, employment, and reproductive freedom.

It's a slippery slope that began in the mid-twentieth century as feminists in this country channeled much of their energy into fighting for equal rights with men and freeing women from the imperative to mother. Emerging from the profamily climate of the 1950s, most feminists wanted to put equality first, break the claim of biology, and "denaturalize" nature. The approach of seeking equal treatment and minimizing gender led to significant gains for women, but by the 1980s its limitations were equally apparent. Equality proved to be more difficult to accomplish than many surmised, and, where gained, it was often not what feminists had bargained for. The National Organization for Women has spent over three decades fighting for equal rights in various fields, under the premise that once all the legislation that discriminates against women is dismantled, the playing field will become level and women would assume their rightful place in society as equal to men. The only flaw in this premise is that by looking to be equal to men, we forgot to fight for the things that make us uniquely women—like our ability to birth, lactate, and produce food for our young. These aspects of motherhood were suppressed for the overall goal of being just like men. By the 1980s even Gloria Steinem, the glamorized feminist leader (who does not have any children), quipped, "We have become the men we wanted to marry." Next came some feminist voices for the "maximizing" approach—that is, celebrating women's differences—which acknowledges that demanding similar treatment gained entry for a few but left the system relatively unchanged. While the fight to access birth control options and have children on our own terms was critical to the movement, the idea of focusing on mothering thereafter instead of returning to work was definitely frowned upon. We were vocal for the right to have children when we wanted, but then what? Leave them as soon as possible and get back to work? Yes, a woman should not be compelled to become a mother, but what if that was her authentic desire? There was no en masse fight for legislation to have a reasonable federal maternity leave policy. Pregnancy accommodation cases, those in which a pregnant woman alleged she was denied a workplace accommodation needed due to pregnancy, such as help with lifting or light duty, have increased 315 percent over the prior decade, according to a 2016 report on family responsibilities discrimination by the Center for WorkLife Law at the University of California Hastings College. Flimsy legal protections for pregnancy and breastfeeding are a byproduct of pushing for a model of work built around men's lives, a model that constantly challenges women to find new ways to fit into that mold. And there are other legal consequences to the push for so-called equality with men. For example, the current law for proving gender discrimination cases requires that you produce a male "comparator" who is of a similar situation to prove unequal treatment. Of course, this is virtually impossible for pregnant and breastfeeding women and courts have used this to dismiss several pregnancy discrimination cases. In 2012 testimony before the Equal Employment Opportunity Commission, Joan C. Williams, director of the Center for WorkLife Law, highlighted two glaring examples of equal rights going terribly wrong. In one case, *Hess-Watson v. Potter*, the plaintiff argued that her employer had held against her the fact that she was on maternity leave in awarding a certain workplace benefit. The court dismissed her suit because she had not identified any man out on maternity leave. Another case involved Kimberly Hern Troupe, who worked at the Lord & Taylor department store in Chicago when she became extremely ill with severe morning sickness. The court awarded summary judgment for the employer on the grounds that the plaintiff had not submitted evidence of a "hypothetical Mr. Troupe" (with severe morning sickness?). The plaintiff's "failure to present any comparison evidence," asserted Judge Richard Posner in the majority opinion, "doomed her case."

When courts hold that women can never prove a discrimination case if they cannot identify a similarly situated man, they embrace a male norm, since we asked for equality, that completely ignores and devalues the extents to which women are different from men. Instead of equal protections, women are protected only to the extent they are like men, while men receive across-the-board protections. This is not meant to be the outcome of feminist efforts. What mothers really need from the feminist movement is a bigger push for federal and workplace policies supporting family caregiving, not support for being away from our babies before we actually want to be. But that's what most women settle into as their "choice."

• • •

It's a cold, wintry day in Chicago and I'm running late to attend an event but in desperate need of some sort of information from the hotel concierge. But the woman in front of me is taking forever. And she's clearly frustrated. She has a FedEx box in her hand, but the concierge is letting her know that she missed the last pickup time for the day. She sounded on the verge of tears. The concierge was calling other locations to find the best place for her to still make the drop-off deadline for a priority overnight shipment. Whatever was in that box was super important. And just as my mind went all judgmental with thoughts of how our microwave-oven, texting society makes us believe everything is urgent, I heard her say it. With her voice cracking, she tells the concierge that in the box is a padded cooler with her breast milk for her baby and she must ship it home for 9 A.M. delivery. She said it took her two hours to pump enough milk and it must be shipped tonight. The concierge found a suitable location but warned that it could be a forty-dollar cab ride to get there. She grabbed her precious box and the paper with the address and, wiping her tears, she turned and walked quickly toward the hotel exit doors. I felt like I had to do something to support her. Forgetting that I was running late myself, I ran behind her. "You're doing a really great thing for your baby,"

I said, and handed her two twenty-dollar bills—all the cash I had in my wallet at the time. She didn't want to accept it, even after my "this is from all mothers and babies" speech, so when her cab pulled up, I quickly gave it directly to the driver as she was getting in and quickly walked away.

She smiled as the cab pulled off.

And there we were, two women with the financial means to support feeding breast milk to an infant despite the absurdities of how our culture is constructed not to support breastfeeding. Being allowed to pump is meant to be the comforting middle ground, but it alienates the food we produce from the nurturance we provide. On social media, women who must travel for work share road-warrior pumping tips ranging from which coolers are easiest to pass through airport security to which hotels make it easiest to get a fridge in your room and how to use room service to freeze your cooler packs overnight. It's a survival mechanism for women caught in the crag between their need to work and their desire to mother. Yet it distances us from our children while providing the illusory feeling that we are still able to provide what's best for our children. Even though that "best" doesn't include our physical presence. Women are supported to pump but not to mother. The value is placed on the milk, not the mothering. Breast milk may be precious, but breastfeeding is another matter.

In the language of feminists, women are empowered by asserting the value of both their productive and reproductive work. But what if that productive work includes producing human milk, which is actually an extension of our reproductive work? While building a feminist movement, there was little consideration of the dynamics of a capitalist society, which created a separation between the product and the producer—a mother and her milk. In the past, these two elements were forced to arrive together. But as improved technology helped make it easier to extract the milk from our bodies, the commodification of breast milk escalated—from for-profit milk-banking companies to novelty ice creams and cheeses. As the value of the milk itself increased, a fertile environment developed for the commercialization of human milk. As researchers discover therapies from human milk, scientists are looking into how breast milk can treat intestinal or infectious diseases and how bodybuilders can use it to build muscle. From informal sharing and sales on Craigslist to Web sites like Eats on Feets and Only the Breast, women are looking to buy and sell breast milk as its value rises. Again, breast milk is rising in value, while the act of breastfeeding is in a valuation tailspin.

Instead of important discussions, we see clamoring over so-called coercion to breastfeed and no understanding of the structural barriers, capitalist forces, and systemic failures that all women face. There's little dialogue over how we were fed the messaging that breastfeeding is difficult and doomed to failure in the first place and then separated from our milk. And since the feminist approach to breastfeeding was founded on cultural mistruths created in part by the same patriarchal structures that feminists claimed to be rebelling against, it is no wonder that profeminist rhetoric has not helped women feel any happier or fulfilled as mothers.

That search for fulfillment, not provided by feminist gains, has certainly benefited commercial interests, which often derive their power and purse from a woman's constantly changing need for identity and the vulnerability of transitioning from an independent, career woman to mother, wife, and caregiver. The uncertainty started in the early to mid-1900s as the role of women began to change. "If a woman is not farming and she's not having a baby every year due to increased birth control methods, then what is she supposed to do? Women began to look for things to do outside the home," says Karin Cadwell, a member of the faculty of the Healthy Children Project who convened Baby-Friendly USA, the organization implementing the UNICEF Baby-Friendly Hospital Initiative in the United States. "There came 'The Woman Problem.'" Women transitioned from occupying a predominantly maternal role to having fewer children and participating in the labor force even after childbirth. This drop in birthrates led to fewer visual images of the breast fulfilling its nutritional function, and the sexual elements of the breast became more prominent.

The so-called woman problem was addressed from all sorts of commercial vantage, from appliances to beauty creams. Women are constantly sold ideas on how to be. In *The Feminine Mystique,* first published in the United States in 1963, Betty Friedan argued that the very word "feminine," which sounded like something every woman wanted to be, actually represented an idealized image and a subversive one that kept women as housewives and discouraged any meaningful work outside the home. Women in the mid-twentieth century were taught to pity "unfeminine" career women. Feminine women did not want things like an education, career, or independence. The media images of happy women were in the home, fixating on properly set dinner tables and shining up the latest appliance.

Commercial interests continue to use advertising to undermine mothers, connecting the "right" to choose between breastfeeding and bottle feeding as a sign of independence—asserting that a woman can achieve identity, self-realization, and fulfillment with the feeding choice for her infant. Feminists agree, arguing that bottle feeding frees women to return to the workforce and to be "independent." Bottle feeding would create more equitable partnerships with men being able to participate, as if feeding is the only parenting task and men can't participate in bathing, diaper changing, burping, and playing with a child. And let's be honest, no woman is ever truly "free" once she becomes a mother. Whether your child is ten days old or ten years old, you will always be constantly consumed with thoughts and worry and angst and joy about your child—forever. You're inextricably linked for a lifetime. Infancy has its demands. The school years have their demands. My parents still worry about me. This is the beauty, not the burden of the mother-child relationship. Not to mention that your status as an independent individual with your own will and desires is for you to define for *all* of your motherhood journey, not just the infancy period. And I assure you that it will shift and twist along the way.

I call it "The Liberation Mystique" for today's generation. It's an equally damaging and subversive message—this idea that we achieve freedom by feeding our babies inferior artificial products and by getting back to working like men. It's an equally powerful malaise of discontent. We will never be fully fulfilled until all of our selves—our maternal selves, our sexual selves, our lactating selves, our career-climbing selves—are acknowledged. Instead of a one-size-fits-all

"liberated" box, we can accept and support all of the variations of "us," allowing women to become the people they want
to be at a given time as they move through different stages of
their lives. Nor can we put all perspectives of motherhood in
the same barrel. Valorizing motherhood is different from an
authentic desire to mother. But there's been little structural
support for the latter and no feminist voices advocating it.

The ultimate connection between breastfeeding and feminism is that in a truly equitable society, women would have
the capacity to pursue both their productive and reproductive work without penalty. In that vein, breastfeeding becomes
the perfect lens to see the misogyny of our culture as it impacts mothers: women are harassed and shamed and illegally
evicted from public spaces for breastfeeding; women are
threatened with losing custody of their children for breastfeeding for "too long"; women are ridiculed and bullied for
trying to pump milk at work; women are described as freak
shows for breastfeeding twins or tandem feeding; women are
called names for breastfeeding; women are told they are sexually abusing their children for breastfeeding; women are
told they're not allowed to keep breast milk in communal
fridges because it's viewed as a bodily secretion and not as
food; women are bullied into stopping breastfeeding because
breasts are the sexual objects of men; women are told that it
is obscene to breastfeed in front of other people's children
or other people's husbands; women are told their bodies are
too fat and too saggy and too veiny to be exposed while breastfeeding; women are told to stay at home with their babies
until they are no longer breastfeeding; women are instructed
to throw blankets over themselves and their babies if they wish

to breastfeed outside the home. The list goes on. This is not the result of some peculiar sensitivity toward babies and small children eating; this does not happen with bottle feeding. This is unique to breastfeeding, and it is about policing women's bodies and lives. You know, exactly the kinds of things feminists used to get riled up about. The fact that women are harassed and shamed for doing something that women's bodies do as a routine part of bearing children is a severe societal flaw that should trouble all feminists.

At times, the language of feminism has led to the undermining of breastfeeding, starting with the word "choice." The mere word conjures up thoughts of women's liberation and reproductive justice and hard-won rights and freedoms earned by the feminist movement. In fact, the very essence of women's liberation was the liberation to make individual choices, whether it be about work, family, or lifestyle. This was most strikingly the case after *Roe v. Wade,* when reproductive politics made the language of choice synonymous with women's liberation. As the feminist writer Summer Wood wrote of "choice" in *Bitch* magazine, "The word's primacy in the arena of reproductive rights has slowly caused the phrase, 'It's my choice' to become synonymous with 'It's a feminist thing to do'—or perhaps more precisely, 'It is anti-feminist to criticize my decision.'" In the so-called mommy wars and specifically in the milk wars, we see the most perverse form of individualism, where individualizing and privatizing choices around motherhood and breastfeeding has created a dangerous environment. What was once the trademark for women's rights has become a consumerist tool being used against women. What began as a highly politicized term, in the context of a right to decide to terminate a pregnancy, has now been depoliticized and used for consumer imperatives, as in the "right" to buy all sorts of products marketed to women, from antidepressants, moisturizers, and diet frozen pizzas to infant formula. Implicit in this tactic is that exercising your choice in these matters is in itself a feminist act.

We see this tactic often in pop culture, such as an episode of the fan favorite *Sex and the City*, where liberated consumer Carrie Bradshaw (in an episode fittingly titled, "A Woman's Right to Shoes") proudly justifies purchasing expensive footwear. The problem with "choice" today is that it has been taken out of the context of women's rights and misconstrued. In its most disgusting reiteration it is being marketed to women and girls by corporate interests. We are being sold on the idea of choice. The combination of aggressive advertising, medical backing, and a love of consumer freedom has led to a free-market paradise where a host of instant foods are readily available and women have been led to believe that the choice between formula feeding and breastfeeding is merely a matter of personal inclination—a feather in the cap of the quest for liberation. And since choices are individual, they have no social consequences; women are therefore relieved of the responsibility of considering the broader implications of their decisions. And once I make my choice, no one is to challenge me.

Lately, choice has taken on a concerning meaning in third-wave feminist circles. One of the new iterations of feminism is called "choice feminism." In contrast to political philosophies that explore the ways in which structural inequality limits freedom, choice feminism tells us that every individual is free to choose and that choice is empowering, no matter what the choice actually is. The result is that the term "choice" is now employed in feminist debates about everything from the sex industry to marriage and makeup to breastfeeding versus formula feeding. Choice feminism dictates that anytime a woman makes a choice, even if it's to engage in prostitution or pole dancing, it is an act of feminism.

This is dangerous thinking when the reality is that our "choice" has more limitations than many think and choices based on uninformed decisions founded on marketing propaganda is not true choice at all. It's particularly dangerous because we fail to differentiate between those who have the privilege of choosing and those who do not, and it avoids any analysis of how race, class, and power actually affect a woman's choice.

For one, choice should be based on equal options. Is having the option of breastfeeding versus formula feeding really a choice when the options are not equal? They are so incongruous that it has taken billions of dollars in research and insidious marketing tactics to build the notion that infant formula is just as good. When one option gives your baby preventive health benefits and the other increases your baby's risk for health problems, then that's not an actual choice. The options are not equal. The options are not equal when the reasons people give for not breastfeeding include returning to work, perceiving formula as more convenient, and fear-based ideas such as it will hurt or that their breasts won't produce enough milk. This is not the choice women need.

It's easy to see why framing breastfeeding versus formula feeding around individualism is a win-win for the formula companies. Doing so means that the idea can't be challenged. So, for example, when breastfeeding or formula feeding is framed as an individual choice, the economic interests of selling formula can be disassociated from the conversation. The billions spent on marketing to create doubt among mothers who are undermined from the day they leave the hospital with a free infant formula bag can be removed from the discussion. If breastfeeding is purely a personal choice, it need not have anything to do with greedy corporations, body politics, or a marketing industry that has sold women damaging messages. If breastfeeding is purely a personal choice, then we don't have to connect the dots between the paltry breastfeeding rates in this country and high levels of childhood allergies, asthma, type 2 diabetes, and obesity.

Think back to reproductive rights. At this point many women see those rights as accessible, but the right to have an abortion is greater than access. It touches on issues such as the wage gap, health care, education—issues that have as much if not greater impact on the real-life choices of women. Similarly, breastfeeding is far greater than a matter of choice when issues such as employer practices, child care, and the lack of federal maternity leave play such a large part in how a mother decides to feed her baby. But continuing to frame the issue around choice allows these greater, more influential factors to remain unmentionables.

Most significantly, keeping breastfeeding as a private choice rather than a public health issue hampers momentum. After all, private choices do not provide the basis for a movement. In fact, framing breastfeeding as a personal choice erases the context of corporate interests and deep-pocketed marketing machines in which it typically occurs. In this context, choice is not liberation. It is suffocation. The dialogue around the real issues that could actually significantly affect our lives, our health, and the health of all infants has been suffocated while we clamor behind choice and use it as a shield to deflect our mommy guilt. Our ability to build conversation and support among ourselves has been stifled because we won't discuss what we have been told is a private matter. It is women and infants who are paying the price for this so-called freedom. As much as we would like to think that it is impossible for a woman to choose her own oppression and that all choices she makes are equal expressions of her freedom, we know that in reality that is not the case. Of course, no woman would knowingly choose her own oppression, but when that oppression has been packaged as "choice," a "lifestyle issue," and "more convenient," women end up responding to, not choosing, influences and end up oppressed. (Remember Twilight Sleep births.)

Mothers will be better served when feminism as a movement accepts that breastfeeding is not a "choice." Breastfeeding is a reproductive right. This is a simple, but remarkably radical, concept. Here's why: when we frame infant feeding as a choice made by individual women, we place the entire responsibility for carrying out that choice on the individual woman. As Bernice Hausman writes in her "Women's Liberation and the Rhetoric of 'Choice' " essay, "In infant feeding debates we position the nursing mother as 'making a consumer decision, rather than exercising a human right.' " This framework weakens legal protections for breastfeeding families. Courts have determined that the Pregnancy Discrimination Act (PDA) does not apply to breastfeeding mothers. Rather than consider it a "related medical condition" with respect to pregnancy, which would give it coverage under the PDA, courts deem breastfeeding to be a choice related to parenting and therefore to be uncovered. "Constructing breastfeeding as a choice that absolves employers from any duty to accommodate it evades the question of whether such choices, when they contribute to the welfare of children, should be supported," writes Maxine Eichner, a professor at the University of North Carolina School of Law and the author of *The Supportive State: Families, Government, and America's Political Ideals.* In that environment, women who have control over their bodies, their time, and their lives—typically highly educated, upper-middle-class women—can choose to breastfeed, but most mothers—hourly workers, women from families that require two incomes to survive, poor women required by law to go back to work or forfeit their federal aid—cannot. The lack of response by feminists to these workplace inequities makes breastfeeding a class-based privilege and, therefore, a social justice issue. When we acknowledge that the benefits of breastfeeding, and not just of breast milk, include the psychological benefits that come from the direct interaction between mother and child, then we can see that the advantages of breastfeeding cannot be matched by merely adding more ingredients to infant formula. A woman is required in the equation.

More strikingly, most of the messaging we receive from commercial marketing, both directly and indirectly, is decidedly antifeminist. Women should never be forced to make a choice between mother work and other work. Yet, across the board, individuals who assume the role of nurturer are punished and discouraged from performing the very tasks that everyone agrees are essential. We are told breastfeeding is too hard, as if we are weak. We are told breastfeeding hurts, while we queue for tattoos and bikini waxes. We are told that breastfeeding distances our men. In this vein, I recently decided that we should stop telling women to go to college. College is very hard. Not to mention trying to carve out a meaningful career as a woman in corporate America. Way too difficult. My mother and father did not go to college and they turned out just fine—they bought a house, always had two cars, and put me through university. College has never been proved to lead to true happiness, and many people who didn't go to college are very successful. When I look at the high rate of divorce, and the number of corporate women who end up single, childless, or otherwise unfulfilled, I'm starting to question the benefit of college and career pursuits.

Truth is, if I ever seriously uttered this idea, an army of feminists would drag me through the streets for treason. But insert the word "breastfeeding" everywhere I said "college," and suddenly it becomes a very acceptable message. Every day women, who fought for independence and autonomy, are being told which pursuits are worth the sacrifice—which areas of our life are "worth" overcoming challenges for and which are not. There is a popular refrain that breastfeeding is hard and too difficult for the payoff. We are fed messages that toned bodies are worth hours of sweating in the gym and the cost of buying expensive products to achieve, but somehow contributing to the long-term health of our children is not worth any committed effort. We encourage each other to crash through glass ceilings, use off-ramps and on-ramps to maintain our career and to "lean in" for greater corporate success—but with breastfeeding we are told to give up and not feel bad. And any impassioned support to continue is misconstrued as pressure. That is deeply troubling, as a feminist.

Women as Real People

At the end of *The Feminine Mystique,* Betty Friedan writes, "If women were really people—no more, no less—then all of the things that kept them from being full people in our society would have to be changed. . . . It would be necessary to change the rules of the game to restructure professions, marriage, the family, the home." Seven years later, as the women's movement gained momentum, she said, "We have to break down the actual barriers that prevent women from being full people in society, and not only end explicit discrimination but build new institutions." To do less, she concluded, would be to make women's movement "all talk."

For women to be truly equal and realize the noble feminist goals, then all the things that still keep us from being equal in our society have to change. These issues transcend breastfeeding. We must redefine "working mom" to be more inclusive so that we stop devaluing the work of mothering. Instead of participating in the so-called mommy wars pitting "stay-at-home moms" against "working moms," we must demand high-quality, affordable child care, flexible work, and paid maternity leave so that each woman can pursue both market work and caring work to the extent that each woman sees fit. We should work to end the structural inconsistencies that undermine mothering, such as the fact that a woman who devotes all of her time to caring for her family does not earn any Social Security benefits, whereas if she gets a paying job and sends her children to day care, she and her day care provider earn credits toward financial security in old age. When advocates for women's rights and advocates for breast-feeding come together, these structural issues should be front and center.

In the feminist effort to neutralize all that ridiculous individualist blaming of women for their choices, we often diminish telling the truth about the significance of their choices to them. We silence the conversation of informing and educating women about the true risks and benefits of their options, so that they have genuinely informed decision making. We quiet the conversation about the structural inequities that undermine us and keep us from having true "choice" anyway. When we say breastfeeding is not all that important, we silence the grief some women feel about not having been able to breast-feed and we take away the sense of achievement other women feel about breastfeeding in spite of multiple obstacles. But possibly worst of all, we undermine the broader message every woman needs to echo, which is that structural and institutional change needs to happen. It's been so terribly easy for a patriarchal culture to put all the responsibility on mothers and not chase the real culprits behind the paltry breast-feeding rates in the United States—deep structural barriers like inflexible workplace policies, the absence of universal maternity leave policies, insufficient antidiscrimination legislation, and hostile societal attitudes toward women's bodies.

The collective failure to properly value and embrace mothering has been a critical failure of the feminist movement. But the breastfeeding movement has had its own blunders. Like the overriding feminist thinking, well-intentioned but misrepresented breastfeeding supporters have also undermined women in several ways.

7

The Problem of No Problem:
The Breastfeeding Movement

The surest way to inoculate a social movement is to keep it embroiled in the matter of choice.

—GOPAL DAYANENI, MOVEMENTGENERATION.ORG

Three simple words: "Breast Is Best." It's been the mantra of the pro-breastfeeding movement for decades. International public health organizations use it. Physicians and nurses use it. On the surface, it's perfect messaging: simple, rhythmic, and to the point. But the phrase has become a loaded one in the breastfeeding movement and representative of its problems.

The strategic focus on evidence-based research and on propping up the scientific benefits when the real struggle is social norms and unsupportive policies makes the movement, led by middle-aged, mostly white and female activists, appear grossly disconnected from the reality of modern-day women's lives. Given changing gender roles, increased economic demands, and less social support, women aren't being shown how to do what's "best" in today's environment, under today's life circumstances, and in the modern context of motherhood, where conflicting ideas about maternal roles and career ambitions loom large. The message hinges on the benefits of breast milk instead of on how women's lives are being materially changed by not having the basic infrastructure to successfully breastfeed for any meaningful duration. It ignores the denial of a basic reproductive right—the right to feed. At times, infant formula makers and physician organizations have colluded to keep this simplistic message intact, knowing its ineffectiveness, even when advocates pressed for something more provocative. Inside the industry, the confusing layers of certification of lactation professionals make it hard for mothers to understand who knows what and what type of credentials really matter for support. Either way, "Breast Is Complicated" may have been a more accurate slogan.

Taking such a simplistic messaging approach to such a complex issue was bound to be risky. Although "Breast Is Best" is factually accurate, it speaks only to the act of breastfeeding and the benefits of human milk, completely ignoring the experience women have when breastfeeding, as if our breasts are disconnected items from our bodies and our bodies aren't affected by the environment in which we exist. I see this problem all the time. When women say breastfeeding is hard, do they mean the act of breastfeeding—the literal process of placing a baby on your breast and your nipple into its mouth—or are they mostly referring to the experience of breastfeeding, that it feels impossible with so many structural and social barriers? Most times, it is the latter. Yes, breast milk may be best, but breastfeeding amid societal pressures and systemic letdowns is the absolute worst. Yet the movement has been, by and large, too focused on benefits messaging for too long, ignoring the emotional toll it takes to deliver such benefits. As a result, the same three words are often used against the movement to question new scientific research and challenge how "best" is best, especially since best can be a culturally derived or personal notion. It also implies that breast milk is best but that infant formula is good enough. The phrase contributes to the dangerous thinking that breast-feeding is just a better parenting choice, like a cloth diaper instead of a disposable one or homemade baby food instead of store-bought, when it is actually a critical public health issue.

The messaging, though well-intentioned, was doomed from the start. It was conceived with a focus on countering the infant formula rhetoric of being "just as good." Instead of attempting to counter a false narrative, the movement, and the women they seek to help, would have been better served by a genuine issue-oriented message that could rally women together. Standing behind a message that is all fact and no emotional affinity creates a fertile ground for the media to corrupt or create their own narrative—and they have, with dangerous implications. Lastly, let's face it. It sounds a little preachy. Women need a message and a movement that engages women as actors, with a role and a mission, not just as an audience.

Ironically, there was a time when the movement attempted to dramatically shift its messaging, but infant formula makers and physicians worked together to stop it. In June 2002, the New York nonprofit Ad Council—renowned for its ability to alter human behavior and attitudes through memorable public service campaigns such as "You Can Learn a Lot from a Dummy" and "Friends Don't Let Friends Drive Drunk"— announced that its next task would be to formulate a campaign to convince Americans of the importance of breastfeeding. Breastfeeding advocates were elated at the prospect that such a highly visible campaign might influence breastfeeding rates as profoundly as the Ad Council has affected other healthy behaviors. The plan was a campaign to show the risks of not breastfeeding. Previous breastfeeding campaigns had always focused on the pros, but after conducting a series of focus groups, the Ad Council and the Department of Health and Human Services decided the ads would be more effective if they warned women, rather than encouraged them, just as ads have strongly warned women of the dangers of smoking or drinking alcohol during pregnancy. One of the more striking ads showed a pregnant woman riding a mechanical bull with a voice-over saying, "If you wouldn't take risks before your baby was born, why start now?" Accompanying the ad was the tag line on the screen: "Babies are born to be breastfed." It was a dramatic change in messaging.

But before the campaign even hit the airwaves, it was mired in controversy over politics and money, as formula companies and the heads of the American Academy of Pediatrics protested the strong language of the campaign. The infant formula makers and AAP leaders took issue with the Ad Council's plans to include statistics published in the past decade showing that formula-fed babies had a higher risk of developing diabetes, leukemia, and other illnesses. They argued that there was not enough hard data to show a direct link to leukemia or diabetes and recommended those two conditions be dropped from the ads. Formula companies focused their opposition on the campaign's cautionary tone. "It could frighten parents," said Mardi Mountford, the executive director for the International Formula Council, an Atlanta-based trade association representing formula interests, in a newspaper article published at the time. The comments suggested parents should be shielded from important information.

The most surprising opposition to the campaign came from the AAP itself. Dr. Joe Sanders, the AAP's executive director at the time, and Dr. Carden Johnston, then its president, sent a letter to Tommy Thompson, then secretary of Health and Human Services, expressing concern about the campaign's strategy and the validity of the science behind the claims. "We don't want to go out there and lose credibility by putting out false data where people will accuse the groups of using a scare tactic," Sanders told one news organization. That letter did not sit well with the academy's own breastfeeding experts, who had been working with the government on the campaign and supported the aggressive approach.

Dr. Lawrence Gartner, the head of the academy's breastfeeding committee, sent his own letter to the Department of Health and Human Services expressing support for the campaign. "To not breastfeed is a risk, that's what the research data show," he says. At a critical juncture for shifting how we talk about breastfeeding, there was infighting at the leading pediatric association—the one publicly supporting breastfeeding as optimal nutrition. It was hard not to question whether AAP leaders had been influenced by their financial entanglements with the formula industry, which has provided significant revenue to the organization over the years. In fact, the year before the ad campaign, Ross Products, the division of Abbott which makes the formula Similac, purchased three hundred thousand copies of the academy's book on breastfeeding, for about $500,000. Soon after the campaign was shelved, the company bought another three hundred thousand copies.

The comments by the AAP insulted women, questioning their strength and intellect. "If a woman can't breastfeed or chooses not to and then her baby develops one of these conditions, what kind of guilt feelings is that going to put on this young mother?" Dr. Sanders continued. These comments are a classic example of the ruse of anti-breastfeeding messaging: comments made ostensibly to protect and support women when, in fact, they are extremely patronizing, implying that women are feeble, weak, and need to be protected from the truth. Those who are ambivalent about breastfeeding often use this bogus claim to justify withholding information instead of viewing women as strong individuals who deserve to be fully informed of the outcomes of their decisions. This dangerous manipulation has been used to undermine women for centuries, even though blatant factual information has been successfully used in other areas of health promotion. Much of the credit for reducing smoking rates, particularly among teens, has been attributed to the highly effective "Truth" ads—the largest national youth-focused antitobacco education campaign ever. It candidly exposed big tobacco's marketing and manufacturing practices, as well as vividly highlighting the real toll of tobacco. If teens can be given accurate information, regardless of how potentially frightening it may be, why not give it to grown men and women? The subtext was beyond reprehensible.

When physicians and infant formula makers aren't intervening, the media has stepped in. Their need for provocative headlines coupled with the breastfeeding movement's weak message and lack of media savvy created fertile ground for the media to dominate and often override the movement's message. The movement became a victim of what is known as the extremist effect. The extremist effect is a strategy to take something virtuous and turn it into a vice by using clever language such as calling it "extremist" or "radical." Researchers wanted to understand how to diminish people who support universally held values (such as wanting a clean environment) without being seen as directly attacking the value itself. The study, published by the International Society of Political Philosophy, showed a common political practice to "vilify opponents as extremists in order to discredit their appeal to common values." Even if the group represents a consensus value like equal opportunity, the extremist label suggests the group's agenda embodies an excessive and uncompromising imposition of this value. Through a series of experiments, the researchers discovered that simply labeling those on the other side as feminists or environmentalists created a significant backlash against them. When the descriptor "radical" was added, the negative reaction was even stronger. The researchers concluded that this "extremist effect" results in negative associations for the audience and is most effective in an environment where the public is unsure about what its priorities should be. The chronic mislabeling of breastfeeding activists as extremists is a clever communication strategy often deployed in the political arena and is designed to undermine their work. And it makes for great headlines.

Enter Courtney Jung, author of *Lactivism: How Feminists and Fundamentalists, Hippies and Yuppies, and Physicians and Politicians Made Breastfeeding Big Business and Bad Policy.* The political science professor at the University of Toronto hit the media mother lode with a book review in *The New York Times* calling her book a "riveting exposé of breastfeeding zealotry." Jung provides no specific examples of how exactly advocates are compelling women to breastfeed. The review on Slate.com had a less subtle headline: "Breastfeeding Extremists Are Even Worse Than You Thought." The tagline said: "Courtney Jung's *Lactivism* shows just how dangerous their cause can be." The emotive nature of the headline mirrored Jung's highly charged tome, which made me question if this was intended to be an academic work or just a political screed by someone with an ax to grind. What's really unfortunate is exploiting an attack on passionate and dedicated advocates for media points or research dollars. In all of Jung's bashing of breastfeeding advocates (even though she breastfed her own children) and belittling of the benefits of breastfeeding, she failed to mention her university's past and present financial connection to breast-milk substitutes. According to the University of Toronto's Web site, in 1930, Frederick Tisdall, Theodore Drake, and Alan Brown of the University of Toronto Faculty of Medicine invented Pablum, the processed food for infants and one of the earliest breast-milk substitutes, used throughout the 1930s. The site continues that Tisdall used his "business savvy" to strike a deal with Mead Johnson Company in Chicago (now maker of Enfamil) to mass produce the first precooked and thoroughly dried baby food. It was a financial success. Tisdall and Drake later worked with the National Dairy Council to enrich milk with vitamin D in the mid-1930s. Today, like many universities, the University of Toronto receives funding from various corporations. Among the companies in the 2014 listing of the $100,000 to $999,999 category are Abbott Labs, Mead Johnson, the Dairy Farmers of Canada, and Nestlé. As a member of the faculty at a school whose founding members were creators of processed infant food and that presently receives donations from a variety of infant formula interests, I can't help but raise the issue of Jung's possible bias, or at least an arguable conflict of interest that should have been disclosed—especially by a member of the Academy. It is unfortunate that the media narrative being shaped about the movement is one of pressure and coercion. In that space, any support is perceived as pressure because that is what you were told to expect. Women are being primed with a false narrative and so any action by well-meaning lactation consultants—most of whom are no more zealous than a doctor repeatedly encouraging you to stop smoking because it is bad for your health or the constant reminders we get about wearing seat belts—will fit into this story.

• • •

Where consultants actually may need to dial back the well-intentioned overzealousness is toward WHO code compliance. The WHO code is an important document and infant formula marketing is indeed more insidious than blatant but still reprehensible. Compliance is critically important. But women don't see it that way. Free samples of everything from laundry detergent to infant formula are viewed as par for the course in American capitalism. Mothers aren't there when their physician is skiing on the dime of the infant formula makers, possibly being influenced by free trips. And in this country, without the stark images of sickly babies, breast-milk-substitute marketing appears to be a victimless crime. Trying to mobilize women around a problem they don't see is counterproductive. In addition, inherent in strict adherence to the WHO code is a dangerous definition of what is considered actually breastfeeding—i.e., at the breast—and what is not. This doesn't unite women, who as a matter of federal policy have very little time to keep a baby at the breast before returning to work anyway. A strident opposition to anyone who makes bottles and nipples, when bottles are necessary for mothers who have to return to work and choose to pump, makes the ones calling out WHO code violators look out of touch. And there are more and more mothers with special circumstances.

"I definitely planned on breastfeeding. I always knew that I would," says Amy Lupold Bair, speaking from her home in the suburbs of Maryland. "I read everything that I could get my hands on before I had my first child, and I understood the health reasons why breast is best. I had taken a leave of absence from my teaching job to be a stay-at-home mom, so I knew that I would have a certain length of time and availability. I just assumed that I would breastfeed and it would just be an easy thing," she says.

Bair is a social media wunderkind of sorts. She created the concept of the Twitter Party and then went on to dominate the field, now charging some $6,000–$8,000 per party and hosting at least three or four per week. You do the math. Her clients are nearly guaranteed to make the coveted trending topics list on Twitter, either in the U.S. or, more likely, world-wide. In July 2008, she launched her award-winning Web site ResourcefulMommy.com, which she saw as a way to write parenting articles for the freelance writing career she hoped to spark, instead of returning to work. And she is the author of *Raising Digital Families for Dummies*. An English teacher by trade, Amy and her husband had a five-year plan that included one child then another two years later, and returning to work three years after that.

But the planned-out motherhood experience Amy had in her head did not materialize. "My daughter was born two months early, so that immediately complicated things. I also had something called hyperemesis gravidarum when pregnant so I had lost thirty pounds and was very sick. So I had my own health issues on top of having an unhealthy newborn. We tried teaching her to latch about forty-eight hours after she was born because there was not an immediate opportunity to feed her. I went to the NICU about thirteen to fourteen hours a day and tried multiple times to breastfeed her. They found that she was burning more calories trying to nurse than she was receiving in milk. On top of that she would stop breathing—due to her preemie-ism she could not suck, swallow, and breathe innately like other babies. I was devastated," Amy says. "A child who feels like they are suffocating when they are nursing because they don't know how to suck, swallow, and breathe pulls away and arches back—it's a survival instinct. So I had this newborn who was pulling away from me frantically when I tried to nurse her and that was a very difficult thing for me to understand as a twenty-six-year-old first-time mother.

"Certainly the focus was on getting my daughter healthy. She was in the hospital for three weeks. It was very critical and touch-and-go with her for a while. Emotionally, it was really terrible. The whole idea of having a big healthy baby that I could hold immediately and would breastfeed happily flew right out of the window," Amy says.

For months Amy agonized over trying to transition her baby to the breast. It never happened. "It was not until I met with the second lactation consultant that I found some relief. She said, "Let's get you on a pump. Let's make life easier for you and just know that you are providing her with some breast milk, which is certainly better than none at all, if that's your goal." It wasn't until she said that that I was able to say, "It's okay. Let it go. It's okay if she never nurses." At that point I was sort of able to relax and I actually went into this mode where I was able to pump more efficiently. Pumping breast milk for eight months, five to six times a day was a nightmare. It was very emotionally draining, but I had the incentive of improving her health. The breast milk that comes in for a premature baby is very different from the milk that comes in for a full-term baby. It has a different quality, caloric amount . . . it even looked different in the nursery fridge from other pumped milk. I understood that it was really important for her health to have that, especially seeing that she was already starting behind because she was two months early, so it was very motivational for me."

Amy ended up with enough milk to provide at least some breast milk through her daughter's entire first year. "But we always had to supplement. We had to supplement in the hospital with milk fortifier and I had some supply issues. When you are exclusively pumping sometimes the body doesn't always provide the supply of breast milk needed. Had we not had things like the milk fortifier, formula, or bottles that had a variety of features like nipple sizes and flow rates, I don't know what would have happened."

Twenty-seven months after her daughter was born, Amy gave birth to her son. "After my experience with my daughter, I already told myself that if this next child does not latch on I don't care if we have to go make him a sandwich, I am not pumping again. I was prepared to go straight to the formula," she says. Like her first delivery, Amy ended up having an emergency C-section and suffering from dehydration. Her newborn son went straight to the NICU. "I didn't even get to touch him. So he actually received a bottle as his first milk and did not have any contact with me for several hours," Amy recalls. "I was concerned that we were going to be in a situation where he wouldn't be able to latch or I would not be able to breastfeed, but actually he rejected the bottle and took to me immediately, so I nursed him for sixteen months," she says. Her son nursed exclusively for six months. "He would not take a bottle. I would pump and have to throw it away. We ended up moving him from the breast to a sippy cup."

Amy's experiences shaped her own sensibilities about the varied experiences of breastfeeding and the need to not have one fixed idea of what is acceptable breastfeeding and what is not. Women like Amy, who wholeheartedly support breastfeeding but also understand the roles of formula, bottles, and teats are not the exception—they are more of the norm. And it is creating fixed lines about what is breastfeeding and what is not that also creates rigid definitions as to who is a breastfeeding supporter or breastfeeding mother and who is not. This is counterproductive to movement building.

Because of her personal story, Amy often works with companies that are technically WHO code violators and has been on the receiving end of serious backlash from breastfeeding supporters for some of these decisions. "To those people I just say that my daughter is alive and healthy because of bottles and because I was able to find a nipple that worked for her. Yes, I want all mothers to breastfeed. But I also want mothers to have support if that is not their story."

• • •

Stories are important. They are how we shape our perception of the world. The stories that shape the breastfeeding world should be multidimensional and complex like the women they seek to attract. Instead, they have been mostly simplistic. Drawing on my communications and messaging expertise, I've identified essentially three story lines that have been dominant in the breastfeeding narrative in the past ten years.

The first is the idyllic-meadow scenario, seen in many parenting magazines, that presents breastfeeding as calming, beautiful, and serene. While that can be the experience of some women, most women face fear and frustration at some point in their breastfeeding journey. Putting out a euphoric visual that is in direct opposition to the experience of most women caused some to stop breastfeeding, concluding that something must be wrong with them if their experience is so different. The second story line is all about the scientific evidence behind breastfeeding, even as "science" became a more confusing field for all. That misstep took an intellectual, fact-based approach to an emotionally charged act—showing once again that the movement did not understand the personal complexities of breastfeeding.

But where the media really dug in and found a place to amplify a dangerous submessage was with the so-called lactivist story line.

"Bristol mother suckers!" the sign said. A woman with a broad smile held the poster up high with her left hand, an umbrella in her right. She had a bright red scarf on her head, tied Rosie the Riveter style. Her baby was snugly in a front-facing carrier, wearing a similarly styled red scarf. The occasion for such colorful outfits and equally colorful language was a breastfeeding flash mob that descended on the Park Street Café in Bristol, England, just days after a twenty-nine-year-old mom was asked to leave when she began breastfeeding her baby. The ousted mom took her anger to the highest court of public opinion, also known as Twitter and Facebook, and in a few days hundreds of breastfeeding supporters rallied to her side on social media and in real life to march to the café, pull out their breasts, and feed in a show of defiance and solidarity. The owner was quick to apologize and reiterate that all mothers are welcome in his establishment. But the nurse-in was on.

It's become an all-too-familiar scene in the U.S. as well. So-called lactivists rallying on social media, staging nurse-ins at cafés, shopping malls, corporate headquarters, and media outlets after a mother has been slighted, shamed, or expelled for breastfeeding in public despite laws in almost fifty states protecting breastfeeding in public. The "defend and protest" refrain has become a common narrative among breastfeeding supporters and a large part of the mother-led, social-media-powered movement to normalize breastfeeding. Much of this organizing occurs on Twitter and Instagram with hashtags such as #NormalizeBreastfeeding or #FreeThe-Nipple that have brought women and men, celebrities and activists together to support nursing moms and end shaming. That's the good news.

The bad news is that every inflammatory headline about an ousted mom sensationalizes breastfeeding and perpetu-ates the notion that breastfeeding puts you at risk of being kicked out of a public place and that you need near activist-level moxie to do it. On the surface, women inciting other women to fight for their right to breastfeed and coming to-gether in a display of sister courage has all the hallmarks of a powerful strategy to mobilize women. But women waving signs like "Bristol mother suckers!" may make breastfeeding look more like a fringe movement or a cult. Names such as the "breastapo" or "mammary militia" are thrown around after these incidents. And who has the time? When I was breast-feeding and heard of nurse-ins, I always wondered who were these women who had extra hours to march to a café and sit there nursing in protest. I had to work. Even while on my ex-tended unpaid maternity leave, I freelanced to keep some money coming in—there was no time for nurse-ins. These dynamics can alienate many women while emboldening a select few. And it adds to the notion that breastfeeding and protecting breastfeeding are the work of the privileged. Something is indeed upside down if not inside out about how we think about our so-called choices when we take to the Internet and to the streets in knee-jerk reactionary ways.

What women need is a well-conceived outlet or campaign for these frustrations that leads to systemic change, not just hashtag activism.

Women also need more institutional support. The United States Breastfeeding Coalition has done commendable work leading the state coalitions to think and act more inclusively and with a broader scope, The W.K. Kellogg Foundation has been the leader in the philanthropic space, funding millions in breastfeeding-supportive activities in line with their mission of supporting early childhood and economic security. Others like the Robert Wood Johnson Foundation have also stepped up. But the dangerous framing of breastfeeding as an individual issue keeps away key funders, who in fact claim to focus on infant and maternal health but don't view breastfeeding as fundamental to improving those outcomes.

Some advocates have gone another route, rallying celebrities to the cause. Bettina Lauf Forbes and Danielle Briggs have built their life's work banking on the power of celebrity being the key driver in shifting cultural norms around breastfeeding. As the founders of the Best of Babes Foundation, they primarily enroll celebrities in the Champions for Moms ad campaign and host events centered on the power of celebrity to advance the breastfeeding movement. They have already enrolled stars such as Kelly Preston, Jenna Elfman, Laila Ali, Kelly Rutherford, and Gabrielle Reece; spurred corporate sponsors to invest in change; and put positive pressure on the media to tell the story of moms who are being prevented from succeeding by what they call Booby Traps.

Their model for helping women and babies is based on the thing no one wants to admit: we follow celebrities. Historically, celebrities and Hollywood have always influenced our ideas about beauty, fashion, and our bodies in general, which play a part in our breastfeeding decisions. We want to buy the strollers and clothing that they use for their own kids. And if celebrities can make leggings and headbands cool, then why not breastfeeding?

"We want to do what Michael Jordan and Nike did for fitness. And what Paris Hilton did for carrying a dog around in a Louis Vuitton bag. Jordan made it cool and hip to exercise. And Paris Hilton transcended socioeconomics. Even if you had a fake Louis Vuitton, you put your dog in it. That's the power of celebrities to set trends," Bettina said in an interview.

Of course, breastfeeding is more complex. And as much as we love celebrities, we also love to hate celebrities and criticize them for their idealized lives, which are far removed from our day-to-day realities. Celebrity can be a double-edged sword.

Still, Hollywood has had a fairly robust parade of breastfeeding supporters: Angelina Jolie, Alanis Morissette, Beyoncé, Alicia Silverstone, Halle Berry, Mayim Bialik, Alyssa Milano, Tori Spelling, Kourtney Kardashian, Miranda Kerr, Gisele Bündchen, Kendra Wilkinson, Selma Hayek, Naomi Watts, Rebecca Romijn, Elisabeth Hasselbeck, Christina Aguilera, Gwen Stefani, Jennifer Garner, Maggie Gyllenhaal, Kate Beckinsale, Mary-Louise Parker, Pink, Ashlee Simpson, Victoria Beckham, Hilary Duff, Jenna Fischer, and Snooki to name a few. All of these mothers have publicly stated that they breastfed or made positive comments about the experience. Snooki even talked candidly about her fear of pain and feeling "like a cow" when pumping, but overall she spoke of loving the experience. Add to this that Ricki Lake, Bialik, and Morissette have also been very vocal supporters of extended breastfeeding and attachment parenting. And alt-rocker Peter Wentz solidified his "cool dad" status by commenting that he had tasted his wife's, Ashlee Simpson's, breast milk, declaring it "soury" and "weird."

With such a long list of celebrity moms and dads talking about breastfeeding, why aren't we there yet? How many more does it take to get our "Nike moment"? For as much as celebrities can help with the "image" of breastfeeding, there is a downside to their spotlight. It's easy to think, well, of course Angelina Jolie is breastfeeding twins—she has the money to buy resources such as nannies, a personal chef, and housekeepers, while the rest of us have to cook our own food and clean up after ourselves (and possibly another child). If I had all of that, I would breastfeed too! Angelina Jolie doesn't have to return to work in three weeks or fret how she will pay the bills. She probably has access to superior health care providers, on-standby lactation consultants, a personal trainer, and money for all the convenience tools. It can deepen the dangerous thinking that you need extraordinary circumstances to breastfeed and, without that, it is just too hard. The use of celebrities may make breastfeeding more attractive to the average woman, but not necessarily more attainable. Is attractive enough?

Bettina and Danielle say yes.

If it becomes attractive enough, then women will push to make it attainable, they assert. Every day we want things we can't afford or seem unreachable for our life circumstances, but many times we make it happen. Mothers will begin to

demand the "luxuries" that should be rights that allow celebrities to breastfeed with ease and leave many everyday
women struggling. Perhaps what we need is not more celebrity
moms endorsing breastfeeding but more celebrities taking
a cue from Snooki and speaking candidly about their challenges, setbacks, and fears. The way to normalize breastfeeding includes normalizing the challenges of breastfeeding.
Then, perhaps, we have to begin to ask more of the celebrities. Breastfeeding does not happen in a vacuum. What
about lending their star power to the myriad of complemen-
tary issues that directly affect breastfeeding, particularly paid
family leave? What if they used their celebrity to get an audience on Capitol Hill to promote better child care options,
flexible work schedules, and more viable part-time work opportunities for women?

My fear is that the movement will never be able to leverage
the scores of breastfeeding mothers in Hollywood because
standing up for women and babies in America can be a dangerous and career-limiting move by Hollywood standards.
Standing up for sick babies in Africa and other underdeveloped countries is socially acceptable and applauded. But in
the United States, the infant feeding conversation is so
wrapped up in the idea of individual choice that any advocacy is often misconstrued as an attack a woman's freedom.

Brazilian supermodel Gisele Bündchen experienced this
firsthand when, soon after giving birth to her son, Benjamin,
in December 2009, she suggested that breastfeeding for six
months should be a law. "Some people here don't think they
have to breastfeed, and I think, 'Are you going to give chemical food to your child when they are so little?' " she said in

an interview in the U.K. *Harper's Bazaar.* "I think there should be a worldwide law, in my opinion, that mothers should breastfeed their babies for the first six months."

Gisele's use of the word "law" was a direct affront to American women's strong connection to freedom and choice, and they let her have it. There was no context that if there was a law, there would also have to be the means and support to comply with it. The media dug it. Gisele became just the latest scapegoat for the cable news networks and the blogosphere. I was one of the women on national television discussing the controversy, attempting to explain the spirit of what Gisele was saying. But the idea of the government interfering with a woman's feeding choice sounded like tyranny, even though state and local governments mandate other areas of infant health such as immunizations all the time. But what women heard was, How dare you with your supermodel body and your Super Bowl husband (she is married to NFL quarterback Tom Brady) talk of imposing laws on everyday women. Gisele was forced to take to her blog and clarify. The damage was done. Gisele never spoke publicly about breastfeeding again.

Powerful celebrities—the ones whose lives and accessories we so dearly want—are silenced by the same forces that stifle conversation and prevent building the kind of momentum that would benefit us all. And I'm not sure that any celebrity is willing to take that on.

The problem of getting it right with breastfeeding messaging goes back to the early 1900s. By 1910, infant deaths reached alarming rates as severe bouts of diarrhea and digestive diseases among artificially fed infants spawned widespread recognition, prompting some of the first breastfeeding promotion campaigns. The culprit was unclean cows' milk, which was being used in many artificial substitutes. What happened next may have changed the course of breastfeeding engagement for decades to come. Two sets of public health campaigns ensued. One designed almost solely by local public health officials urged mothers to breastfeed for as long as possible. The other—involving public health departments and a much wider array of supporters, including concerned citizens, municipal governments, medical charities, settlement houses, private physicians, and newspapers—crusaded for clean cows' milk. Both campaigns had noble and useful goals, but the latter, with its broader array of supporters, had greater exposure. It also created an unintended consequence to the breastfeeding culture.

Public health officials around the country hung posters in urban neighborhoods urging mothers to breastfeed or to avoid feeding their babies the spoiled, adulterated cows' milk that pervaded U.S. cities. The language on the posters was direct and to the point. One commanded, "To lessen baby deaths let us have more mother-fed babies. You can't improve on God's plan. For your baby's sake—nurse it!" Another, which explained the importance of home pasteurization and keeping cows' milk on ice if a mother did not breastfeed, pleaded, "Give the Bottle-Fed Baby a Chance for Its Life!" The campaign efforts focused on immigrant communities, and posters appeared in English, Bohemian, Croatian, German, Italian, Lithuanian, Polish, Serbian, Swedish, and Yiddish.

But the broader "clean up the milk" efforts had deeper media support. Calling pure cows' milk "one of the essentials of daily living," urban newspapers decried "the diluted, adulterated, and harmful quality of milk" common in U.S. cities. As the country's infant death rate garnered unprecedented concern, journalists charged that cows' milk "plays no small part in this colossal crime of infanticide." A *Chicago Tribune* headline from September 1892 read "Scarcely Any Pure Milk" and another "Stop the Bogus Milk Traffic." Reformers fought for more than thirty years for pasteurized milk gathered from healthy cows, processed under sanitary conditions, sealed in individual bottles, and shipped in refrigerated railroad cars. While urban reformers focused on cleaning up cows' milk, human milk advocates concentrated on keeping babies at the breast.

By the late 1920s, with laws in most municipalities mandating the pasteurization and hygienic handling of cows' milk, the urban breastfeeding campaigns disappeared. The outcry that unclean cows' milk was the culprit for the high number of infant deaths drowned out the need to breastfeed regardless of the quality of cows' milk. Although low breastfeeding rates continued to generate public health problems, the link between human milk and infant health was less obvious. As a result, breastfeeding never became the cornerstone of preventive medicine that so many early-twentieth-century physicians recommended. Instead, the lay and medical communities came to believe that pasteurization nullified the differences between human and cows' milk. With readily available clean cows' milk, breastfeeding crusades and breastfeeding itself seemed antiquated and unnecessary, as mothers sought artificial milks as they continued to work more outside the home. By the early 1930s, a new generation of doctors belittled human milk as "nothing . . . sacred." Unlike their breastfeeding-activist predecessors, these pediatricians never witnessed the rampant death of infants by spoiled and adulterated cows' milk and so came to place more faith in the efficacy of cows' milk than human milk.

By presenting breast milk as the best and safest compared with cows' milk, the true benefits of breast milk were lost in the messaging. Breast milk should not have been compared with anything. With the advent of pasteurization, cows' milk was considered safe. And human milk substitutes made from cows' milk were also considered safe. But safe does not mean better. Technically, Spam, the canned, precooked meat product made by Hormel, is safe. But no one would tout its health benefits and agree that children should be fed a steady diet of the factory-manufactured stuff. Yet with cows' milk being technically safe, the fundamental reason why health officials told mothers to breastfeed had now disappeared. Breast milk lost its competitive advantage and never regained its rightful place as the best nutrition for infants—hands down—and its rightful determination as preventive medicine. Instead, artificial milks were viewed as "as good as" breast milk.

The results were disastrous. From 1930 to the early 1970s, after several failed attempts at breastfeeding marketing campaigns and with the collusion of physicians, not only did mothers continue to supplement their breast milk with cows' milk and wean infants in the first few weeks and months of life, but more and more mothers did not breastfeed at all. Breastfeeding in America was nearly eradicated. It was a low point for the movement. By 1966, just 18 percent of babies were breastfed when they left the hospital—an all-time low in the United States—and fewer for more than a few weeks after that. Not until later in the 1970s did the women's health reform movement rekindle interest in breastfeeding. Even as more women in the 1970s nursed their infants, the medical community never deemed breastfeeding as the gold standard of care. Instead, formula feeding became the norm and nursing became the "best" thing to do—a nice cost-effective choice, but not necessary. Between 1984 and 1989, breastfeeding initiation rates declined 13 percent from almost 60 percent to 52 percent. Not until 1995 did these rates return to a high of 60 percent. In 2001 69.5% of U.S. mothers initiated breastfeeding.

Today, the movement is faced with a different, but still troublesome, challenge. While initiation rates have reached 75 percent in the United States, only about 13 percent of babies are exclusively breastfed for six months, according to the Centers for Disease Control and Prevention. Compare that to South Asia, where 44 percent of babies are exclusively breastfed for six months. Meanwhile, supplementation rates continue to rise, with an increasing percentage of mothers introducing formula just days after leaving the hospital. Fifty-three percent of lactating mothers introduce formula before their babies are a week old, 68 percent do so by two months, and 81 percent by four months, according to the latest CDC data.

Well-intentioned health organizations and government agencies have spent considerable time, money, and effort trying to fix the breastfeeding problem. In 2000 the Department of Health and Human Services (HHS) published a bold booklet titled *HHS Blueprint for Action on Breastfeeding.* The first sentence said it all: "Breastfeeding is one of the most important contributors to infant health." The language was reminiscent of the early-twentieth-century public health campaigns' insistence that having been breastfed was the single most powerful predictor of an infant's ability to survive childhood. HHS called the lack of exclusive and prolonged breastfeeding in the United States "a public health challenge" and urged health care providers, employers, and child care facilities to formulate policies supportive of extended breastfeeding. HHS also called for a social marketing effort to explain to the public the importance of human milk and the dangers of formula feeding.

In early 2011, U.S. Surgeon General Regina M. Benjamin issued "Call to Action to Support Breastfeeding," an unprecedented report urging mothers to breastfeed longer and pushing for the removal of key barriers to breastfeeding. Dr. Benjamin, a MacArthur "Genius" Grant recipient, was a rising star in the medical community. In 1995 she was the first African-American woman to be elected to the American Medical Association board of trustees. She gained notoriety following Hurricane Katrina as one of the only physicians treating patients in her Katrina-ravaged community of Bayou La Batre in Alabama. Her nomination was a boon for family medicine. "Call to Action" laid out steps for hospitals, physicians, nurses, and lactation consultants for community engagement. Advocates cheered that "America's Doctor" was a breastfeeding ally and rallied around "Call to Action," but the report was directed more toward policy makers and institutions. And a call to action is not a mandate or law. Yes, it provided more evidence to push for policy change, but without the groundswell of women demanding change, policy can seem like a solution to an issue with no problem.

Forget the *Feminine Mystique*; for years breastfeeding has been the problem without a name. The problem that was not a problem. Infant formula companies heralded the nutritional quality and safety of their products—creating no reason to complain. By promoting the idea that babies were just fine and mothers were just fine, there was no outrage and no need to fix anything. This is very dangerous from the perspective of shifting cultural norms. Social movements are, by definition, collective actions in which the populace is alerted, educated, and mobilized, over time, to challenge the power holders to redress social problems or grievances and restore critical social values. Sometimes social problems are as blatantly obvious as police brutality or domestic violence. Those are problems people actually see with vivid images, bruises, bloodshed, and, in these days, footage from a cell phone camera posted on YouTube. Though the Internet did not yet exist in the 1970s, similar tactics were used then to mount one of the most successful movements in breastfeeding history, created in response to the unnecessary deaths of infants in Africa and other developing nations, where babies were literally dying from infant formula. In 1974 the British charity War on Want published *The Baby Killer,* in which the journalist Mike Muller wrote a dramatic account of the tactics used by formula companies to capture their market. *The Baby Killer* had a powerful cover picture, showing a severely malnourished child trapped inside a baby bottle. The report also included other tragic images of impoverished and malnourished infants. Other reports and studies followed, including a critical Consumer's Union investigation of food and pharmaceutical industries and a book, *The Nutrition Factor*, by the Brookings Institution scholar Alan Berg. These damning reports prompted the World Health Organization to call for a review of corporate sales practices and to advise member governments to consider action in 1974. In 1975 a documentary called *Bottle Babies* was released. Filmed in Kenya, it was filled with powerful visual images of starving, malnourished, bottle-fed infants. In one scene, a mother is shown scooping water from a filthy puddle and mixing it with baby formula. Another scene showed a graveyard full of infants with their graves marked with bottle and formula cans. In Kenya, as in other parts of the world, it is customary to bury the infant with their most valued possession—and the formula was it. The film was a critical step in the global movement to curb inappropriate marketing of infant formula and was a highly effective tool in creating awareness of the health problems created by bottle feeding.

One researcher defines social movements as the "collective enterprises to establish a new order of life." In that regard, the push to limit infant formula marketing in developing countries was a success. But by that same rubric, we also see the gaping hole in the U.S. breastfeeding movement. For if you to want a new order, you have to see something wrong with your current order. Here in the well-heeled U.S.A., it was hard to frame the problem of breastfeeding. Babies weren't visibly dying. There were no heart-wrenching optics of sick and malnourished babies. No picture of an American mother collecting dirty water with which to feed formula to her baby. On the contrary, technological advances made milk substitutes safer. Formula-fed babies were plump. In fact, the infant formula companies made sure of that by creating and sponsoring infant growth charts based on typical weight gain for formula-fed babies, often making breastfed babies look underweight. Women couldn't see a problem. Most mothers today still do not. This was particularly difficult since the framing of the problem had long been co-opted by the physicians and pharmaceutical companies, who made the unpredictable nature of breastfeeding the problem.

But there was a very serious public health problem. However, instead of making women aware of the structural barriers and the very real dangers of having a commercial entity control what you feed your baby, women were messaged about the benefits of breast milk. The movement saw educating women with medical information instead of rallying them around the structural barriers to breastfeeding as the solution to the problem. Many of the barriers are so woven into the fiber of our existence that we no longer recognize them as odd. We take them as normal. Karl Marx called on workers to become aware of their oppressed status and to develop a class consciousness. He also held that a social movement would require leaders to sharpen the awareness of the oppressed. They would need to help workers overcome feelings of false consciousness, or attitudes that do not reflect workers' objective position, in order to organize a revolutionary movement. Similarly, one of the challenges faced by women's liberation activists of the late 1960s and early 1970s was to convince women that they were being deprived of their rights and of socially valued resources.

But breastfeeding isn't viewed or framed as a societal

problem. As we discussed in the previous chapter, breastfeeding has not been included in the reproductive rights conversation. As women fought to figure out how to have control over when they have children, there was never any conversation about the right to feed the children that we did have.

What will it take to transform breastfeeding into a broadly supported social movement? Social scientists say mobilizing people for action requires three main characteristics. To start, there needs to be a level of discontent with the way things are, based mainly on how people perceive their situation. Then, people must feel that they have a *right* to their goals, that they deserve better than what they have. And lastly, there needs to be a shared perception that members can end their relative deprivation only through collective action.

Gopal Dayaneni knows something about movement building. He also knows about breastfeeding. In his native India, he was breastfed until he was four years old, and he remembers the experience. Gopal is on staff of MovementGeneration .org and serves on the board of the International Accountability Project. He is considered one of the key architects of the modern-day art of strategic movement building. He has a long career, a highly regarded reputation, and several active roles providing strategic communications to progressive organizations looking to win the battle of ideas. Gopal, who is a work-at-home dad to his two daughters, says that, despite his vast expertise in the field, he finds the current state of breastfeeding affairs in the United States very confusing. It wasn't long into our conversation before Gopal identified the fatal flaw in breastfeeding messaging. "The surest way to inoculate a social movement is to keep it embroiled in the

matter of choice. It's precisely how to keep a social movement stuck in the cultural space. And it masks what actually
is going on," he says. So, to be clear, from a movement building experts' opinion, the pro-breastfeeding efforts are in the
worst state possible.

Clearly, the well-intentioned forebears of the breastfeeding message were not movement-building specialists. If they
had been, they likely would not have been complicit in ring-
ing the movement death knell of "choice." They sought to encourage women to choose to breastfeed by arming them with
facts. Those facts included information about what's wrong
with formula but not what's wrong with society. They courted
women as the sole decision makers on infant feeding without
considering how women were being influenced by societal
barriers, partners, relatives, and marketing influences. These
forebears armed women with the information without showing women how they were being impeded from exercising a
very basic right. A review of women's history reveals that linking controversial topics like abortion to generally accepted
values and basic rights has been extremely effective.

I am back to Gopal and the steady hum of his voice.
"Movements need to be organized around identities that are
important to the audience," he said. This is an important
insight, because, really, is mother an identity that we rally
around? Yes, it's an important identity, but our social norms
push us to prove that we are not solely mothers—that we
haven't "lost ourselves" in motherhood. Women shy away from
rallying around that identity because we've been told mothering is demeaning work. And when we do rally, we're often
in defensive mode justifying our choices.

The movement has tried to mobilize women around scientific facts about the benefits of breastfeeding instead of organizing them around the quality of their life, around the fact that women have basic reproductive rights, and around their status as potential change agents more broadly. These are lives that lack paid maternity leave, affordable child care, and financially viable part-time work, to name a few. Those two approaches to building support among women are very different with very different outcomes—and have been critical missteps in the overall failure of the breastfeeding leadership throughout the years to fully meet its own goals.

From a communication perspective, the movement has suffered from an overreliance on scientists and medical experts, as if feeding decisions were purely rational and based on facts only. But mothers are suffering from expert overload, and modern mothers' concept of who is the authority on motherhood has transitioned from professionals to peers. The industry's heavy leaning on scientific research also discounts the complicated relationship that some communities of color have with the medical profession. For example, between 1932 and 1972, the government conducted a forty-year study that intentionally left six hundred black men untreated for syphilis in the well-documented Tuskegee Experiment. The men had no idea that they were involved in a study and were told they were being treated for "bad blood," when, in fact, the only data being collected was from their autopsies. Thus, in one of the most horrible scandals of the medical industry, they were deliberately left to degenerate and die from the effects of advanced syphilis, which include tumors, blindness, and heart disease. Even the surgeon general of the

United States participated in enticing the men to stay in the experiment, sending them certificates of appreciation after twenty-five years in the study. In 1997 President Bill Clinton apologized to the country and the eight remaining survivors, calling the experiment "morally wrong" and "racist." The Tuskegee Experiment is an often-referenced point in African Americans' widespread distrust of the medical community and the government. The cultural nuances of who trusts the medical and scientific community is often missed in breast-feeding messaging.

Common messaging also refers to nursing rooms as "accommodations," as if employers are doing women some special favor for facilitating a biological need. As a cultural norm, men urinate standing up, but a urinal is not considered an "accommodation" for men—it is just the standard. This is exactly what women deserve: lactation facilities as the norm, instead of being made to feel they are being done a favor because of their unique biological needs.

Physician, Heal Thyself

The breastfeeding leadership is not without its own problems. The national breastfeeding committees, state coalitions, lactation-industry associations, major public health departments, national WIC, advocates, and allies must be mobilized as well. However, instead of leading women, they have in many ways come to mimic the problem—divided, frustrated, and with a gaping racial disparity in their professional ranks. The infighting is often exacerbated as the lactation industry begins to resemble the medical industry and as the multiple layers of certifications for lactation professionals get in the way of mass mobilization. At the top of the professional heap are International Board Certified Lactation Consultants (IBCLC); then there are Certified Lactation Consultants (CLC) and Lactation Consultants (LC); then there are peer counselors. IBCLCs are considered the gold standard for lactation support, and the certification requires advanced medical classes, ninety "clock" hours of lactation education, a thousand hours of supervised clinical experience, and eight college courses to then take a lengthy and costly exam. The process for certification is confusing: three "pathways" are offered, and the rules change often. As one physician who is also an IBCLC quipped, "compared to becoming an IBCLC, becoming a medical doctor was easy." The changing rules create barriers for newer, younger, and more diverse women to enter the field, particularly as the cost of access to this elite rank rises. Without a doubt, when dealing with preemies or serious lactation problems, such as tongue-tie in an infant or breast infections, an IBCLC is the professional you need. But for the most common of lactation challenges, one of the lower levels of certification such as an LC, CLC, or peer counselor just may do. This realization, that most lactation problems are not medical but emotional or psychological, is not always welcomed by all IBCLCs. There's also a big push for mother-led support, as more moms look to peers for advice, which is being resisted by some certified lactation professionals. Jobs for IBCLCs are growing but still limited compared with other health jobs. Nonprofits focused on breastfeeding scramble for limited funding. As a result, instead of leading with vision, they often lead with fear—warning women about risks instead of showing them the way forward. Grassroots organizations and nonprofits are in dread of losing funding. Lactation professionals are in dread of losing "ownership" of breastfeeding as more players are brought into the field, yet opportunities remain limited. And in that space, it is hard to create the kind of vision that is needed to effectively mobilize women and men for widespread societal change.

The clock is ticking. Any movement-building strategist worth his protest sign will tell you that social movements have life cycles. There are often only small windows of opportunity to act—such as with Rosa Parks refusing to sit in the back of the bus. Those are critical moments to motivate collective action. But those windows close quickly, and no one knows when they may open again. I strongly believe that we are at one of those times. Yes, there are sizable challenges to overcome. Many are systemic and deeply rooted.

Two of them are right in front of us, literally.

8

Boob Control: The Sexualization of Breastfeeding

Scientists now believe that the primary biological function of breasts is to make males stupid.

—DAVE BARRY

It was the nipple that changed life as we know it. The half-time show at Super Bowl XXXVIII easily goes down in history as one of the most memorable incidents since the creation of television. The 2004 show was a collaboration by the year's top pop stars, including Kid Rock, Britney Spears, Justin Timberlake, and Janet Jackson. But the performance took a sharp turn from a PG rating when Justin Timberlake neared the end of his single "Rock Your Body" and tore off a piece of Janet's bustier, apparently intending to leave the red lace bra underneath intact. Instead, he grabbed both the bustier and bra, and her nipple was inadvertently exposed to over 140 million viewers. Shock and horror ensued over "Nipplegate." It was one thing to have Jackson's breast pushed all the way up, but a darkened nipple for American families to see? This was too much. The crime against America's most unifying form of entertainment lasted for all of 9/16ths of a second, but the FCC received a record-setting 1.4 million complaints, and the episode provoked national outrage. The FCC and all the producing entities involved, including the NFL and MTV, immediately changed their policies for working with artists in live settings. A legal battle ensued between CBS and the FCC, with CBS ultimately being fined $550,000. The expression "wardrobe malfunction" entered the American vernacular, and by 2008 the *Chambers Dictionary* acknowledged the term. Janet Jackson's nipple literally changed the world.

That's no hyperbole. For the millions that did see the infamous wardrobe malfunction, there were still millions more who did not. At that time, there was no way to go back and rewatch the show unless you had taped it. The media frenzy over Nipplegate and the scores who did not see it led to an uptick in TiVo subscriptions. But it also inspired three tech guys, who missed out on the salacious event and couldn't find any videos of the incident online, to start working on the code to create a site where people could upload their own content for all to see. That site ended up being YouTube, a current staple of modern-day existence, which launched not long after. Much of YouTube's initial success was in part due to people looking for clips of Janet and Justin's performance and, more specifically, Janet's breast. In just one year, Google saw the potential of the site and purchased it for over $1.5 billion plus Google stock, making the founders very wealthy. Indeed, the sensationalization of the nipple has changed cultural history.

Never before had communication commissions, culture critics, columnists, and California tech start-ups paid so much attention to one nipple. Suffice it to say, our culture is still overly obsessed with voyeurism as it relates to the female breast. It's worth noting that men have breasts too—including breast tissue, a nipple, and areola. The only difference is that women's breast tissue grows larger and produces milk. Yet the female areola is the most sexualized circular body part in the United States.

Women's breasts are exposed everywhere, in television, films, magazines, and constantly in advertising. Every day society continues to serve up a poisonous diet of images that fragment women into mere body parts, starting with breasts. They are readily used to sell chicken wings, burgers, and beer, but the potential of exposing a breast while breast-feeding changes everything. As a result, nursing in public is mostly tolerated only in private rooms or under cover, and mothers are still being harassed or asked to leave restaurants, malls, movie theaters, and even airplanes for breastfeeding their babies—even though breastfeeding is a protected act in nearly all states and not subject to indecency laws. Rarely do several weeks pass before there is another media story of a security guard, bus driver, flight attendant, retail employee, or manager booting out a breastfeeding mom. A woman from Texas was told to leave a Victoria's Secret, of all places, and nurse in an alley beside the store so that nobody would see her breastfeed. The mother was obviously shocked to learn that a store that caters to female parts and sells push-up bras would not be accommodating toward a woman wanting to use her breasts to feed her hungry child. That is, instead of dressing them up in lacy material for visual pleasure.

Oddly enough, the sexualization of the female breast has

not always been the case. Nor did the change come from nature. It was society that sexualized the breast. The slow turn of events was accelerated by the World War II pinup-girl poster, postwar soft porn such as *Playboy* magazine, and the popularity of such Hollywood icons as Marilyn Monroe. Society's very complex relationship with breasts complicates breastfeeding, which involves attaching an infant to the most provocative and highly sexualized female body part. It creates an incongruity: the breast is also a source of infant nutrition. Breastfeeding is not just a biological process but also a culturally determined behavior strongly influenced by the environment it occurs in. And when that culture constantly dictates that breasts are sexual objects, the consequences are dangerous. As breasts became more sexualized, they became less functional: more the purview of men and sexual objects and less in service of infants and a source of food. This hypersexualization of breasts has alienated many women and caused some mothers not only to fear breastfeeding in public but also to rethink breastfeeding altogether.

As the transformation of the breast from food to fun continued, the idea of breastfeeding in public became more abnormal and taboo. It became a socially acceptable notion that breastfeeding should be hidden from the view of others, that it is a private act using sexual parts. This put breastfeeding in the unique position of being both a private act, shrouded in individualism and personal choice, and, at the same time, a very public matter that opens mothers up to scrutiny and shaming from strangers. Breastfeeding began as a public matter because of an appropriate public health interest in infant health and survival. As infant health and mortality rates improved, breastfeeding was framed more as a mother's personal preference, but the public involvement continued. The scientific advances of human milk substitutes freed the breast from feeding to focus more on pleasuring men. Since the breast also represents femaleness, this public health concern for the health of babies warped into other anxieties about women's bodies, including their sexuality and the physicality of feeding at the breast. Undercurrents of body politics, such as which women's bodies deserve to be seen as pure or trustworthy versus which bodies need to be controlled also emerged in the conversation. These issues provide an important lens to how all women's bodies have historically and continuously been involved in culturally derived conflicts. From a sociological standpoint, the underlying notion tells us a lot about how people see and understand women and their breasts. The answer: as sex objects. We are all affected by the double standard to body politics, whether we are mothers or not.

At every turn, women are fed messages that breastfeeding ruins your breasts or that a baby will bite your breasts or that, God forbid, your breasts will be less desirable to a man because of breastfeeding. Some women fear that breastfeeding will permanently change the shape of their breasts, so they don't do it. A UK magazine called *Mother & Baby* came under fire when the deputy editor told readers that she bottle-fed her baby because, "I wanted my body back and to give my boobs at least a chance to stay on my chest rather than dangling around my stomach. They're part of my sexuality too, and when you have that attitude, seeing your teeny, tiny, innocent baby latching on where only a lover has been before it feels, well, a little creepy." The anti-breastfeeding overtone of her words resulted in six complaints to the British Press Complaints Commission and prompted a heated debate. However, many moms, including Beyoncé, have also publicly stated that they stopped breastfeeding because they "wanted their body back." The message behind the refrain is that I want my breasts back as sex objects. I want to return my breasts to men. I want my body back to diet and lose weight to meet some standard of postbaby aesthetics. All of which sound more like continued female repression than some forward-thinking self-expression.

Even some modern-day feminists promote this "breastfeeding kills your sexy" view. In "The Conflict," French feminist philosopher Élisabeth Badinter warns of the "ayatollahs of breast-feeding" (in reference to the La Leche League) and writes of the "despotism of an insatiable child" and the "tyranny of maternal duty." But she also suggests that a nursing mother "is not necessarily an object of desire for the father watching her" and condemns nursing as an activity that "may well obliterate the woman-as-lover and endanger the couple." Women feel forced to choose between their maternal bodies, which belong to their babies, or their sexual bodies, which belong to their male partner. It sends a confusing and contradictory message to women because breastfeeding is often associated with the ideals of being a "good" mother. Yet breasts are sexualized, and women desire to make them attractive to men. That leaves women in a can't-win paradox: they either breastfeed and prepare to be ostracized for using sexual objects for feeding or they feed their child formula and deal with the stigma of being labeled a "bad" mother. They can either fear they will be less desirable to male partners or fear they will be judged by other women. Either way, women are caught in the crosshairs.

The consequences of body politics are hard to ignore. For example, for years, physicians, scientists, and behaviorists have recognized the importance of the bonding benefits of breastfeeding for strengthening the mother-child dyad and for child development. Yet when this acknowledged bonding and developmental need collides with the sexuality of women's bodies, there are dangerous attempts to measure and control how this attachment should be executed. Where should this happen? And, for how long?

The need to limit and determine how long a woman's breast can be used for mothering was apparent in May 2012, when *Time* magazine ran one of its most provocative covers in recent history. It featured Jamie Lynne Grumet, a twenty-six-year-old Los Angeles mother pictured breastfeeding her three-year-old son while he was standing on a chair to nurse on his mother's exposed breast. The headline: Are You Mom Enough? The cover story is actually about attachment parenting, a growing trend that includes extended breastfeeding, cosleeping, and baby wearing, but the cover photo with a child who looks too grown to be breastfed and Grumet's defiant look sent the Internet and social media ablaze. Commenters warned that the child would be psychologically scarred from nursing at such an age.

This cultural obsession with breasts on the part of men and women alike is also very damaging to the promotion of breastfeeding. Campaigns that may help further normalize breastfeeding are often hindered by societal hang-ups about breasts. A few years ago, an organization commissioned clever breastfeeding posters for a public health campaign complete with photos of mothers with babies at their breasts. The posters said fun things like, "Fast food outlets. Two convenient locations" and "Sometimes it's okay to suck up to the boss" but were deemed "offensive" and inappropriate for public display by local public health officials.

Yet many public health campaigns for breast cancer awareness actually leverage the sexual nature of the breast, with campaigns like "Save the Ta-Tas." The T-shirts had slogans like, "Caught you lookin' at my ta-tas" and "I love my big ta-tas." In Toronto, Canada, there's an annual Booby Ball to benefit Rethinking Breast Cancer, which included a public service announcement that proclaimed, "You know you like them / now it's time to save the boobs." These campaigns, though well-intended, send the message that breast cancer is worthy of our attention because the breast is so desirable to men. And that if we stop breast cancer, then we protect women's desirability and the male connection to the female body. All of these campaigns draw on a long-term sexualization of the breast and the association between femininity and the intact breast.

You can also see this connection in the focus on breast reconstruction after a mastectomy. New breasts are often jokingly referred to as the "consolation prize" of breast cancer surgery, only furthering the breast-fixated perspective. It's as if a woman can only be whole, complete, and sexy again if she has two full breasts. Way too much pink has been adorned to save breasts from disease or replace diseased breasts but little is done to help breasts perform their normal biological function—lactation. Both efforts often reduce women to their body parts without considering the whole woman. In both scenarios, breastfeeding and breast cancer, women often report feeling helpless and not in control of their bodies.

Seeing breasts as sex objects also prevents us from having a deeper understanding of and appreciation for the breast. "Breasts are the only organ that does not have its own medical specialty, even though it is the most cancer ridden organ of our body, besides for skin," says Florence Williams, a mother, science journalist, and author of the groundbreaking book, *Breasts: A Natural and Unnatural History.*

The damage of sexualizing breasts often falls squarely along racial lines. There's a strong historical legacy of denigrating the bodies of African-American women. Not only do black women suffer from sexual objectification, but the ways in which they are objectified is linked to how they have been racially depicted as "exotic" and as "hypersexual." During slavery, black women labored liked men but were also valued for their ability to "breed" and "feed," enriching the stock of plantation owners by producing more slaves and benefiting the slave owner's family by wet-nursing their babies. Historical records document that black women were often forced to stop breastfeeding their own children to nurse the children of the white slave owner. Black women's breasts were examined and graded at slave auctions as if they were livestock. During the slavery era, their status as property meant that black women could legally not be raped, so the frequent sexual abuse by their white owners was passed off as licentious behavior on their own part. If the breast is sexualized, the totality of black women's bodies has been hypersexualized. The fixation on the black breast became a legendary historical moment when Sojourner Truth, the six-foot-tall women's rights and antislavery activist and former slave, most known for her impassioned and impromptu "Ain't I a Woman?" speech at a women's convention in Ohio in 1851, was challenged on her femaleness. Truth, who had at least three of her children sold away from her while enslaved, was addressing a white audience that included a group of proslavery men. The men challenged her honor and questioned her claim to be a woman, demanding that she show her breast to the women in the audience. According to an article in *The Liberator* newspaper in 1838:

> Sojourner told them that her breasts has suckled many a white babe, to the exclusion of her own offspring; that some of those white babies had grown [and] . . . although they had suckled her colored breasts, they were, in her estimation, far more manly than they (her prosecutors) appeared to be; and she quietly asked them, as she disrobed her bosom, if they too wished to suck! . . . she told them that . . . it was not to her shame that she uncovered her breast before them, but to their shame.

The unique controversy surrounding black women's breasts goes back to a history of Africans being labeled as primitive, subhuman, and animal-like because they lived naturally in their native continent. This was twisted into a justification for the capture, enslavement, and oppression of Africans in America, who were deemed unworthy of humane treatment. Ever since then, the idea of whose breasts and bodies need to

be controlled and which are valued has had racial implications. Today, breastfeeding is marketed as "natural," which
often backfires with black women because it negatively con-
notes stereotyping and subjugation.

This continued politics around black women's breasts became blatantly evident in the summer of 2014 when a friend
of Karlesha Thurman, twenty-five, who just earned her ac-
counting degree from California State University, posted a
photo of Karlesha wearing her cap and gown and breastfeeding her three-month-old daughter while at graduation. The
picture went viral, setting off an international media and
social media firestorm. The headlines used words such as
"provocative photo," "fury erupts," and "stirs controversy."
The negative and insulting comments Thurman received are
too many and too vulgar to mention here. Thurman appeared
on the *Today* show to address the unwanted attention and
unexplainable cruelty. Four months later, a white Austra-
lian woman, Jacci Sharkey, sent a picture of herself also with
her baby at her left breast, to the University of the Sunshine
Coast as a thank-you for helping her graduate while juggling
two children. The university found the photo so "amazing,"
they posted it to their own Facebook page. Her picture, too,
went viral, amassing over 275,000 likes and being shared
more than nine thousand times. Buzzfeed ran the story of an
"adorable" breastfeeding mom. These two very different reactions by the public and the media to a black woman and a white
woman engaging in the exact same activity must be noted.
The media referred to the white woman's photo as "adorable" and held it up as proof that "women are the greatest." If,
indeed, all women's bodies have been sexualized, black

women's bodies have been hypersexualized. And many times white women are able to overcome the sexualization. Only one of the two women was called "adorable" by the media and portrayed with girlish innocence, and it wasn't the black one. These responses play into historical ideas of whose bodies need to be controlled and whose bodies are dangerous.

Socioeconomics plays a part. Many studies have identified a significant correlation between low maternal education and the hypersexualization of breasts as a key barrier to breastfeeding. A study in Quebec, published in the September 2013 issue of *Health & Place,* found that middle-class women were more able to overcome the hypersexualization of the breast. As the study explored, these women have various sources of cultural capital, including more education, and share the value of scientific knowledge as it relates to parental practices. But low-income women may have less access to education and scientific knowledge as sources of cultural capital and may rely more heavily on the power of being viewed as attractive. Poor mothers lacked access to the power required to negotiate these barriers in their social space. "Women living in poverty tend to have less power via their total capital to challenge and negotiate the gaze of others when they engage in field of power of different public spaces," the study authors wrote.

"On the other hand, one source of social power they did have was physical attractiveness. In this paradigm, the perceived loss of physical attractiveness some low-income women associated with increased breastfeeding—believing it would damage the shape and tone of the breasts—is a loss of social capital that they are not willing to risk. Our results suggest that poor mothers do not rely predominantly on scientific knowledge to guide their infant feeding decisions but tend to rely more on competing experiential knowledge of their family and peers, including the prototypical infant feeding experiences of their families," the report concluded.

This thinking is also seen on social media—a common go-to resource for breastfeeding support. For years, Facebook allowed videos of shootings and decapitations, but women were constantly being booted off Facebook when other users flagged their breastfeeding photos as indecent. By 2013, Facebook made an about-face, changing its community standards to say that it aspires "to respect people's right to share content of personal importance, whether are photos of a sculpture like Michelangelo's David or family photos of a child breastfeeding." However, the areola is the boundary for indecency. If it is visible, the image is verboten. The official announcement, posted under Facebook's Community Standards reads: "We restrict some images of female breasts if they include the nipple, but we always allow photos of women actively engaged in breastfeeding or showing breasts with post-mastectomy scarring."

The truth is the breast is not inherently sexual. "There is an assumption that breasts are sexy and that they are sexual signals. But that wasn't always the case," said Florence Williams in an interview. However, Williams also notes that there's no real historical evidence that breasts are universally considered sexy or that there is a particular size and shape that is universally desired. "In fact, there are many cultures and many times in our history where breasts just weren't that big of a deal. The strange preoccupation with breasts as sex objects in the West is very unique. This is not universal," she says. For much of human history, female and male breasts were treated the same. For centuries, women went topless in most parts of Africa, Asia, and the Americas. Stroll through Europe, and there are countless statues of women's bare breasts and women breastfeeding. They were the subject of many paintings and other beautiful artworks. As late as the fifteenth century, going topless wasn't viewed as inappropriate since breasts were more associated with children and motherhood—not sex. But it was the spread of Christianity and missionary work in developing countries that changed the cultural norms, equating toplessness with uncivilized and ungodly behavior.

So breasts went undercover. But the fact they were covered created more mystery, curiosity, and schoolboyish, Monty Python–like behavior. Keeping breasts in the dirty and taboo pool has its own set of consequences. It's ironic that covering breasts up has likely done more to sexualize them than when they were exposed. New cottage industries have been created and billions have been made and paid in the quest to see an uncovered female breast. Web sites feature popular and extensive photo galleries of celebrity boob shots, "nip slip" moments, side boobage, awkward moments getting out of cars, and other costume slippages. Some young actresses anxious to prolong their celebrity sometimes intentionally dress to qualify for these boob-obsessed and highly trafficked series. At the 85th annual Academy Awards in 2013, comedian and host Seth MacFarlane opened the show with the song, "We Saw Your Boobs," in which he rattled off famous actresses and the movies in which they disrobed. The Oscar host mentioned actresses like Charlize Theron, Kristen Stewart, Kate Winslet, and Jodie Foster. Some saw it as a classic satire of an industry obsessed with breasts; others took offense. Our breast obsession is beyond schoolboyish, it's downright embarrassing. And it allows viewers to happily forget the primary function of breasts and focus solely on the sexual one.

Interestingly, at one point, the male nipple was also sexualized and banned from public view. But men fought back, protesting and going topless until the culture changed. The revolution ignited in 1930 when four guys were arrested in Coney Island for going shirtless on a beach. Then Hollywood icon Clark Gable stripped off his shirt in *It Happened One Night,* marking the scandalous debut of a man's uncensored nipples in American cinema. In 1935 New Jersey hit back with a mass arrest of forty-two topless men in Atlantic City. After years of protest and outrage, New York lifted the male topless ban in 1936, and suddenly a man's nipples were no longer "obscene" in society but, rather, commonplace and natural.

What about women? In 2015 the *Free the Nipple* movie and social media campaign were launched all over the world. Women went topless in the streets to protest the hypocrisy of men's ability to bare their nipples when women were disallowed from doing so. On social media, the hashtag #FreeThe-Nipple trended for days as celebrities such as Miley Cyrus bared their breasts in Twitter pics in solidarity. Scout Willis, the daughter of Bruce Willis and Demi Moore, walked around New York City topless to highlight the inequality of women's bodies. Women recognized the captivity of the nipple as symptomatic of the continued objectification of women's bodies. Momentum is building, but the nipple is not yet free. Can the breast ever be moved out of the sexual category and therefore freed to feed babies? It's hard to see how.

Then there's the men—the partners or husbands who are clearly inextricably involved in the breastfeeding equation. Any analysis of the forces influencing breastfeeding must include the men, who historically have owned women and their bodies. They have contributed to the problem but also may be part of the solution. In the old days, the marriage contract was used to grant men the right of sexual access and ownership. Expressions like, "Why buy the cow if you can get the milk for free?" still show that sexual access should be limited and withheld until "ownership"—that is, marriage. When women's bodies belong to men, that includes the breast. A man's claims to the breast come in direct conflict with a child's needs, and women are stuck in the middle. Women are often uncomfortable nursing in public because of the anticipation of a male gaze. In some neighborhoods, the idea of nursing in public and bringing unwanted male attention to your breasts is a safety issue. In other cultures, men oppose breastfeeding because of their fears of other men looking at their wife in a sexual way. Some breastfeeding or infant formula ads support the male-gaze viewpoint, showing a man watching his wife breastfeed. Your assumption is that his focus is on the child. But he may be thinking, "Hey kid, when am I going to get that back?"

Perhaps the greatest consequence of the breast as a sex object is that it prevents us from talking about the many ways breastfeeding feels good. Yes, breastfeeding is pleasurable. That is not conjecture; that is biology. The suckling of an infant

produces the release of the pleasure-inducing hormones prolactin and oxytocin—the same ones released during orgasm.
It is also released in large amounts during labor. During breastfeeding, the oxytocin is responsible for the milk-ejection reflex, known as the "letdown." Oxytocin's documented effect
on calmness and well-being have earned it the nicknames the
"cuddle chemical," the "bonding hormone," and the "love
hormone." But conflating breasts with sexuality and sensuality
and the idea that an infant can produce the same biological
response as a man is too much for the male psyche and patriarchal structures to handle. Perhaps this is one area where the
La Leche League had it right. A 1992 member magazine nailed
it when it said, "the human race would not have survived if
breastfeeding was not enjoyable for mothers."

Mothers daring to speak of the pleasure of breastfeeding
have faced serious repercussions. Take the example of Denise
Perrigo, a white single mother of one, who in January 1991
was arrested on charges of sexually abusing her child and had
her two-year-old taken away from her and put into foster care
for a year. The charge was "mouth to breast contact." Perrigo
practiced extended breastfeeding. One day while nursing her
daughter, Perrigo experienced a "sexual kind of feeling," she
said. Alarmed by this, she called a local community volunteer
center and asked to be put in touch with the local La Leche
League office. But when the volunteers heard "sexual arousal,"
they directed Perrigo to the rape counsel center instead of
La Leche League. The counselor at the center heard Perrigo's story and deemed it "child sexual abuse." She said
that, because a child was involved, she needed to get her
supervisor on the phone, but had already told the supervisor

that it was a case of child abuse. While on the phone, the supervisor asked questions that fit her preconceived ideas. For example, she asked Perrigo where her daughter was right then. Perrigo responded that she was in her bed. Although Perrigo was in another room on the phone to the supervisor while her daughter was in her bed, the supervisor wrote down that Perrigo was in bed with her daughter.

While she was on the phone arguing with the supervisor, the supervisor contacted the rape crisis "hotline," which sent the local police to arrest Perrigo. Press coverage cast Perrigo as a victim of the "national hysteria" over incest. La Leche League assisted Perrigo by providing expert testimony and lawyer referrals, as well as local leaders' emotional support. The criminal charges were eventually dropped, but social services filed charges of sexual abuse and neglect, and Perrigo was allowed only biweekly supervised visits with her daughter during an almost one-year separation.

The message was clear: breastfeeding is not meant to be a pleasurable experience. And if you experience pleasure, you dare not speak of it. In fact, some La Leche League materials advised never confiding in unfamiliar professionals, especially when extended breastfeeding, who may interpret it as "pathological." To make sure women were not demonized for the actual biology of their bodies, breastfeeding became hypersterilized over the years and idealized in order to separate it from the sexual breast.

There is no doubt in my mind that breastfeeding is pleasurable. Yes, the early days can be awkward and uncomfortable, but after you get the rhythm, something else happens. I remember how, after a long day at work, there was nothing more relaxing and comforting than to lie down and enjoy a slow nursing session with my son. The tingling sensation of the letdown was followed by a very calming feeling. That sensation feels good. I'm not sure if it ever felt sexual for me, but it was certainly sensual, in some way. But we don't talk about that because breastfeeding has been culturally redefined as an asexual experience. That redefinition was related to women's oppression and our desexualization as maternal beings—our inability to be fully expressed as both sexual beings and maternal beings. So we focus on the medical benefits and not the pleasurable feelings of breastfeeding because we are afraid of societal taboos of an already hypersexualized breast. If only Perrigo had known that her feelings were normal, not deviant, perhaps she would not have made that fateful call. Instead of the pleasure of breastfeeding, pain is assigned to the experience with an infant, saving pleasure for the male or sexual role. We have been told that any sensual feelings must come from a man or lover and that anything else is wrong. That turns any pleasurable feelings while breastfeeding into pathology or a source of shame for women. There is no safe place for a mother to enjoy breastfeeding and experience it in a way that counters the dominant narrative.

This is extremely dangerous to the advancement of women and the promotion of breastfeeding. Limiting the maternal benefits of breastfeeding to only the medical advantages contributes to the dangerous "mother as martyr" and "sacrificial lamb" ideology that is attacked by modern-day feminists like Badinter. Instead, what if breastfeeding was touted for the pleasurable feelings it creates for mothers and the benefits of releasing the "love hormone" multiple times a day? Oxytocin is a multifunctional hormone. It regulates appetite through receptors in the brain. Oxytocin is a natural antibiotic, attacking hostile bacteria and decreasing susceptibility to uterine infection. Stress increases prolactin secretion, and excessive prolactin can enhance the risk of breast cancer, brain tumors, and leukemia. But oxytocin regulates the secretion of prolactin, so it has many health benefits.

From a promotional perspective, every marketing expert will tell you that focusing on the feeling of the product or the experience of using it is how you engage audiences and create affinity. Instead of touting their own platitudes on the superiority of their product, even brand titans like Coke and Pepsi have shifted to focusing on the feelings users get from their beverages. "Coke is it!" changed into "open happiness." What could it mean for the promotion of breastfeeding to talk more about the happiness and pleasure women experience while breastfeeding?

Hollywood and the Breast

A lot of this tunnel-vision view of breasts is perpetuated in advertising, on television, and in the media. The Hollywood entertainment industry, to be exact, has been very influential in shaping our ideas of beauty, sexuality, and most notably, our breasts, for years. Believe it or not, there was a time when Hollywood was concerned with "showing too much," and breasts were just a tease. They were shimmying under sheer silk chemises. They were covered with the appropriately placed sequins. But by the 1960s, that all changed. Not to mention the growth of pornography. Then came *Baywatch* and the superstardom of Pamela Anderson, who built her Hollywood fame squarely on top of her DD breast implants.

Television shows influence what people see as normal behavior; this we know. When people are exposed to a consistent set of messages on the television, they incorporate those messages into their understanding of the world around them. For example, one study showed that television portrayals tend to underrepresent older persons, which has led to people underestimating the size of the elderly population. On the other hand, I think we all can agree that television shows like *Will & Grace* and *Modern Family* have played a huge role in broadening acceptance of gay and lesbian lifestyles and normalizing same-sex marriage. Knowing its power to shape cultural norms, television has been strategically used to foster messages about smoking and wearing seat belts, helping to normalize these behaviors in subtle ways. The potential impact of television on public health goals is so significant that the Centers for Disease Control and Prevention helps fund the University of Southern California's Hollywood, Health & Society program, which connects medical experts with screenwriters in an effort to minimize misinformation on screen. HHS has worked on various issues from promoting condom use to normalizing the disabled.

What of breastfeeding? A study published in the journal *Health Communication* found many television characters are still often portrayed as uncomfortable in the presence of a breastfeeding mother. For example, there's a scene in the sitcom *Two and a Half Men* in which one of the lead characters, Alan (played by Jon Cryer), dates a single mom who breastfeeds in the restaurant, causing Alan to have trouble eating. On a *Sex and the City* episode, Miranda breastfeeds her son, Brady, and Carrie can't help shockingly exclaiming, "Your breasts are huge!" The study found fifty-three representations of breastfeeding, spanning from 1974 to 2012, with portrayals of breastfeeding clearly becoming more acceptable after 1998. (Forty-eight of the fifty-three examples were found since then.) The shows ran the gamut from dramas such as *ER* to sitcoms like *Friends, The Big Bang Theory,* and *The Office.* Most of the time, writers folded a "learning to breast-feed" plotline into stories about characters having babies. In *The Office,* for example, the characters Jim and Pam had their first child and had difficulty with nursing. This was played for laughs when their hospital's lactation consultant was revealed to be male, making Jim uncomfortable. Characters almost never breastfeed in public, and, when they do, other characters comment on it with discomfort. For example, the study noted one episode of *Friends* where characters Joey and Chandler become uncomfortable when Ross's ex-wife, Carol, breastfed her son. Ross berated Joey and Chandler for their insensitivity, but wouldn't it be better to let public breastfeeding pass without comment? In most instances, breastfeeding is used as comic fodder—someone is squeamish or someone gets squirted with breast milk. The portrayal perpetuates the idea that women using their breasts for anything other than men's pleasure is somehow wrong, uncomfortable, or worthy of note. Instead of the highly trumpeted "Breast Is Best" message, the more pervasive message emanating from big- and small-screen portrayals is more like "Breast Is Awkward." The study also called out the cable network TLC, which has an array of baby-related programming, as "horrible" at conveying good breastfeeding information, citing large advertising dollars from formula companies.

In the movie *The Hangover* there's a scene when a stripper played by Heather Graham is nursing her baby while talking to the three leading men—all of whom appear visibly uncomfortable yet at the same time unable to look away from her exposed breasts. Mostly, it's the extended breastfeeding that takes the brunt of the joking. On an episode of *Two Broke Girls,* the staff at the diner are disgusted by the fact that a customer is breastfeeding her son, who is certainly older than the age when American moms typically stop nursing. "Some mothers tend to breastfeed for a lot longer these days. It's called attachment parenting," waitress Caroline explains to Max, Han, and Earl, who were watching the mom and child. Max then says, "When the kid's that big, it's called dating." This trend of public shaming parental decisions about breastfeeding, as depicted in this scene, only adds to the stigma. In the movie *Grown Ups,* Maria Bello's character breastfeeds her four-year-old son, inciting judgmental looks, jokes, and comments from the other parents. Her nursing is a source of tension between the mom and her husband, who later hands his son a carton of milk to make him "wean."

More recently, a spate of "housewife" and other reality shows that feature younger mothers and a new sitcom preoccupation with family has created new avenues for talking and laughing about breastfeeding. Snooki talked about breastfeeding. Kim Kardashian is seen on reality television breastfeeding. Before her, her sister, Kourtney, was also frequently seen breastfeeding. There were episodes where breast milk was tasted and the infamous "pump and dump" episode after Kourtney had a few drinks. And I'll never forget Kim Zolciak-Biermann on the *Real Housewives of Atlanta*, who was filmed pumping while driving. A later *RHOA* cast member, Phaedra Parks, famously carried her breast-pump bag to all the "girls" outings, bragging about her "liquid gold."

While breastfeeding is getting more reality airtime, the bigger-is-better idea about breasts still prevails. Breast augmentation still ranks as the number one surgical procedure among women, according to the American Society of Plastic Surgeons—a position it's held since the FDA ended the silicone-gel implant moratorium in 2006. However, in 2012, the number of women undergoing this procedure declined 7 percent from the year before, with just over 286,000 breast enhancements performed compared to 307,180 in 2011. Women deserve to have their bodies accepted as they are and to not feel compelled to go under a surgical knife to reach some ideal body.

For most of these women, how the quest for big breasts affects breastfeeding is not even a thought—until years later when they become mothers. Some women can breastfeed after augmentation surgery, while others cannot. Plastic surgeons are quick to tell women that they can still breastfeed with implants, depending on where the implant is placed. As one board-certified plastic surgeon explained, the key is to avoid a nipple incision and instead put the implants under the breast crease or under the muscle of the chest wall. Nipple incisions are usually preferred by surgeons because it's very cosmetic and because it's right where the pigment of the skin changes so the scar is not as noticeable. But that is also where all the milk ducts that drain the different lobes or sections of the breast convene. And there's a risk of accidentally cutting milk ducts or the nerve that sends the signal to your brain to release more hormones that then helps you produce more milk. Cutting a nerve accidentally during a breast augmentation surgery could also result in the nipple's becoming oversensitive, which would also make breastfeeding difficult no matter how much milk a woman is able to produce.

According to Dr. Miriam Labbok, breastfeeding after breast implants is not always easy. The less pressure that is put on a woman's mammary glands by an implant, the better the chances to produce milk later. "The mammary gland, like any other gland, performs normally when it has blood supply and space to grow," Labbok said in an interview. "But when you put continued pressure on any gland in the body you risk it malfunctioning and compromising lactation."

Once again, lactation is compromised by cultural notions about breasts. Women are taking the risk of surgical augmentation out of dissatisfaction with how their breasts look because we have a culture where men judge a woman's value based on the size of her breast. Add to that a widespread misunderstanding of the primary function of the breast, and breastfeeding ends up being viewed in a sexual context. Women are told they must choose their sexual body or their maternal one. Can't we have our cake and eat it too? The costs of these cultural beliefs, in terms of maternal health and self-esteem and infant health, are too high to pay.

9

Ending the Letdown:
The Way Forward

In the end, we are all looking for solutions. But what if the solution is actually the problem? In fact, what exactly is the bigger issue here: the problem itself or the solution it requires? This is not my attempt at some Yogi Berra approach to fixing the broken breastfeeding landscape but, rather, at offering what is perhaps a critical insight into understanding the way forward, courtesy of some recent research. In November 2014 a study in the *Journal of Personality and Social Psychology* delved into why people can often be so divided over a particular issue, especially in the face of a solid body of scientific proof. Scientists have long suggested that psychological motivations often direct reasoning. But in this study, researchers Troy Campbell and Aaron Kay, of the Duke University Fuqua School of Business, explore a new dimension of this "motivated skepticism," showing the source of the motivation is not necessarily an aversion to the problem, per se, but an aversion to the solutions with the problem. This "solutions aversion" model says that people will be skeptical of the evidence supporting the existence of a problem, if it "directly implies solutions that threaten a person's

cherished beliefs and ideological motives." The model suggests that certain solutions associated with the problem are
more aversive and threatening to individuals who hold an
ideology that is incompatible with the solution. News of the
study went viral. National media and social media went wild
covering this latest development. The study directly applied
the theory to the issue of climate change, and the extreme
polarization across Republican/conservative and Democratic
lines. Yet immediately the study's findings were applied to
technology, education, social movements, and everyday life.
"Have you ever thought about going on a run but then
thought, 'Cardio isn't that important'? This may be Solution
Aversion," one blog post said.

What does this have to do with breastfeeding? Well, imagine for a moment that all of the players in the infant feeding
theater are suffering from solution aversion. Medical doctors
don't want to accept that they are not above the influence of
infant formula education and sponsorship and that they are
indeed woefully ignorant about an important biological
process. The feminist movement doesn't want to acknowledge forty years of misdirecting women and undermining
motherhood to the detriment of infant health. Pharmaceutical companies and other profit makers certainly don't want
to let go of their fat bottom lines. Scientists don't want to admit that funding has corrupted their objectivity and that they
have put out bad science at the expense of vulnerable women.

And what of women? Are women battling, belittling, and
denying the scientific evidence of breastfeeding because fighting on the Internet is easier than doing the important work of

dismantling the many structural barriers that seem insurmountable? We continue fighting over our choices instead of fighting for better options from which to choose. Fighting over choice is easy. We can do that online from the comfort of our home computers—posting comments on blogs, signing petitions, retweeting catchy maxims, or clicking the LIKE button on social media pages that empower us. The alternative is much messier. That's because choice occurs in relation to other people—your mother, your spouse, sisters, friends, colleagues. We don't have to be at odds with our mother who didn't breastfeed, our sister who only breastfed one week, or our friend who breastfed for three years. We are freed from potentially damaging relationships with people we love and care about. By not articulating our opinions, judgments, observations, and conclusions, we avoid conflict.

Not only does hiding behind choice offer us an easy way out of conflict with others, we are also offered an easy out from the conflict we experience within ourselves. We are relieved of the burden of being consistently feminist or "empowered" ourselves: We do not have to struggle to bring our own lives into line with a demanding set of principles. We do not have to deal with the inner conflict we may feel around choosing motherhood versus a career or the guilt of having to leave our babies six to eight weeks after birthing them. We don't have to articulate the frustrations of modern motherhood and modern partnership when we simply and dangerously convince ourselves that what we have done is just a matter of free choice. Is "choice" our solution-aversion mechanism? Fighting for better options would require the hard work of changing the fundamental structure of our society and, quite frankly, women are overburdened with responsibilities and expectations as it is.

Given that backdrop, perhaps the problem of breastfeeding is not the problem at all. The true problem is the sheer monstrous nature of the multilevel solutions needed to effectively shift the landscape. I admit, the "fix" is daunting. Therefore, it is critical that any blueprint that has any real potential at finally righting the course and discourse of breastfeeding must include strategies that abate resistance or skepticism about the solutions.

To do that, solution-aversion theorists agree, requires the strategic messaging and communication to accomplish three things: reducing ambiguity, reducing threat, and offering people a reason to want to believe. Solution aversion runs high when ambiguity is high. There needs to be irrefutable facts to help reduce any wiggle room for debate. That means leveling the playing field of scientific research to make sure breastfeeding is used as the normative behavior.

Reducing threat means helping people be less averse to the solution by making the problem appear more solvable in a nonaversive way. That means simplifying the solution and removing the individualistic nature of breastfeeding that leaves women burdened with both the problem of and the solution for breastfeeding. Instead, we need a framework for collective action. The truth is, there is little evidence that isolated initiatives are the best way to solve the many social problems in today's complex and interdependent world. No single individual or organization has ever been responsible for solving any major social problem. However, women collectively, as a social organization of sorts, can build relationships in a systemic approach based on a shared objective—a truly level playing field for all infant feeding decisions. Breast. Bottle. Or whatever lies in between. In this scenario, collective responsibility is also joint responsibility, meaning that each member of the group is individually and morally responsible for the outcome of the joint action and that responsibility is shared with others. In effect, I am my sister's keeper. With this mind-set, women could actually harness their collective will to solve today's most serious public health problem with the resources we already have at our disposal. Instead of creating more options that are not really options, we can work collectively to transform the experience of all mothers.

• • •

To start, we should take a lesson from spaghetti sauce. Or, more specifically, what Howard Moskowitz learned about spaghetti sauce. Moskowitz, a Harvard-educated psychophysicist who had a penchant for measuring things, made his mark in market research. One of his first client assignments came from the beverage giant Pepsi. As the legend goes, most famously told by Malcolm Gladwell, author of *Blink* and *The Tipping Point,* around the time that aspartame was becoming popular, Pepsi was looking for the perfect formula for Diet Pepsi. How much aspartame should be in each can of Diet Pepsi in order to create the perfect diet soda? Pepsi thought it was somewhere between 8 and 12 percent and wanted Moskowitz to figure it out exactly by creating an experimental batch of Pepsi at every degree of sweetness, taste testing it among thousands of people, and taking the most popular

concentration. It sounded simple, until Moskowitz's expecta-
tion of a bell curve of results showing the most popular concentration never materialized. In fact, the data was all over
the place. Moskowitz wasn't satisfied with merely making an
educated guess somewhere right in the middle, and the question lingered with him for years. As Gladwell relates the story
(as he does frequently in speaking engagements), one day the
answer hit Moskowitz like a lightning bolt. The Pepsi folks
were asking the wrong question in their experiment, he concluded. They were looking for the perfect Pepsi, when they
should have been looking for the perfect Pepsis, he declared.
At the time, everyone thought this was sheer lunacy, but his
thinking turned out to be one of the most brilliant breakthroughs in food science. Moskowitz traveled the country
telling his story, and nobody would listen to him or hire
him. Until he got a big break with Campbell's Soup, makers
of Prego spaghetti sauce, which at the time was struggling
next to Ragú—the dominant sauce of the industry for much
of the '70s and '80s. They asked Moskowitz to fix the Prego
problem. And he did, by first creating some forty-five varieties of spaghetti sauce and varying them in every conceiv-
able way—by sweetness, by garlic flavor, by sourness, and by
tomatoey-ness, and so on and so on. Several months and
tons of data later, Moskowitz had his "Aha!" moment, which is
especially relevant to the topic of breastfeeding. He realized
that most Americans fall into one of three groups—you
either like your spaghetti sauce plain, spicy, or extra chunky.
The chunky discovery was particularly significant because
at the time you could not find extra chunky on the shelves of
the supermarket. Prego went back and reformulated their

sauces and came out with a line of extra chunky sauces that immediately and completely took over the spaghetti-sauce business, earning over $600 million over the next ten years. This was revolutionary because it showed the food industry that they didn't really understand their consumers and had been approaching them all wrong. In his quest to transform spaghetti sauce, Moskowitz knew that companies worked off the flawed premise that you need to ask a consumer what she or he wants. But he realized that consumers didn't actually know what they wanted. They didn't know that chunky spaghetti sauce was their preference until someone gave it to them. Their choices were based on what they knew, what they had in front of them. And I'm convinced that our approach to motherhood has been equally flawed strategically. Women only see the options in front of them and society has yet to show us the chunky. Nor have we fully imagined the "chunky" for ourselves. This is our work—to reimagine the world and then go make it happen. We did it before and we can do it again.

Moskowitz shattered a system that was based on searching for universals and showed us that the secret sauce is in the variability. Other fields have already embraced this concept. For example, now the great revolution in medical science is not just to understand how cancer works but to understand how cancer works specifically in my body, with my genetic code and my physiology. If we can understand the importance of variability in our sauces, what of motherhood? How do we actually create a society that embraces all the variabilities of motherhood and in turn, breastfeeding? Here are seven super important starting points:

1. **Policy is paramount.** We can't continue to call ourselves a world leader when we are the biggest laggard when it comes to meaningful paid family leave and other supportive policies as a government-mandated right.

2. **Science needs to step up.** Scientists must level the playing field for breastfeeding research using breast milk as the normative behavior and setting funding limits on the infant formula industry. As a group, the scientific community has to be held to higher standards to effectively deal with conflicts of interest, opportunities for bias, and to be responsible for reporting openly and honestly to the public to make their work understood. This is the very least we should expect, particularly from research that impacts our youngest and most fragile citizens. Those scientists who dilute the body of scientific evidence with flimsy research, knowing that the research may be used to shape critical public policy that affects millions of Americans, must be held accountable.

3. **Medicine must be separate from industry.** The medical field needs to end their historic financial entanglement with the pharmaceutical industry, and work to rectify the damage this relationship has caused. That means holding our pediatricians accountable for being proficient in lactation management, and knowing how breastfeeding works. Medical schools must teach lactation as a basic biological function.

4. **Policy is important but so are people.** Ultimately policy change must lead to and be accompanied by cultural change—and that shift needs to be woman-powered, from the ground up. For the movement to be truly successful on a wide scale, we have to give women something to believe in and ensure that they feel seen, heard, and understood. Instead of focusing on building a case of scientific facts, build emotional affinity and a connection to the right to a better food system for infants. Yes, breastfeeding is already an emotional issue, but much of the emotional messaging we receive is the anger of so-called lactivists or the pain of shamed mothers. The positive messages we do see are connected to the act of breastfeeding (blissfully in a meadow) but not about the lived experience of breastfeeding in the context of modern-day America. Breastfeeding needs an empowerment message more akin to how Nike makes us feel we can do the impossible. Do not deny that breastfeeding is difficult and try to sell "easy." Embrace the difficult—show women the personal pride and sense of accomplishment that comes from breastfeeding, just like running a marathon or scaling a mountain. I have never run a marathon in my life, and probably never will, but those Nike commercials make me believe that I can because I'm connected to their message of overcoming obstacles, defying stereotypes and naysayers, and female empowerment. We've done facts. Let's get women connected to empowering feelings.

5. **Disrupt the "choice" narrative and add context.** The concept of choice is critical to our American and feminist ideals, but context is everything. The choices we actually have are framed by the context in which we live. For example, the so-called choice for women to quit their jobs and become stay-at-home mothers is shaped by the current U.S. tax code, which penalizes two-career married couples, and the high costs of child care, which for some families means that monthly day care costs are nearly equal to one month's salary; when you factor in commuting, food, and work-clothing expenses, one parent might as well stay home. The "choice" to become a supermom is framed by a historically contingent cult of motherhood with roots in child psychology, an inner conflict between education and career and motherhood, and a conservative backlash against feminism. The "choice" to have cosmetic surgery to meet a porn-star ideal of beauty and to learn to striptease are produced by the commodification of a narrow range of sexual behaviors that are sold to women as sexual liberation. This is the fundamental problem with our infant feeding choice: it occurs within a context that appears fair and untainted but most definitely is not. Dismantling the language of choice by exposing all the ways it does not truly exist is the next step in the process.

6. **Lactating may be biological, but breastfeeding is behavioral.** Studying behaviors is different from studying breasts. Does the movement need a better

understanding of lactation or a better understanding of women and how they truly live and experience breastfeeding? I'd argue for the latter. Understanding behaviors deepens our knowledge of decision making. For example, we tend to believe that these decisions are exhaustively researched. We view decision making as a scale, with evidence and reasons weighed equally on each side. The side with the weightier proof wins. This feels more normal for us. But, increasingly, the research about how our brains work indicates that because of this process we're likely to miss the connection between cause and effect when there is a mismatch in size—when the less heavy side of the scale actually wins. A better understanding of behaviors can help the movement improve its messaging. Which leads me to . . .

7. **Sweat the small stuff.** While the big ideas about breastfeeding are important, we can't forget some of the smaller areas of life that ultimately impact the social acceptance of breastfeeding. Our ideas about breastfeeding aren't shaped solely by our knowledge of the medical benefits or scientific findings. Sometimes they are shaped by our sense of self, body ideals, sexual history, and cultural influences. Increasingly behavioral scientists, mathematicians, and other researchers are opening up our understanding of how we make decisions, and what they are finding supports the idea that the small things—whether they are body-image issues or school curriculums that don't teach how human mammals feed their young—may be

just as important as the next blockbuster study in regards to how women view breastfeeding. And so the following things that may seem small really aren't: an entire market of baby dolls that only come with bottles; the formula-maker-provided growth chart at pediatricians' offices; swag bags from the maternity ward with free infant formula inside and coupons for more; the coffee mug or pen with the infant formula company logo at your ob-gyn's office that we begin seeing at age fifteen. Are these truly small? Our attitudes about mothering and breastfeeding do not occur in a vacuum or in the space of forty weeks of pregnancy; they are part of a continuum of life that is influenced by our family structure, community, and societal norms. We need a long-term approach to changing cultural norms about breastfeeding, not just to target women during the nine months of pregnancy and expect change. As we learned in this book, the formula companies are also targeting them during pregnancy so we need to start sooner. This includes rethinking what children are taught in biology and nutrition classes and teaching the next generation how human mammals feed their young.

. . .

These are important starting points. Ambitious, yes, but not unattainable. Moskowitz's work democratized the concept of taste—proving that there is no one way to be. Perhaps this could happen for breastfeeding. It, too, could be democratized to include the full spectrum of each woman's varying breastfeeding experience with varying layers of support. Everyone will find their chunky! Such that, whether your motherhood experience is a metaphorical garden chunky or three cheese, there is easily accessible education and multi-layered support on the policy, hospital, medical, and community levels, just waiting on the shelf for you. When society embraces the broad diversity of our mothering experiences and our breastfeeding experiences, then we will win. Our children will win with healthier lives. Society wins with reduced rates of diet-related disease and chronic illnesses. Ultimately, every woman wins the freedom to actually, truly choose her mothering experience. Then and only then will we be able to finally end the big letdown.

Acknowledgments

Books, like breastfeeding, require a lot of support. Thankfully, I received so much in so many ways. First, I'd like to thank the tireless breastfeeding advocates who, armed solely with their passion, skills, and love for mothers and babies, have achieved amazing success against remarkable odds. I applaud you and thank everyone who shared their thoughts, ideas, time, sources, and research with me. This work is yours as much as it is mine. I want to thank my children, Kayla and Michael-Jaden, my two greatest cheerleaders and my two favorite teachers, who continue to support my work—even when it takes me away from them—and continue to motivate me to be my best self. For the moments I was not fully present, dinner was not fully cooked, or you were not exactly on time for a practice or lesson and you did not complain, thank you. Mothering you two is my greatest joy. I hope you see the beautiful struggle of chasing a dream as you embark on your own one day with everything you've got.

I'm very grateful to my wonderful parents, Alma and James Seals, who have come to my rescue over and over again to give me writing time, mental breaks, child care on work trips, and everything in between. Thank you for always supporting my interests, even as a kid who was into bird-watching, taping my own radio show where I played the host and guest, writing poems, and playing violin—you never let me think I was weird. (I'm not exactly sure how you pulled that off, but thank you.) My brother, Jeffrey Seals, and my sister, Katrina Seals Ruiz, thank you both for always having my back. My uncle James Billy and my cousins Schmoll Reaves-Bey and Khalebo Harris, thank you for believing in me and for the unconditional support. I want to thank my secret brain trust for generously sharing your genius with me when needed: Shadan Deleveaux, Dionne Grayman, Julian Curry, Simran Noor, and Marion Rice. My fellow Food & Community Fellows—an incomparable group of food advocates who welcomed and embraced me and my work and gave me a most incredible two-year lesson about friends, food, and food systems. Our time together inspired the seeds of the book, and I want to give a special thanks to Raj Patel, for early feedback that helped set me on the right course, and to Nina Ichikawa, who was never too busy to send me a link to an article she thought was relevant. Thank you, Tonya Lewis Lee for the check-ins and empathy. Ken, Keiva, Asim, Owen—the laughs and encouragement was always right on time. And to Matthew, who reminded my heart how to skip a beat.

Of course, none of this would have been possible without the ongoing support of my agent, Stacey Glick from Dystel & Goderich, who responds to all of my high-energy calls and e-mails with coolness and steadiness and is a great strategic partner. To my editor, Nichole Argyres—this has been a true journey and I thank you for pushing me to be a better writer and helping me get to where I needed to be. You believed in this project from the beginning and I deeply appreciate your vision and stewardship.

Lastly, I want to thank "the process." The process of writing a book often seems sexy to outsiders, but it is a decidedly un-sexy marathon—a don't-stop, long-haul, sweaty, want-to-give-up, do-it-over-and-over-again marathon. Even on your fifth book. And just as a marathon refines you, clears your mind, takes your mental acumen to another level, I am aware of and grateful for how the process of writing this book has helped me grow as a writer, mother, human, and a voice for women. Like a marathon, the process can be painful and overwhelming—there are sores, scars, and stretched muscles—but when I reflect on my personal growth and character refinement, I will be forever grateful to the journey. And everyone I met along the way.

Notes

Introduction

5 *data available from the Centers for Disease Control* Center for Disease Control, "Progress in Increasing Breastfeeding and Reducing Racial/Ethnic Differences: United States, 2000–2008 births," *Morbidity and Mortality Weekly Report* 62, no. 5 (2013): 77–80; Center for Disease Control, "Breastfeeding Report Card: United States/2014," National Center for Chronic Disease Prevention and Health Promotion, 2014.

6 *Compare that to Sweden, where the exclusive breastfeeding rate* K. M. Michaelsen, L. Weaver, F. Branca, and A. Robertson, "Feeding and Nutrition of Infants and Young Children: Guidelines for the WHO European Region with Emphasis on the Former Soviet Countries," *WHO Regional Publications, European Series* 87 (World Health Organization, 2000).

10 *treating water as a universal human right* http://action .storyofstuff.org/sign/nestle_water_privatization_push/.

1. Doctor Who? The Medical Field's Influence on Mothers

17 *Then researchers set to find out if this should be classified as some* K. G. Dewey, M. J. Heinig, L. A. Nommsen, J. M. Peerson, and B. Lönnerdal, "Growth of Breast-Fed and Formula-Fed Infants from 0 to 18 Months: The DARLING Study," *Pediatrics* 89, no. 6 (1992): 1035–41.

17 *One key study by DARLING* K. G. Dewey, M. J. Heinig, L. A. Nommsen, and B. Lönnerdal, "Adequacy of Energy Intake among Breast-Fed Infants in the DARLING Study Relation-

ships to Growth Velocity, Morbidity, and Activity Levels," *Journal of Pediatrics* 119, no. 4 (1991): 538–47.

17 *"Arguably, the current obesity epidemic in many developed countries*   "Child Growth Standards: How Different are the New Standards from the Old Growth Charts?" WHO.int, last modified 2016; see also http://www.who.int/childgrowth/faqs/how_different/en/.

19 *Every year Perrigo Nutritionals*   "Survey Finds Infant Feeding Tops List of Questions New Parents Ask Pediatricians," PerrigoNutritionals.com, last modified August 13, 2014; see also http://www.perrigonutritionals.com/press.aspx?ID=418.

19 *despite the fact that the American Academy*   "Divesting from formula marketing in pediatric care," Resolution 67SC (2012).

20 *A 2000 study published in* Obstetrics and Gynecology   C. Howard, F. Howard, R. Lawrence, E. Andresen, E. DeBlieck, and M. Weitzman, "Office Prenatal Formula Advertising and Its Effect on Breast-Feeding Patterns," *Obstetrics and Gynecology* 95, no. 2 (2000): 296–303.

20 *In a study of obstetricians and patients at a multispecialty*   A. Stuebe, "The Risks of Not Breastfeeding for Mothers and Infants," *Reviews in Obstetrics and Gynecology* 2, no. 4 (2009): 222–31.

22 *Most medical schools don't have*   L. S. Davis, "Is the Medical Community Failing Breastfeeding Moms?" healthland.time.com, last modified January 2, 2013.

23 *Every year, the Abbott Nutrition Institute*   "Conference Summaries," ani.org, last modified 2016.

23 *Researchers at the Robert Wood Johnson*   L. Feldman-Winter, L. Barone, B. Milcarek, K. Hunter, J. Meek, J. Morton, T. Williams, A. Naylor, and R. A. Lawrence, "Residency Curriculum Improves Breastfeeding Care," *Pediatrics* 126 (2010): 289–97.

25 *"Treating only children*   Jacqueline H. Wolf, "Pediatrics, Obstetrics, and Shrinking Maternal Authority," in *Beyond Health, Beyond Choice: Breastfeeding Constraints and Realities*, ed. P. H. Smith, B. Hausman, and M. Labbok, 87–97 (New Jersey: Rutgers University Press, 2012).

28 *In 1893, Dr. Rotch wrote*   T. M. Rotch, "The General Principles

Underlying All Good Methods of Infant-Feeding," *Medical News: A Weekly Medical Journal* 63 (1893): 600–02.

29 *In 1923 Mead Johnson, maker of Enfamil* S. Johnson, "A Glimpse of Mead Johnson," in *Mothers and Medicine: A Social History of Infant Feeding, 1890–1950*, ed. R. D. Apple (Wisconsin: University of Wisconsin, 1987).

30 *The authors of a 1991 Scandinavian study* G. Nylander, R. Lindemann, E. Helsing, and E. Bendvold, "Unsupplemented Breastfeeding in the Maternity Ward Positive Long-Term Effects," *Acta obstetricia et gynecologica Scandinavica* 70, no. 3 (1991): 205–09.

33 *The 1914 article sparked a call* M. Tracy and C. Leupp, "Painless Childbirth," *McClure's Magazine*, vol. xlii, no. 2 (June 1914): 37–52. Accessed on https://books.google.com.

35 *The 1914* New York Medical Journal C. E. Sajous and C. L. Wheeler, "New York Medical Journal: A Weekly Review of Medicine," 100(C) (1914).

37 *In 1971, the year I* G. E. Hendershot, "Trends in Breastfeeding," *Vital and Health Statistics of the National Center for Health Statistics* 59, 1–7 (1980).

37 *in 2015 it was 32.7 percent* A. Almendrala, "U.S. C-section Rate Is Double What WHO Recommends," *Huffpost Parents*, last modified April 16, 2015; see also J. A. Martin, B. E. Hamilton, and M. J. K. Osterman, "Births in the United States (2013)," NCHS Data Brief, 175, 2014, 1–8.

2. Milk Money: The Big Business of Bodies, Breasts, and Babies

38 *"If the [cow's] milk cannot be obtained,"* J. B. Lyman and L. E. Lyman, *How to Live, or, the Philosophy of Housekeeping: A Scientific and Practical Manual* (Philadelphia: W. H. Thompson, 1869).

41 *Researchers believe that the taste preferences* G. K. Beauchamp and Julie A. Mennella, "Early Flavor Learning and Its Impact on Later Feeding Behavior," *Journal of Pediatric Gastroenterology and Nutrition* 48 (2009): S25–S30; L. L. Birch, and Jennifer O. Fisher, "Development of Eating Behaviors among Children and Adolescents," *Pediatrics* 101 (supp. 2) (1998): 539–49.

43 *a 1995 study*   J. W. White and M. Wolraich, "Effect of Sugar on Behavior and Mental Performance," *American Journal of Clinical Nutrition* 62, no. 1 (1995): 242S–247S.

44 *An infant diet that is high in sugar*   C. Sheikh and P. R. Erickson, "Evaluation of Plaque pH Changes Following Oral Rinse with Eight Infant Formulas," *Pediatric Dentistry* 18 (1996): 200–204.

44 *The American Academy of Pediatrics*   R. Murray and J. J. S. Bhatia, "Snacks, Sweetened Beverages, Added Sugars, and Schools," *Pediatrics* 135, no. 3 (2015).

44 *According to a 2000 report by the American Diabetes Association*   American Diabetes Association, "Type 2 Diabetes in Children and Adolescents," *Diabetes Care* 23, no. 3 (2000): 381–89.

45 *Dr. Francine Ratner Kaufman*   F. R. Kaufman, "Type 2 Diabetes in Children and Young Adults: A 'New Epidemic,'" *Clinical Diabetes* 20, no. 4 (2002): 217–18.

51 *earning $19.4 million in total compensation*   http://www.equilar .com/reports/37-2-associated-press-pay-study-2016.html.

51 *such as The Vanguard Group*   https://finance.yahoo.com/quote /ABT/holders?ltr=1.

52 *Warren Buffett, owns a 25 percent stake (valued at over $22 billion in March 2016) in Kraft Heinz*   http://www.investopedia.com /articles/investing/022716/warren-buffetts-portfolio-3-reasons -kraft-heinz-co.asp.

54 *As far back as the 1940s*   "Commercial of the Week," *Jet*, Dec. 4, 1952, 17.

56 *By the mid-1970s, over 75 percent of American babies*   S. J. Fomon, "Infant Feeding in the 20th Century: Formula and Beikost," *Journal of Nutrition* 131, no. 2 (2001): 409S–420S.

61 *A 1982 report by the Action for Corporate Accountability*   "Organization Records," *Action for Corporate Accountability: An Inventory of its Records at the Minnesota Historical Society* MNHS.org; see also http://www2.mnhs.org/library/findaids/00374.xml.

61 *One proposal from Ross Laboratories*   S. Solomon, "The Controversy Over Infant Formula," *New York Times*, Dec. 6, 1981.

65 *In 2013 the Academy of Breastfeeding Medicine*   "Academy of

Breastfeeding Medicine Urges AAP to End Formula Marketing Partnership," https://bfmed.wordpress.com/2013/12/27 /academy-of-breastfeeding-medicine-urges-aap-to-end -formula-marketing-partnership/, last modified December 27, 2013.

66 *In the summer of 2012, the AAP* C. Lewis, "Formula Markets Put Pediatric Academy in the Bag," womensenews.org; see also http://womensenews.org/2013/12/formula-marketers-put -pediatric-academy-in-the-bag/.

66 *This designation was changed* M. Meadows, "A Century of Ensuring Safe Foods and Cosmetics," fda.gov, last modified January-February 2006.

69 *Several meetings of the Food Advisory Committee* "FDA Takes Final Step on Infant Formula Protections," fda.gov, last modified June 9, 2014.

70 *Since 2000 the price of regular infant formula has increased 100 percent* http://www.ers.usda.gov/media/892137/efan02001f _002.pdf.

71 *Dairy industry subsidies totaled $5.6 billion* https://farm.ewg .org/progdetail.php?fips=00000&progcode=dairy.

73 *the guidance was still accepted as is* http://www.idfa.org/news -views/headline-news/article/2016/06/02/who-proposal -passes-with-some-positive-provisions-for-dairy.

76 *United States incurs 13 billion* M. Bartick and A. Reinhold, "The Burden of Suboptimal Breastfeeding in the United States: A Pediatric Cost Analysis," *Pediatrics* 125, no. 5 (2010).

3. Scientific Breakthroughs or Breakdowns?

80 *Doubt is our product* Smoking and Health Proposal, 1969, BN:680561778, Legacy Tobacco Documents Library

88 *by the age of three* D. W. Teele, J. O. Klein, and B. Rosner, "Epidemiology of Otitis Media During the First Seven Years of Life in Children in Greater Boston: A Prospective, Cohort Study," *Journal of Infectious Diseases* 160(1) (1989): 83–94. Available from: http://dx.doi.org/10.1093/infdis/160.1.83.

92 *In 2012 the American Academy of Pediatrics acknowledged* A. I.

Eidelman and R. J. Schanler, "Breastfeeding and the Use of Human Milk: Section on Breastfeeding," *Pediatrics* 129, no. 3 (2012).

93 *A 2010 analysis shows*   R. Li, S. B. Fein, and L. M. Grummer-Strawn, "Do Infants Fed from Bottles Lack Self-Regulation of Milk Intake Compared with Directly Breastfed Infants?" *Pediatrics* 125, no. 6 (2010): 1386–93.

94 *Research has confirmed*   T. Saarela, J. Kokkonen, and M. Koivisto, "Macronutrient and Energy Contents of Human Milk Fractions During the First Six Months of Lactation," *Acta Paediatrica* (Oslo, Norway: 1992) 94, no. 9 (2005): 1176–81; O. Ballard and A. L. Morrow, "Human Milk Composition: Nutrients and Bioactive Factors," *Pediatric Clinics of North America* 60, no. 1 (2013): 49–74.

95 *made big headlines*   N. Bakalar, "Is Breastfeeding Really Better?" *New York Times*, March 4, 2014, well.blogs.nytimes.com.

95 *A follow-up*   J. Grose, "New Study Confirms It: Breast-feeding Benefits Have Been Drastically Overstated," Slate.com, last modified February 27, 2014.

95 *Colen's study*   C. G. Colen and D. M. Ramey, "Is Breast Truly Best? Estimating the Effect of Breastfeeding on Long-Term Child Wellbeing in the United States Using Sibling Comparisons," *Social Science and Medicine* 109 (2014): 55–65.

99 *In January 2013* The New England Journal of Medicine   K. Casazza, K. R. Fontaine, A. Astrup, L. L. Birch, A. W. Brown, M. M. Bohan Brown, N. Durant, et al., "Myths, Presumptions, and Facts about Obesity," *New England Journal of Medicine* 368, no. 5 (2013): 446–54.

103 *on peer review fraud published in* NEJM *in December 2015*   http://www.nejm.org/doi/full/10.1056/NEJMp1512330#t=article.

103 *There are several studies*   M. W. Gillman and C. S. Mantzoros, "Commentary: Breast-Feeding, Adipokines, and Childhood Obesity," *Epidemiology* 18, no. 6 (2007): 730–32; I. M. Paul, C. J. Bartok, D. S. Downs, C. A. Stifter, A. K. Ventura, L. L. Birch, "Opportunities for the Primary Prevention of Obesity During Infancy," *Advances in Pediatrics* 56, no. 1 (2009): 107–33.

103 *One study comparing the milk of humans*   L. Hambraeus, "Proprietary Milk versus Human Breast Milk in Infant Feeding: A

Critical Appraisal from the Nutritional Point of View," *Pediatric Clinics of North America* 24, no. 1 (1977): 17; O. T. Oftedal and S. J. Iverson, "Comparative Analysis of Nonhuman Milks: Phylogenetic Variation in the Gross Composition of Milks," in R. G. Jensen, ed. *Handbook of Milk Composition* (San Diego: Academic Press, 1995): 749–89.

103 *recognize feelings of satiety* A. Brown and M. Lee, "Breastfeeding During the First Year Promotes Satiety Responsiveness in Children Aged 18–24 Months," *Pediatric Obesity* 7, no. 5 (2012): 382–90.

104 *In one study published in the journal* Pediatrics J. A. Mennella, C. P. Jagnow, G. K. Beauchamp, "Prenatal and Postnatal Flavor Learning by Human Infants," *Pediatrics* 107, no. 6 (2001): E88.

109 *An extensive review of synthetic* M. Hamosh, "Introduction: Should Infant Formulas Be Supplemented with Bioactive Components and Conditionally Essential Nutrients Present in Human Milk?" *Journal of Nutrition* 127, no. 5 (1997): 971S–974S.

109 *The algae DHA is not* D. J. Raiten, J. M. Talbot, and J. H. Waters, eds., "Executive Summary for the Report: Assessment of Nutrient Requirements for Infant Formulas," *Journal of Nutrition* 128 (11S) (1998).

110 *convened by the Institute of Medicine* Committee on the Evaluation of the Addition of Ingredients New to Infant Formula, "Infant Formula: Evaluating the Safety of New Ingredients" (Washington, DC: National Academies Press, 2004); see also C. Vallaeys, "Replacing mother—Imitating Human Breast Milk in the Laboratory" (Cornucopia Institutes, January 2008).

110 *International Baby Food Action* Y. J. Kean and A. Allain, "Breaking the Rules, Stretching the Rules 2004: Evidence of Violation of the International Code of Marketing of Breast Milk Substitutes and Subsequent Resolutions" (International Baby Food Action Network, 2004).

111 *Mead Johnson based its IQ claims* E. E. Birch, S. Garfield, Y. Castañeda, D. Hughbanks-Wheaton, R. Uauy, and D. Hoffman, "Visual Acuity and Cognitive Outcomes at 4 Years of Age in

a Double-Blind, Randomized Trial of Long-Chain Polyunsaturated Fatty Acid-Supplemented Infant Formula," *Early
Human Development* 83, no. 5 (2007): 279–84.

112 *as part of their Organic Integrity Project* Cornucopia Institute,
"Questions and Answers about DHA/ARA and Infant For-
mula," cornucopia.org, http://cornucopia.org/DHA/DHA
_QuestionsAnswers.pdf.

4. The Things Unseen: Battling Structural Barriers

125 *According to the Park Slope Parents 2015 Nanny Compensation
Survey* http://cdn.parkslopeparents.com/images/2015Nanny
SurveyResults_FINAL.pdf.

128 *Compare that to Sweden's* Sweden and Finland: International Labour Office Geneva, "Maternity at Work: A Review of National
Legislation, 2nd ed." (Geneva: International Labour Organization, 2012).

130 *In 2012 nearly one quarter* "Family and medical leave in 2012:
Detailed results appendix," (September 6, 2012); see also,
http://www.dol.gov/asp/evaluation/fmla/FMLA-Detailed
-Results-Appendix.pdf.

130 *correlation between death rates and paid leave* C. J. Ruhm, "Parental Leave and Child Health," *Journal of Health Economics* 19,
no. 6 (2000): 931–60.

131 *decline in depressive symptoms* M. Rossin-Slater, C. J. Ruhm,
and J. Waldfogel, "The Effects of California's Paid Family
Leave Program on Mothers' Leave-Taking and Subsequent
Labor Market Outcomes," *NBER Working Paper* 1771 (Decem-
ber 2011); P. Chatterji and S. Markowitz, "Does the Length of
Maternity Leave Affect Maternal Health?" *NBER Working Pa-
per* 10206 (January 2004); P. Chatterji and S. Markowitz,
"Family Leave after Childbirth and the Mental Health of New
Mothers," *Journal of Mental Health Policy and Economics* 15
(2012): 61–76.

131 *access to any form of paid family leave* U.S. Department of Labor,
Bureau of Labor Statistics, "National Compensation Survey:

Employee Benefits in the United States, March 2014" (U.S. Department of Labor, September 2014).

132 *The highest-paid workers* U.S. Department of Labor, Bureau of Labor Statistics, "National Compensation Survey: Employee Benefits in the United States, March 2014" (U.S. Department of Labor, September 2014).

135 *shows the scope of the legal letdown women face* http://www.leagle .com/decision/In%20FDCO%2020160401B39/ALLEN -BROWN%20v.%20DISTRICT%20OF%20COLUMBIA.

139 *Women now make up more* U.S. Census Bureau, Current Population Survey, DataFerrett, Monthly Microdata (December 2014); see also Department for Professional Employees, "Women in the Professional Workforce," dpeaflcio.org, last modified February 2015.

139 *Over the past forty years* R. M. Spalter-Roth and H. I. Harmann, "Increasing Working Mothers' Earnings: Executive Summary," U.S. Department of Labor, Women's Bureau (November 1991).

139 *number of part-time jobs* R. Valletta and L. Bengali, "What's Behind the Increase in Part-Time Work?" *Economic Research* (August 26, 2013).

139 *a study of working mothers by the Pew Research Center* K. Parker, "Women, Work, and Motherhood: A Sampler of Recent Pew Research Survey Findings," pewsocialtrends.org, last modified April 13, 2012, http://www.pewsocialtrends.org/2012/04/13 /women-work-and-motherhood/.

141 *two economic researchers at Washington University* J. Compton and R. A. Pollak, "Proximity and Coresidence of Adult Children and Their Parents: Description and Correlates," University of Michigan Retirement Research Center, Working Paper 2009–215 (2009).

143 *In 2015, Abbott Labs spent* http://www.opensecrets.org/lobby /clientsum.php?id=D000000383&year=2015.

147 *"On the one hand, wet nursing* Wilma A. Dunaway, *The African-American Family in Slavery and Emancipation* (Cambridge: Cambridge University Press, 2003).

148 *historian Michele Mock* M. Mock, "Spitting Out the Seed: Ownership of Mother, Child, Breasts, Milk, and Voice in Toni Morrison's *Beloved*," *College Literature* 23, no. 3 (1996): 117–26.

5. Nipple-omics and the Value of Motherhood

154 *Women are paid 23 percent less* C. DeNavas-Walt and B. D. Proctor, "Income and Poverty in the United States: 2014: Current Population Reports, P60-252" (Washington, DC: U.S. Government Printing Office, 2015).

157 New York *magazine featured* J. Senior, "All Joy and No Fun: Why Parents Hate Parenting," nymag.com, last modified July 4, 2010.

163 *U.S. women still work more hours* R. Blundell, A. Bozio, and G. Laroque, "Extensive and Intensive Margins of Labour Supply: Work and Working Hours in the US, the UK and France," *Fiscal Studies* 34, no. 1 (2013): 1–29.

166 *As George D. Sussman writes* George D. Sussman, *Selling Mothers' Milk: The Wet-Nursing Business in France, 1715–1914* (Champaign, IL: University of Illinois Press, 1982).

166 *Zelizer famously surmised* V. A. Zelizer, *Pricing the Priceless Child: The Changing Social Value of Children* (New Jersey: Princeton University Press, 1985).

6. The Feminist Fallacy

170 *easier to control cows* E. F. Brush, "How to Produce Milk for Infant Feeding," read at Fifty-Fifth Annual Session of American Medical Association, *Journal of the American Medical Association*, volume 43 (1904): 1385.

174 *the plaintiff argued that* https://www.eeoc.gov/eeoc/meetings /2-15-12/williams.cfm#fn4.

174 *"failure to present any comparison evidence* http://law.justia.com /cases/federal/appellate-courts/F3/20/734/522956/.

186 *Constructing breastfeeding as a choice* M. Eichner, "Parenting and the Workplace: The Construction of Parenting Protections in United States Law," *International Breastfeeding Journal* 3:14 (2008),

https://internationalbreastfeedingjournal.biomedcentral
.com/articles/10.1186/1746-4358-3-14.

7. The Problem of No Problem: The Breastfeeding Movement

198 New York Times *calling her book a "riveting exposé of breastfeeding*
http://www.nytimes.com/2015/12/20/books/review/lactivism
-by-courtney-jung.html.

198 *The review on Slate.com*   http://www.slate.com/articles/double
_x/doublex/2015/12/the_breast_feeding_extremists_who
_put_lactivism_ahead_of_protecting_babies.html.

8. Boob Control: The Sexualization of Breastfeeding

227 *A legal battle ensued*   Federal Communications Commission,
"FCC Proposes Statutory Maximum Fine of $550,000 against
Viacom-Owned CBS Affiliates for Apparent Violation of Inde-
cency Rules during Broadcast of Super Bowl Halftime Show,"
(September 22, 2004).

230 *UK magazine called* Mother & Baby   A. Jamieson, "Breastfeeding Is 'Creepy' Says Parenting Magazine," telegraph.co.uk, last
modified June 27, 2010.

231 *"ayatollahs of breast-feeding"*   Élisabeth Badinter, *The Conflict:
How Modern Motherhood Undermines the Status of Women* (New
York: Metropolitan Books, 2012).

232 *importance of the bonding benefits*   N. M. Else-Quest, J. S. Hyde,
and R. Clark, "Breastfeeding, Bonding, and the Mother-Infant
Relationship," *Merrill-Palmer Quarterly* (2003): 495–517; J. R.
Britton, H. L. Britton, and V. Gronwaldt, "Breastfeeding, Sensitivity, and Attachment," *Pediatrics* 118, no. 5 (2006): e1436–e1443.

234 *"Breasts are the only organ*   F. Williams, *Breasts: A Natural and
Unnatural History* (New York: Norton, 2012).

234 *Historical records document that black women*   W. A. Dunaway,
The African-American Family in Slavery and Emancipation
(Cambridge: Cambridge University Press, 2003); R. Hamad,
"A Tale of Two Breastfeeding Pictures," dailylife.com.au, last
modified Nov. 7, 2014; A. E. B. Crawford, *Hope in the Holler: A*

Womanist Theology (London: Westminster John Knox Press, 2002).

239 *For centuries, women went topless* S. S. Hughes and B. Hughes, *Women in World History*, vol. 1, *Readings from Prehistory to 1500* (New York: Routledge, 2015); J. Schreindl, "Why 'Free the Nipple Is Key to Women's Equality," rolereboot.org, last modified May 15, 2015.

242 *Oxytocin's documented effect* L. Garfield, C. Giurgescu, C. S. Carter, D. Holditch-Davis, B. L. McFarlin, D. Schwertz, J. S. Seng, and R. White-Traut, "Depressive Symptoms in the Second Trimester Relate to Low Oxytocin Levels in African-American Women: A Pilot Study," *Archives of Women's Mental Health* 18, no. 1 (2015): 123–29; M. Mokkonen and B. J. Crespi, "Genomic Conflicts and Sexual Antagonism in Human Health: Insights from Oxytocin and Testosterone," *Evolutionary Applications* 8, no. 4 (2015): 307–25.

242 *A 1992 member magazine* J. M. Riordan and E. T. Rapp, "Pleasure and Purpose the Sensuousness of Breastfeeding." *Journal of Obstetric, Gynecologic, and Neonatal Nursing* 9, no. 2 (1980): 109–12.

246 *journal* Health Communication *found many television* K. A. Foss, " 'That's Not a Beer Bong, It's a Breast Pump!' Representations of Breastfeeding in Primetime Fictional Television," *Health Communication* 28, no. 4 (2013): 329–40.

9. Ending the Letdown: The Way Forward

251 *In November 2014* T. Campbell and A. Kay, "Solution Aversion: On the Relation Between Ideology and Motivated Disbelief," *Journal of Personality and Social Psychology* 107(5) (2014): 809–824.

Index

CPSIA information can be obtained
at www.ICGtesting.com
Printed in the USA
LVHW091451080421
683829LV00003B/7/J